BABY X

Detective Sergeant Harry Keeble has almost twenty years' experience in inner-city pro-active policing. He joined the Met after leaving university in 1989. In 1999, Harry joined Haringey drugs squad as a uniformed sergeant and spent the following twelve months planning and leading 100 raids on fortified crack houses. Appalled at the number of abused children he encountered, and in particular by the senseless death of Victoria Climbié, Harry joined Hackney's Child Protection Team. He spent the following five years bringing dozens of child abusers to justice, managing several international police investigations related to child abuse across Europe, Africa and the Caribbean. He has prosecuted major drug dealers, rapists and child abusers at the Old Bailey and currently works for Specialist Operations at New Scotland Yard.

Kris Hollington is a freelance journalist and author living and working in London. He has written for the *Sunday Times*, *Guardian*, *Mail on Sunday*, *Evening Standard*, *News of the World*, *Loaded* and *Arena*, among others. Kris is the author of five books including, also with Harry Keeble, *Crack House*, published by Simon & Schuster.

BABY X

BRITAIN'S CHILD ABUSERS BROUGHT TO JUSTICE

HARRY KEEBLE *with*
KRIS HOLLINGTON

POCKET
BOOKS

LONDON • SYDNEY • NEW YORK • TORONTO

First published in Great Britain by Pocket Books, 2010
An imprint of Simon & Schuster
A CBS COMPANY

1 3 5 7 9 10 8 6 4 2

Simon & Schuster UK Ltd
1st Floor
222 Gray's Inn Road
London WC1X 8HB

www.simonandschuster.co.uk

Simon & Schuster Australia
Sydney

A CIP catalogue record for this book is available
from the British Library.

ISBN: 978-1-47112-705-2

Typeset by M Rules
Printed and bound by CPI Group (UK) Ltd, Croydon, CR0 4YY

For all the Baby Xs

CONTENTS

AUTHOR'S NOTE

It is important to ensure that the details of some of the individuals encountered through my work (witnesses, police officers, social workers, teachers, etc.) are not set out in a manner that would enable people to recognize them. It is of course also necessary to protect the identities of children and the parents whose stories are detailed in this book. The authors have, with the exception of names that are in the public domain, protected the identities of these people by changing names and altering some background details. Those cases that are a matter of public record are reported in their original detail.

ACKNOWLEDGEMENTS

I can only hope that I have done justice to the stories of the abused children in this book. The bravery of the children and those adult victims who confronted their traumatic past cannot be praised enough.

Special thanks goes to Rob and later Byron for their leadership and support of Hackney Police Child Protection Team as well as all the officers I served with for providing me with such an enjoyable and challenging posting.

Rob, my mentor and my very good friend, deserves additional praise for handling impossible tasks so incredibly well. I can think of no one better to work on the serious case review of Baby Peter.

To all those at Hackney Social Services, thank you for all your constructive advice, your courage and for being such a pleasure to work with.

To Detective Chief Superintendent Peter Spindler and Detective Superintendent Chris Bourlet, I am forever grateful for your unstinting support of front-line Child Protection officers.

My gratitude goes out to the Crown Prosecution Service who supported victims and our department through many very challenging trials.

Finally, for those who wish to contact me to discuss any issues raised in this book, then I am available via email: harrykeeble@btinternet.com

CHAPTER ONE

SIEGE MENTALITY

'That's the last time I leave you idiots in charge!' my boss Rob yelled down the phone. Bloody hell. This was supposed to be an easy one. Practically my first job and I'd kicked off a full-blown siege and a thirty-strong lynch mob was ready to rip our suspect to pieces. I'd had better Monday mornings.

I glanced up at the windows of the council house in Hackney's heartland. Somewhere behind the glass was our man, armed with a knife, threatening suicide. I shivered in the January drizzle as the van full of officers in riot gear pulled up. What was keeping the hostage negotiator? He'd been talking to the bloke for ages.

A white guy with a mullet was the most vocal of the growing mob. 'Scum!' he yelled at the house. 'Castrate the bastard!' About thirty neighbours and passers-by had joined him in the street. Pure hatred radiated from them to the house.

James and Simon were both giving me daggers. 'What? It's not my fault the guy's a fruit loop.' But I knew my gung-ho approach hadn't helped. When I joined Hackney's Child Protection Team at the end of 2001, I thought I had all of the answers to their many problems.

I was rapidly finding out that this was not the case.

The Child Protection Team (now called the Child Abuse Investigation Team or CAIT) investigates all forms of abuse (whether physical, mental, sexual or emotional) of a child by family members, extended family members, main carers, baby-sitters, youth workers and teachers – because in most cases of child abuse, that is exactly who's responsible. In this case it was an uncle accused of molesting his nine-year-old nephew.

When my colleagues heard I had applied to join Child Protection they asked me, 'What the hell are you going there for?' It was a fair question. Nobody wanted to join the 'Cardigan Squad' – so-called because Child Protection officers were seen as woolly, glorified social workers that mopped up after domestics. It was the least glamorous department in the Met, a real career cul-de-sac. Ambitious officers were expected to fight drug-dealers and terrorists, the exciting big-budget departments with cool gadgets and massive, prestigious operations.

Not me. I wanted to be out on the streets, fighting crime, get-ting my hands dirty.

My hard-hitting approach had worked wonders at my previ-ous posting, as a uniformed sergeant in charge of the five-man Haringey Drugs Squad. My team and I decided that the only way to return the streets to the community was to fight a war against crack. Our mission was to eliminate all one hundred crack houses in our borough in one year. It should have been impossi-ble. But we did it. As a direct result all black-on-black killings in Haringey were halted for the following twelve months.

About six months into our marathon, we crashed into a crack house in Tottenham. By this time we were pretty much immune to the sight of prostitutes and their clients in a filthy stinking room but this time we were brought up short by a sight that absolutely stunned us – in one of the bedrooms we found two terrified kids hiding under the bed. One was six years old, the other eleven. The older child asked me if they could still go to school. Christ, I thought. What chance have they got? I made sure they were handed over to the care of Child Protection.

A few weeks later, as I took one dealer into custody, a little girl walked past me in the company of two adults – she looked terrified. I wondered what her life would be like, growing up surrounded by violence and horror. I hated the fact that, more than any other age group, drugs seemed to hurt children the most.

I didn't know it then, but living just a few doors away was another little girl who was about to change my life.

Her name was Victoria Climbié.

From July 1999, the moment she arrived in Tottenham from the Ivory Coast, eight-year-old Victoria was tortured by her 'aunt' Marie Kouao and her boyfriend, Carl Manning, who believed she was possessed. To exorcize the 'evil spirits' she was beaten with belt buckles, bicycle chains, coat hangers and shoes. Razor blades were taken to her fingers and a hammer to her toes. She was burned with cigarettes, had boiling water poured over her and slept on a bin bag in the bath.

She died on 25 February 2000, of hypothermia, severe neglect and malnutrition. Her body had 128 injuries. According to the official inquiry that followed, a large part of the blame fell on the 'blinding incompetence' of Haringey social workers who missed twelve chances to save her. The police hadn't fared much better; one officer from Haringey's Child Protection Team decided not to visit Victoria's home because she was worried about catching scabies.[1]

When the news of this reached me I was, like most, utterly stunned. I was horrified that this had happened round the corner from where we'd been closing crack houses. I'd been so close.

I wondered how on earth the Child Protection Service could have let this happen. I soon found out why. They had hardly any trained officers and no budget to speak of. I was amazed to discover that detectives investigating serious offences against children weren't actually trained detectives. They were simply regular police officers with a job title.

Our little drug squad didn't have any computer technology to speak of but Child Protection was supposed to be a serious department with countless cases requiring major resources. Yet their software was slow and unwieldy; it could take all day just to research four or five cases when they should have been able to do that many an hour.

Worst of all, no less than fifteen children had died in recent years in the London Borough of Haringey *while in care*. Nine children had died while they were either in council-run children's homes or with council-approved foster parents or adoptive parents.[2] Haringey council had also unknowingly recruited child molesters, two of whom worked as caretakers in the borough's primary schools.[3]

And most worryingly, these examples weren't restricted to Haringey – they were cropping up all over London and the UK. In one of the worst cases a mother rang social services and told them she was going to harm her two children aged eight and nine (who were already on their 'at-risk' register). She was ignored. The next morning she set fire to her house and both of her kids burned to death. A six-year-old girl was murdered, smothered to death after her stepfather stabbed her crack-addicted mother in the heart, killing her. In another case, a ten-week-old baby was on the child protection register when she died in agony from blood poisoning caused by severe nappy rash. She had been seen by social workers twenty-eight times in the weeks leading up to her death but was allowed to remain with her crack-addicted mother.

As I looked at the files, I realized I was staring at the faces of kids we'd 'rescued' from the horrors of crack cocaine. What was the point of handing them over to Child Protection Teams only for them to disappear, eventually showing up years later as crack addicts and prostitutes?

I was, like most, utterly stunned. Along with everyone else, I wondered how on earth the Met's Child Protection Service could have let this happen. Unlike almost everyone else, I was in a position to do something about it. So, instead of accepting an offer to head up part of a major new glamorous drugs task force, I transferred to Child Protection.

I believed that the department lacked passion, had no sense of urgency – after all, something was desperately wrong if they didn't have the money or manpower to save a little girl from being murdered while I was successfully busting all the crack houses in the neighbourhood. As far as I was concerned, they needed a boot up the arse.

But it was never going to be that straightforward.

There was no time for official training at the understaffed department, so I was magically transformed from a uniform into a detective overnight – a process which normally takes between four and seven years.

With barely enough time for a hello to the fifteen-strong team, I found myself standing on a Hackney doorstep, dressed in a suit, freezing my backside off on a wet January morning. The man inside was accused of sexually abusing his nine-year-old nephew. I knocked.

'Fuck off! I'm not coming out,' came the reply.

Idiot.

The sensible thing would have been for him to come out and play the game. Our chances of getting this guy locked up were slim to none. The allegation hadn't been corroborated and his family didn't even want to take it to court. But a complaint had been made, so the plan was to arrest and interview him in the vain hope he'd break down and confess under questioning. It was what was referred to as a 'never to return'. In other words we bailed them, but because of the lack of evidence and willingness to prosecute from the family, they'd never be asked back.

My partners for the day were James and Simon. James was a real rarity, a lifelong detective constable, experienced in major inquiries. Like me, James had asked to come to Child Protection and was determined to make a difference. Simon had joined the squad around the same time as me. A natty dresser, he'd made a couple of million buying and selling property and came from the murder squad; his experience there would prove to be invaluable later. Many of his fellow officers wondered why he'd decided to stay in the Force, let alone sign up for the Cardigan Squad. (I for one was mortgaged to the hilt, with wife, three kids and two horses.) He jogged round the rear of the house, just in case our man made a run for it.

The plan was to nick the guy and head back to 'Stokie', Stoke Newington police station. Then we'd have a leisurely breakfast at the local Turkish cafe while we waited for the solicitor to show up.

Determined to have him come quietly, I turned on the charm but our suspect wouldn't budge. We were freezing; our empty stomachs rumbled. I gave the flimsy blue door a push; it was on a piddly Yale lock. Sod it. We're going in – Harry style.

I'd given the door a couple of warning kicks to alert him to the fact that we were about to crash through when James produced a shovel he'd found round the back and suggested we use it to prise the door open.

It worked. I held the door open while James wandered inside, me right behind him. The house was untidy but looked fairly normal, nothing that screamed 'child molester'.

There was a 'clunk' from upstairs and Simon ran up. As I followed him our suspect screamed, 'Get back!' and suddenly Simon turned tail and bounded down the stairs towards me at top speed, screaming, 'He's got a knife!' I wanted to run up and spank the idiot but Simon shoved me outside, slamming the door shut behind us.

'Bloody hell!' he cursed, catching his breath.

James tapped me on the back. 'Erm . . . where did that lot come from?'

A small crowd of about fifteen people had gathered. Some of them knew or were related to our suspect and were angry at what they saw as our heavy-handedness.

A woman joined the crowd. She went up to a tall bloke with a mullet who was in the middle of chastising us and said: 'You should let 'em 'ave 'im. He's a bloody paedo.'

'What?'

'Yeah, I've just been talking to Jill who'd met Kieran's mum and she told her that he'd "touched" her son; he's a pervert!'

The mood changed as they realized their friend, neighbour and relative was a 'monster'. People think that child molesters are fiends who abduct kids. They aren't. They're the nice ones, the clever ones who persuade you to invite them inside your house. They're a father, uncle, friend, brother, the helpful neighbour, the dedicated youth worker, the schoolteacher.

Now the crowd *hated* him.

Oh God. Oh no, no, no. I suddenly saw where this was going.

The crowd grew. And the larger it got the more people came to see what was going on.

We put our standard tactics into place. We surrounded the house and put in cordons. I started to shiver. No coat, and no hope of breakfast thanks to this fool.

We should have been on our fourth coffee and going through the paperwork. Instead we were stood around with blue noses while the hostage negotiator tried to talk our suspected paedophile out of killing himself. I couldn't help but cough out a bitter laugh as I wondered what the angry mob would make of that.

The negotiator tapped me on the shoulder. 'He's lost it. Very likely he's going to kill himself. You should go in.'

Great.

At least I was on familiar ground here. 'No problem,' I told the negotiator, 'this should be a piece of cake.' I'd been used to facing mob-handed suspects, dealers and addicts armed with every kind of weapon, but here we had just one puny guy with a knife who only wanted to harm himself.

After a quick scout round the outside of the house, I briefed officers from the Territorial Support Group (TSG). These are the Met's muscle; they patrol the capital in vans with six or more officers ready to rush to any incident. They formed up on the pavement and, on my signal, stormed the house, much to the excitement of the crowd.

With rising horror, I watched as the mob, who had been whipping each other up into an outraged frenzy, stormed our cordon and charged after the TSG, mullet-man at their head crying the battle-charge: 'Get the fucking paedo!'

Just when I thought this day couldn't get any worse.

I sprinted back to the doorway and blocked it, pushing the mullet-man back. 'Get back! Get the fuck back! I need some help here!' The TSG started coming back out of the house, yelling for calm. I prayed that no one was taking pictures. An image of the TSG in full body armour looking like they're about to charge a bunch of innocent civilians would be on the front page of the *Evening Standard* in a flash.

'Bastard! Kill the paedo! Castrate the bastard!'

Meanwhile, our suspect, screaming all the way, had fled for his life out of the back door, straight into the arms of the waiting TSG officers. Foolishly, he decided against surrendering; not smart – especially when the TSG know you're armed with a knife. He disappeared underneath a wave of blue overalls and NATO helmets. After a couple of well-placed thumps, our suspect was cuffed and carried, wriggling and screaming, into the van – yet another stupid move. The baying mob darted away from the front of the house and towards the van. Luckily the TSG were able to form an immovable wall and held the hordes at bay amid much shouting for calm and the occasional wallop.

After all that, once we got back to the station all I got was a brick wall of denial.

'Bastards!' the suspect shouted at me, his eyes red, his voice hoarse. 'How can you think that?! I can't believe that you think I did it . . . whoever did this is sick.'

'I'm not getting anywhere,' I told Rob when I stepped outside. 'Perhaps he is innocent, after all.'

Rob, who'd been listening in, sank back against his chair, which creaked under his massive frame. He pushed his glasses back onto his balding head. 'No, Harry. You need to be able to pick these people apart. Within his denials are evasions; they give you something to work with, no matter how small. He was objecting to the question, answering a question with a question, saying he can't *believe* – not that he didn't do it – and uses projection: he doesn't believe he's sick. He thinks what he did was acceptable.'

I looked back at the suspect. He was forty-something, had a big, round face and was short and skinny. Definitely the runt of the litter.

'Even the way they speak can tell you all you need to know,' Rob continued. 'Their words may sound truthful but their voice pitch may rise or perhaps they make a gesture which is out of synch with what they are saying. There are always microexpressions of anger, no matter how hard they try and control it. Admittedly he's good at lying but he's been lying to his family for the last God-knows-how-many years. He's practised for the moment when he's caught for months, years even.'

Even with Rob's advice, I wasn't able to get anything more

out of the suspect. As it was just his word against the kid's, and as the family didn't want to see him cross-examined, we had to turn our suspect loose.

He turned pale when I told him. 'What? Back *there*?' he gestured, jerking his thumb over his shoulder. 'With that mob?'

As I escorted him out of the station, I tried to hide my grin and said, in my most reassuring voice, 'Oh, don't worry, I'll be keeping a *very* close eye on you.'

After our dejected suspect had left to face whatever awaited him back home, we headed off to the Turkish cafe for a very belated lunch. I'd lost my appetite and poked at my food dejectedly. Rob leaned across the table and pushed his specs back on his head. 'Don't worry,' he said sympathetically, 'it's a bit different from kicking in crack house doors, but you'll get there.'

I wasn't so sure.

CHAPTER TWO

CARDIGAN SQUAD

'Don't come here expecting any glory,' Rob had told me, 'the boys upstairs only want to know when we've screwed up. So we don't screw up and they leave us alone.' Easier said than done.

The one massive plus was that after Victoria Climbié, money was (almost) no object and we were expected to pursue the accused using every inch of the long arm of the law without thinking about cost. The problem was that apart from a few exceptionally hardy and deeply dedicated officers, no one wanted to join us and we remained extremely short-staffed and underqualified. I felt very uneasy about my sudden elevation; certain skills and knowledge were supposed to come with the title of detective and I didn't even yet know what they were, let alone have them.

Of course, the Cardigan Squad was anything but woolly. We were operating in one of the most challenging environments the UK had to offer. Hackney, home to about 205,000 people (according to the 2001 census, but the true figure was probably higher), remains one of the most deprived areas in Europe with 47 per cent of kids living on or below the poverty line.[4] There was an extreme lack of affordable housing and the Met's own crime figures for 2000 to 2001 revealed that burglary figures were almost three times the national average, while robbery levels were an astonishing eight times higher.

Personally, I loved the area. Although I now lived with my family in a leafy part of Hertfordshire, I had cut my police teeth in Hackney, working as a beat officer. This was where the action was, where impossible challenges awaited us every day. I knew the people, criminals and local officials. I knew the make-up of almost every street, where the drugs gangs were, where the Turkish Cypriots drew their territorial lines, where the Somalis bought their khat, which schools had gang problems, and I felt totally at home.

Besides, Hackney was far from being entirely bad. Plenty of people of all colours and creeds were enjoying life there. The buoyant housing market meant that many wealthy and middle-class people had seen Hackney's potential and had started investing in the area, which was only a few minutes' commute from the City.

Unfortunately, Hackney also had the distinction of being the place where you were more likely to hear the sound of gunshots than anywhere else in Britain. The area running between Lower and Upper Clapton was known as 'Murder Mile', and shortly after I arrived murders and shootings were at their peak. Gunmen pursued their victims in broad daylight, finishing them off at point-blank range in streets packed with witnesses.

For example, on 27 March 2000, a man tried to use a stolen credit card at the Shell petrol station on Lower Clapton Road. When the attendant refused to hand it back to him, he returned with a handgun and opened fire. Fortunately, the thick glass saved the terrified attendant's life.

Two months later, on 25 May 2000, Memet Adiguzel, thirty-seven, was shot six times in front of dozens of witnesses in broad daylight as he sat in his car in Upper Clapton Road. Three weeks after that, a man in an Afro wig shot another man waiting out-side a West Indian cafe called Too Sweet, close to Lower Clapton Road. The victim survived. Five days later, Meneliek Robinson was driving his red BMW convertible along Upper Clapton Road, when a motorbike rider fired several shots through the window. Robinson staggered from the car and col-lapsed on the street, dying of massive blood loss. A few weeks after this, John Nugent, forty-six, was beaten unconscious by a group of men and pushed under a bus. He was pronounced dead on arrival at Homerton Hospital.

The next week . . . well, I'm sure you get the point by now. The official number of shooting incidents, beatings and knifings was high but the reality was even higher – a huge number went completely unreported. If you look at the call-out records for the ARVs (armed response vehicles), you'll find they go to Hackney more than anywhere else. In fact, if they are at a loose end, they always hang around in Hackney because sooner or later, the call will come.

Locals were used to it and simply went about their business. Some people even brought their children to look at the police cordons. And that was the point, of course. Many of these deal-ers, hit-men, robbers and crack prostitutes all had families, girlfriends, wives and kids – kids that needed to be saved from that violence if they were to have a shot at a decent life. The kids most at risk lived in rough estates with aggressive, some-times drug-addicted parents, some of whom were armed. Occasionally we'd find ourselves trying to gain access to the homes of some of London's toughest gangsters so we could take their kids away.

And there was no shortage of cases to investigate. Several hundred kids were on our radar at any one time and I soon had twenty-two on my own list to deal with.

We had fifteen staff led by our Detective Inspector, Robert

aka 'Rob', or the 'Fat Controller'. He grasped my hand warmly and I immediately took a liking to him. But for the obligatory cigar and shotgun under the desk, he looked exactly like every TV show's rough-round-the-edges, I-miss-the-mean-streets police chief. Rob was the unit's rock, always 100 per cent behind us no matter what crap we ended up dumping on his desk. He went on to write the serious case review for Baby Peter, an indication of just how highly regarded he is.

He was always at work by 6 a.m., worked at least twelve hours, glasses pushed back on his balding head. He never wore a suit because he wanted to appear relaxed and approachable. He refused to stay in a separate office, working instead among us, right in the thick of things. As a salaried detective inspector, he didn't have to work so hard but he couldn't help it. It was in his blood. Rob was a totally committed and experienced detective who made sure we did absolutely everything we could to protect children. He inspired confidence and formed the bedrock of our fantastic working environment.

Our brand-new, spacious and modern offices were in Stoke Newington and weren't bad at all. Much better than the stock cupboard that had once been Haringey Drug Squad's office. Until recently the Child Protection Teams across London were housed in rather scruffy accommodation with poor facilities.

'Not everything's perfect, Harry,' Rob said, 'for some reason we've only been allocated one vehicle between fifteen of us, but,' he added proudly, 'the important stuff, the environment we can now offer children is second to none.'

He took me on a guided tour of the cosy flat with mini doctor's surgery and discreet CCTV lounge where we interviewed children. The flat had its own secluded entrance to the police station, unaffected by the hustle and bustle of a busy North London nick.

Also inside this section of the building was the SOIT (Sexual

Offence Investigation Trained) suite. This was where victims of serious sexual assault were taken. 'Here's the lounge,' Rob said, 'TV, DVD-player, comfy sofas and plenty of toys for all ages.' It was just like an ordinary family lounge; no clue that you were inside one of London's largest police stations. The decor was ten years out of date but tasteful. Decent prints on the mellow-coloured walls; the furniture looked warm and cosy. Everything was done to try and make those brave children who stepped through our door as comfortable as possible.

The interview room, very similar to the lounge, was opposite. The one difference was that it contained tiny cameras, one in each corner. These fed images to a small control room.

Interviewing children is one of the most difficult things a police officer can do and took anything from a few minutes to several hours. I had kids of my own and had already interviewed some youngsters from my drugs squad days but I wondered whether I had the skills to cope with abused kids. I was counting on Rob and the rest of the team to show me how.

'I typically start with a gentle chat about favourite sports, TV shows and school,' Rob told me, 'before tackling the questions about abuse. We don't use dolls but sometimes the kids like to write or draw.'

The two remaining rooms were the witness statement suite and the forensic medical examiner's room. This looked similar to the nurse's room at a GP's surgery and was a great facility, with a very large, comfy examination table. It proved so attractive that one unknown idiot cop got too drunk down at the local boozer to stagger home and so slept on it – after urinating in the flowerpot. After that, the security arrangements were updated.

The child protection process works like this. After a teacher, doctor or concerned relative contacts social services to raise concerns about the well-being of a child, a social worker will decide whether the case comes under Section 47 of the Children Act (1989). This is the key legislative document for children and families. It places a duty on local authorities to safeguard children, and Section 47 states that a 'Local Authority has a duty to investigate when there is reasonable cause to suspect that a child is suffering, or is likely to suffer, significant harm'.

Once an S47 is launched then we get involved and, along with all the relevant agencies, we look at the evidence and a child protection conference is held to decide whether or not the child is placed on the child protection register. This confidential list is only available to professionals, indicating that the child is at risk of significant harm and there is a plan in place to address the harm. The plan of action is decided by a Core Group, formed by various agencies, and follow-up conferences then take place at three-month, then six-month intervals to review progress. In a nutshell: 'The child protection service is a framework of mechanisms that exist to identify significant harm, formulate actions to address harm, carry out the plan and review progress towards the objective of making a child safe as soon as possible and adjusting the plan as required to meet this goal.'[5]

Each London borough has a Police Child Protection team and since Victoria Climbié's death they are controlled centrally from the Metropolitan Police's Child Protection Command, based in Cobalt Square in South London. The big boss was Detective Chief Superintendent Peter Spindler, who, I'm pleased to say, drove forward the principles of aggressive case investigation coupled with the sensitive handling of victims.

Knowing all this made Child Protection a great place to work. We all knew that we had the full confidence of our superiors and that we would be allowed to pursue every investigative lead. As an added bonus, we knew that we also had strong support from the Crown Prosecution Service (CPS). This was thanks to Rob, who'd wisely identified that early consultation with the CPS in child protection cases is a highly effective way of helping to secure convictions. This early consultation process has since been rolled out across the UK.

We relied heavily on members of the public and professionals who worked with children such as teachers, nurses and council officials to refer cases. The main pooling point for all the information that came through Hackney at this time was Duty and Assessment at Downham Road, run by social services. Any information that came in was logged into a computer and assessed there. They then referred cases to us by fax.

When the fax arrived at Stoke Newington, it was logged and a yellow form was added. Some basic checks were made and, after a telephone discussion with social services, it was decided whether we should act together or separately. Rob had decided that at Hackney we should log our decision-making, again a wise move that has been replicated across the Metropolitan Police Service.

We scored cases according to four types of abuse (Emotional, Physical, Sexual, Neglect) and we then held a strategy discussion with caseworkers, managers and sometimes parents. This very formal but extremely dramatic process was where massive decisions were made that affected the child's life for ever. Of course, although it sounds simple, there were always complications and sometimes serious communication and cooperation problems between most of the bodies involved in child protection.

The following quote came from an inquiry into child protection held by the London Borough of Greenwich Council, published in 1987. 'The report of the inquiry into the circumstances surrounding the death of Kimberley Carlik in June 1986 showed clearly that no system of exchanging information among the relevant agencies existed.' Kimberley was starved and beaten to death by her stepfather, Nigel Hall. He was given life for her murder while her mother was given twelve years for

assault and cruelty. The inquiry found that her death was avoid-
able and concluded that four key social work and health staff in
Greenwich failed to apply the necessary skill, judgement, care
and communication.

Sixteen years later and another report into the murder of a
child was published.

[She] was known to no less than two further housing authorities, four social services departments, two Child Protection
teams of the Metropolitan Police Service, a specialist centre
managed by the NSPCC and she was admitted to two different hospitals because of suspected deliberate harm. The
dreadful reality was that these services knew little or nothing
more about Victoria [Climbié] at the end of the process than
they did when she was first referred to Ealing Social Services
by the Homeless Persons' Unit in April 1999.

Time and again, year after year, there had been far too many
communication breakdowns meaning that crucial information
had not been passed on, or acted on, when it had been received.
Amazingly, this problem had been addressed way back in 1990,
when, in an enlightened experiment, a North London Police
Child Protection unit and a team of social workers were housed
together in Havering. This made perfect sense to me. We would
have loved to have had rapidly organized face-to-face formal and
informal meetings, information exchanges, and to travel
together on visits but, for whatever reason, it was judged by the
powers that be as a failure and was forever forgotten.

Shortly after I'd applied to join Child Protection, I'd been
on attachment with Haringey's Child Protection Team. This
was a temporary assignment designed to give me a feel for the
type of work that went on in that department, to see if this was
what I really wanted to do. I spent it with Ricky Budd, one of

the sergeants who worked on the Victoria Climbié Inquiry. When we travelled down to the offices of the social services department, we were met by a very pleasant social worker, who explained very politely that we were not allowed inside their office and would have to stay in another area. Ricky explained that this was because one of the managers didn't like the police! This was exactly the sort of attitude that drove me, and many others, totally nuts. We need to work together to protect kids – how could we hope to do that if we're not even allowed in their bloody office!?

There have been at least seventy public inquiries into tragic failures in the British child protection system. Inevitably Lord Laming's report on the murder of Victoria Climbié repeated many of their recommendations. Including his report, sixteen inquiries out of the thirty-six held since 1973 have called for improved communications among the staff and services involved in safeguarding children. The key points remain:

Lack of inter-agency communication.
Lack of multi-agency communication.
Lack of training (no time).
Lack of supervision (no time).
Unqualified social work staff undertaking complex assessments.

As far as I could tell at this early stage, many of these problems lay at the door of social services. I relished the challenge of dealing with them and looked forward to 'communicating' until I was blue in the face.

As we finished my tour, Rob introduced me to the rest of the team. There was millionaire Simon, the detective sergeant who joined me on the disastrous siege and who eventually became my best mate on the unit. We never grew tired of teasing him about his wage slips being ice cream money and, although he had no financial reason to stay in the police, as he said, he didn't want to become a 'fat useless tosser sitting in a Benidorm villa, sipping pina coladas all day'.

As we chatted, Simon suddenly looked over my shoulder. 'Oh crap, not *again*,' he said. I followed his gaze and spotted what was a basic flaw in inter-departmental communication. It sat looking distinctly out of place in our modern office. An antiquated fax machine. 'Should've realized, the bloody thing's been too quiet,' Simon added.

Rob saw my puzzlement and explained. 'All the referrals arrive from social services via fax. Sadly, their budget doesn't allow for a half-decent IT system with email.'

The team gathered round the machine as it started to spew sheet after sheet of paper. Rob said: 'The problem is that the bloody thing runs out of paper very quickly and they often jam.'

'Then we get this after the fault's been discovered,' Simon added, 'a nasty white-knuckle ride where we learn whether we should have been rescuing some poor kid half an hour ago.'

Rob went on to tell me that it was not unheard of for some-one to accidentally hit redial or press a wrong digit and a child's sad history would whirr out of a random fax machine anywhere in the UK. Unbelievably, it took until February 2009 before this antiquated system was replaced by email.

As Simon checked the referrals, Rob carried on with the rest of the intros. Craig, a detective constable, came from the streets; he had been a uniform officer in East London. He took work very seriously and was a tenacious and dedicated investigator. He felt, like many, that the change from walking the beat on a Friday afternoon in uniform to investigating child rape in a suit on Monday was a travesty but he had the courage and determination to see it through.

Patrick was also a former uniformed constable. A great story-teller, he was built like a tank, very useful when visiting some of Hackney's rougher estates. I was delighted to see a familiar face sat next to them – Clara, the office manageress. I knew her from my days as a PC at Stoke Newington. That was perfect; I knew she would help bolster my reputation with the rest of the team. They would hear from her that I was a solid, committed cop that could be trusted. A local girl, she took no nonsense and was well respected by all. Although Rob was king, Clara kept the shop floor in order.

Part of the reason we were known as the Cardigan Squad was due to the false perception that most of our officers were female and part-time officers with their own families who zipped out the door faster than a jack-rabbit at 5 p.m. every day, with no regard for the cases they left sitting on their desks.

As far as our squad was concerned nothing could have been further from the truth. Any investigating officer in Child Protection wanting to work nine to five from Monday to Friday is in the wrong job. Lucy, a uniformed officer, was a fantastic role model and showed us how it was possible to balance home life and work – even though her son had several medical problems requiring a great deal of attention.

Lucy would never say: 'I've got to be at the hospital, goodbye.' She'd solve the issue first, saying something like: 'I've got to be at hospital this afternoon, but I'll ring the victim tonight and when I'm done I'll write it up from my local nick.'

Lucy's work was always done and her son kept all his appointments. I know this seems like common sense but in my experience many people don't seem to behave as well as this in real life. Lucy didn't need supervising, because she balanced everything and came to managers with solutions, not problems.

Another former uniformed officer was Sarah, who was the sharpest, toughest tool in the box. Again, she was the type that didn't need supervising. Deeply passionate about her work, she always spent considerable time analysing her cases in great depth and never went home until absolutely certain everything had been done correctly. Sarah was always at the forefront of the many heated discussions and debates we had about the best way to protect a particular child. This was exactly as it should have been. She was never afraid to tell me when she thought I was wrong about something – and she was often proved to be right. I soon developed a huge respect for her and we ended up working closely together on several difficult cases.

James was the extraordinary detective who'd also joined me on the siege. He was exceptional, utterly determined to make a difference. Karl was nearing retirement and had been a uniform constable for his entire career. He'd seen it all, from the days when the police rule book collected dust from lack of use, to the politically correct, form-filled world of today. He often made it robustly clear which era he preferred. He was like a pit bull, once he got his teeth into a case he couldn't ever let it go, a trait that some thought would be too difficult to live with in Child Protection. I thought he was just what a post-Climbié Child Protection Team needed; someone who would really push the boat out to protect children, say what he thought and who would get things done through dogged detective work – as he would later demonstrate.

And then there was me: thirty-five, six foot four, skinny as a rake with a strange resemblance to the rubber-faced Hollywood actor Jim Carrey, determined to prove that the Cardigan Squad were anything but woolly. I was on a mission to take down every last child abuser on our patch; anyone with me on their case needed to be very afraid. It was, of course, never going to be that easy. Bashing down the doors of crack houses was simple, dealing with the minds of paedophiles and child abusers, as I was about to discover, was a very different and very complicated kettle of fish indeed.

CHAPTER THREE

SKELETONS IN THE CUPBOARD

So here I was, not long after nearly kicking off a full-scale riot, ready to knock on the very respectable-looking door of a suspected paedophile, the first on my very long list. I still hadn't got used to wearing a suit on the job; it felt awkward.

Normally a 'raid' to me meant running at the door full pelt with a battering ram and forcing the occupants into submission. This felt far too civilized; once again I wondered whether I'd done the right thing, turning down a prestigious post on a swanky new drugs task force.

The fact that the address looked so decent had really thrown me; the immaculate front garden packed full of expensive plants; the perfect front door, statues on either side; the bay windows with original shutters.

Inside, the family were no doubt going about their morning routine. I took a breath. I was about to rip their lives apart. Within twenty-four hours the man will be jobless, friendless, possibly homeless, facing the public humiliation of being dragged through the courts for this most terrible of offences. Some kill themselves before they make it to court.

But I knew what he'd been watching. Out went any sympathy.

Think of the kids. My stomach knotted, my neck muscles hardened.

Here goes . . .

A young man answered the door. He was in his late twenties, looked normal. No obvious signs of perversion (although I had no idea what I was expecting).

I introduced myself; he asked us in, offering a seat and a cuppa. 'How can I help?' This polite greeting made me feel even more uncomfortable. I was more used to the cold shoulder, verbal abuse or a broom handle through the letter box – I knew where I was with that, but his casual civility threw me. He looked and behaved just like one of the guys from my circle of friends: middle class, ambitious and clean living.

The house was spotless; beautiful stripped-pine floors with furniture to match. 'Have a seat,' he repeated as we arrived in the lounge. I just couldn't do it; I just couldn't sit down.

He confirmed his name. This was my suspect, so I took a breath and explained why I was there. He'd accessed child pornography on the Internet, along with 7,250 other British people whose credit card details and Internet provider addresses were uncovered by the Dallas Police Department in the United States. The colour drained from his face. He wasn't going to deny it.

'This is bad,' he said. 'My girlfriend's upstairs, she's pregnant.'

Oh God. That's three lives I'm about to shatter. How am I supposed to play this? I started to say: 'I can tell her—'

'No! No way. I'll do it, if you'll let me go upstairs.'

I nodded.

She came down a couple of minutes later, ashen-faced, and asked me if she could leave. Yes, but not without a search. Luckily, Lucy was with me; she performed a quick, professional check and the man's girlfriend left without another word, an innocent victim, her life suddenly trashed.

Our suspect, John, was carted off to Stokie, where he was interviewed. He was bailed for six months, due to a huge backlog in computer examinations. This backlog was thanks to Operation Ore, Britain's biggest child pornography investigation, one small part of the world's largest child pornography investigation – Operation Avalanche. In 1999, US investigators stumbled across an online child porn empire stretching across three continents, with some 250,000 subscribers and a turnover of $1.4 million a month.

The usual excuse people tried on us first was that they'd stumbled upon child porn by accident but in this case there was no question of their guilt. For those who knew how to access the portal that led them to a network of 5,700 child porn sites, owned by a company called Landslide Promotions, there was no hiding what was on offer. On the homepage there was a button that said 'For child porn click here'. And if you clicked on that button, that's exactly what you got (after handing over your credit card details).

Users were able to download and share pornography with other paedophiles all around the world. All the subscribers had to provide a credit card number, so once the authorities cracked the code scrambling the numbers, they started tracking down the owners of the cards – and the links that took them to Landslide Promotions' front door. The owner of Landslide, Thomas Reedy, was found guilty of eighty-nine charges in December 2000, including sexual exploitation of minors and distribution of child porn. He was sentenced to 1,335 years in prison (reduced to 180 years on appeal).

Once the UK list was ready we had to prioritize and take out those who worked with children or worked in law enforcement. This included judges, solicitors, social workers and police officers.

This taught me a useful early lesson. Paedophiles are everywhere – they are computer programmers, truck drivers, company directors, accountants, actors, pop stars and the unemployed. They are in their twenties to seventies. They live in small council flats on problem estates and in detached houses with long drives and pools. They live on their own, with their parents, or had a loving wife and children.

They had nothing in common except for a shared set of fantasies that was for many of them their central driving force in life. They shared a bond that transcended social class, economic grouping, family background and education, and they sought each other out over the Internet. They formed clubs, secret societies with chat rooms to exchange fantasies and experiences. They were obsessive collectors of photos.

In all, 4,283 homes were searched, 3,744 people were arrested and 1,848 were charged resulting in 1,451 convictions and 493 cautions. Some 140 children were removed from suspected dangerous situations and at the time of writing over 850 investigations are still under way.

We were given the names of a new batch of people linked to Operation Ore every few weeks. There were so many requiring verification that they couldn't all be done at once. Some of these men were the innocent victims of credit card theft and fraud but the overwhelming majority were guilty. The police unit that was supposed to go through their computers was so overwhelmed with a two-year backlog we had to use private companies, so the PC belonging to this man John was sent to a company based in Oxford.

At the next address, a 1930s semi, once again everything screamed respectability: a pint of milk on the doorstep below the 1950s door with frosted glass, which was opened by a lady in her late sixties wearing slippers. The door opened and stopped as the chainlock kicked in. She looked at me with some concern – not surprising really, I'm six feet four and don't wear suits well. I plastered what I hoped was a friendly smile on my face, showed her my warrant and introduced myself. 'May we come in?'

She smiled at my card. 'I wouldn't know what a real one looks like anyway, dear.'

Patrick and I stepped over the threshold. The house was of eat-your-dinner-off-the-floor standard. No horrible smells had smacked us in the face, always a welcome relief. We continued to smile as she took us through to the kitchen diner.

'I hope it's nothing too dramatic,' she said, 'only my husband can't take too much excitement, he's just out of hospital after heart surgery.'

I tried to recall the most up-to-date procedures for CPR, as she introduced us and offered us tea. The search warrant was now red-hot in my pocket.

I declined the tea. They asked me how they could help. Not the guarded 'What do you want?' of the guilty or mistrustful. Something was very wrong here. I looked at her husband. Am I about to destroy a decades-long relationship? Am I about to kill the old man?

Clearing my throat, I said: 'We need your help with a delicate inquiry.'

'But of course,' came the answer, 'anything we can do.'

'Does anyone else live here?' I asked hopefully.

'Only our son,' the husband said, looking over my shoulder. Patrick and I turned.

Relief washed over me. No one should ever stereotype what a paedophile looks like but in this case he fitted the bill perfectly. In his mid-thirties, he had long lank hair, patchy stubble, a grey-ish pallor, bad teeth and I could smell him from across the room. You look like you've just walked out of a cave, mate, I thought. I had no idea how close to the truth I was.

Now more confident, but still wary of the old man's dicky ticker, I waffled quite a bit, trying to get across the information with the minimum of shock for the innocent couple sat before me. But of course this was impossible. This is the dreadful part of being a cop. As I reached the part where I said we had a warrant to search the house for indecent images of children, they crumbled from the inside. Things would never be the same for them again.

The snag was that the only computer was in a downstairs room. If the son didn't confess here and now, then we'd have to drag the parents down to the station for an interview under caution. This couple, who'd been good citizens all their lives, would have to face mandatory questions about drug taking and the state of their mental health from custody officers.

We searched the house, starting with the most logical place, the son's room. I pushed the door but it would only open slightly; there was something behind it. The smell of stale sweat seeped out into the hallway. 'Bloody hell!' Patrick said, holding his nose. I'd seen some pretty horrendous rooms busting crack houses, but this was something else.

There was no natural light. In the centre of the room was a filthy cot bed. There was no other furniture. Instead, surrounding the bed, from floor to ceiling and stacked several feet deep were thousands upon thousands of magazines, about half of which were in advanced stages of decomposition. They were dusty, mouldy and were all different shades of dirty yellow and grey. Not one square inch of the walls was visible. It was, in effect, a cave.

By the time we came back downstairs, the son had decided to do the decent thing and confessed to spending his nights surfing for child porn. His parents were no longer able to look me in the eye. We seized the computer, arrested the son and left the elderly couple to have one of the most difficult conversations of their lives.

Just before I was about to give the briefing for the very next raid, Rob introduced me to a familiar-looking female face. She was in her forties with long, wild, reddish-brown hair and was extremely confident and relaxed as she reached over to shake my hand in a firm grip.

'Hi, I'm Anita.'

Bloody hell, it was only Anita Roddick, the founder of The Body Shop!

She'd won an auction at some posh charity do. Her prize was to spend a day with any police department she liked and she'd chosen us. I was flattered and flummoxed; most people haven't even heard of us, let alone wanted to spend a day hunting paedophiles and child abusers.

We were about to raid a trendy apartment in Hackney for child porn. Anita sat in on the briefing, looking on interestedly and taking notes as I talked. I stated the aims of the raid, how we were going to achieve it, the risks involved. I finished with the usual question.

'Is anyone unclear about their role?'

Anita's hand shot up.

'Can I come?'

I looked at Rob, who nodded almost imperceptibly. 'Fine by me,' I said. I considered the complications of bringing an internationally famous person on the trip. 'We won't say anything unless anyone recognizes you. Any other questions?'

Anita's hand shot up.

'If we find child pornography, what will happen to them?'

'They'll be arrested and we'll bring them here for questioning, after which we'll charge them and if successful they'll end up in jail and on the sex offenders' register.'

'What is the register, exactly?'

'Good question,' I replied, trying to stay calm. I hadn't been in the unit long and suddenly my knowledge was being tested by a renowned business leader in front of my fellow officers.

'It contains the details of anyone convicted, cautioned or

released from prison for sexual offences against children or adults since September 1997, when it was set up. About 29,000 people are on it.'

'How long will they be on the register?'

'It depends on the offence,' I said, now perspiring freely. 'Those given a jail sentence of more than thirty months for a sexual offence are placed on the register indefinitely. Those sent down for between six and thirty months remain on it for ten years, or five years if they are under eighteen. Those sentenced for six months or less are placed on the register for seven years, or three and a half years if under eighteen. Those cautioned for a sexual offence are put on the register for two years, or one year if under eighteen.'

From the back of the room, Rob gave me the thumbs-up. Phew.

'If you find pictures and films, do you try and find the kids that are in them?'

'Absolutely. We'll look for clues in the background of the pictures as to their location and will question the suspect as to where they came from, what they know about the supplier and so on.' Finally satisfied, Anita nodded and looked around.

'Right,' I said, with no little relief, 'time to go to work.'

We drew up outside the apartment and marched to the door. A man in his late twenties answered and appeared nonplussed when I explained who we were.

His girlfriend appeared behind him and asked: 'Who is it?'

When he told her who we were she didn't seem so surprised. Anita looked at me knowingly. I guess you don't get to own a global business empire without learning when someone is hiding something. The couple didn't recognize Anita and so, without further ado, I explained what we were looking for and we got stuck in. Anita couldn't help herself and soon took on a supervisory role, directing us to areas we might have missed. 'Have a go yourself,' I said, and sure enough she did, rummaging around like a pro.

The first lead came from Sarah. She called me over and showed me two A4 pages of handwritten stories of child abuse fantasy. This is not classed as an offence in itself but was a clear sign we were on the right track. It also made good evidence.

I picked up their digital camera. I started to scan through the images and realized that they were building up to girl-on-girl action, our suspect's girlfriend with another woman, on the kitchen table. I asked the girl if she would prefer a WPC to review the material. She nodded and so I passed it over to Sarah. A few moments later she said, 'All clear, Harry.' Their computer was seized and sent off for examination.

I returned to my car to find a parking ticket flapping away on it. Typical. Thankfully, all it takes is one form signed by Rob to make it disappear in a puff of smoke.

As usual, once all the evidence was processed we sat down at Bodrum's in Stoke Newington High Street for our Turkish breakfast. Anita quizzed and quizzed us about all aspects of Child Protection. Me being the newbie and having already done my part at the briefing, I let Rob do most of the talking. Anita started by asking, 'Are you finding more child pornography these days?'

'Yes,' Rob replied, nodding with no little passion, 'the Internet has a lot to answer for. Men can find perversions on the net they never knew they had; they discover sides to their character they might have gone to their graves without knowing. Twenty years ago, the paedophile was isolated, sitting alone with magazines imported at considerable risk from the continent and too frightened to even try and make contact with others like him.

'Thanks to the Internet, the floodgates have opened and

people can exchange porn and chat with no worries about border control. They can find others like them in seconds. On the upside, from our viewpoint, by using the Internet ourselves we've been able to identify and prosecute hundreds of paedophiles and have been able to rescue dozens of children.'

'Would you agree that pornography helps to reduce the number of actual attacks on children?'

'If only,' Rob replied, looking round the caff. 'Generally people don't like to pay for porn off the Net as it requires the divulging of traceable credit card details. So instead they swap it. To have some swappable porn that no one else will have means making your own and exchanging it. On the lower end of the scale, men take photos of their own kids in the bath and send them round the world. And then there are the ones driven to produce the most abhorrent, disturbing films you can imagine.'

Inevitably, the conversation turned towards the sexual abuse of children by those closest to them.

'Sexual abusers are most often very close to the child's family if not a relative, step-relative or in-law. They are narcissistic opportunists, paranoid and antisocial. They understand social interactions are necessary to achieve their aim but they don't enjoy being sociable; they tell people what they want to hear simply as a means to an end.'

'Surely they must stand out like a sore thumb?'

'No, no, not at all. Most of the time they're apparently very law-abiding and people often refuse to believe that they're child abusers. Abusers are supposed to be anorak-wearing monsters, with greasy hair and wonky teeth, aren't they?'

Anita nodded.

'Some are but the monsters who travel the country kidnapping kids are the exception. The ones that fit in can molest children hundreds of times before they're caught. These are more common by far because it's so easy for them. They're the surrogate uncle who offers to babysit without charge, the community worker who devotes an extraordinary amount of time to kids' projects, the Boy Scout leader, teachers, doctors, all of these people are close to us and we instinctively trust them. They go the extra mile; they pick litter, visit the elderly, take part in fundraising and give generously to charities. Their reputation is second to none.

'One paedophile said he would target church groups because they were so open and accepting and prepared to overlook his social shortcomings; then he would volunteer for any project that related to children. They appear altruistic and we welcome them into our homes but really they're evil selfish bastards grooming kids to satisfy their own needs.'

Rob stirred his coffee. 'What bothers me is that it's the public's lack of knowledge that gives them such an edge. Parents believe them over their kids. Kids don't often tell, especially on an adult who their parents respect, or if it's their own father. Besides, for most people the possibility is just too horrible to seriously consider.'

'What do they say when they're caught? What's their defence?'

'If an adult civilian confronts them, they act confident. They know all the moves, they can look you in the eye and say: "Look, I'm telling you the truth, and I don't know what these people are trying to prove, but I haven't done any of this. I don't know why they're doing this. You can check my records. I've never been in any trouble." When their liberty is at stake they will have no qualms about lying to us.

'When we get hold of them, they sometimes tell us what nobody else gets to hear, what compels them to hunt out children, 'cos that's what it is, hunting. Some of them are proud and can't help but boast. Others justify their acts by claiming they were consensual, the child encouraged them; wanted them to do it. They don't accept just how much this "pleasure" had scarred their victims for life. They are intellectual and emotional bullies who, despite their claim to love children, are committing a crime that will negatively affect the child's life for ever.'

'Is it something that's getting worse?'

'It's a massive problem, much bigger than anyone realizes. My officers are always amazed when they join the team. They ask me: "Why is there so much abuse here?" I tell them it's like this all over.

'Many of these paedophiles have suffered horrendous abuse themselves as kids. The research is by no means definitive but one theory is that one in eight of all abused kids will themselves become child abusers. This is exasperating to the countless adult survivors of abuse who'd rather die than see a child suffer as they did but there does seem to be some credence to the idea that abuse fosters abuse.'

'Isn't there some way of preventing that?'

'Extended therapy can help but that's only available to a few lucky ones – and the best therapy is only available in prison. It's a question of money and resources failing to match demand. I don't know of any cure for paedophilia, apart from the easy answer of castration. Several have been touted and some behavioural therapies have had a limited success but this is not something that's going to go away. We have to face the fact that a significant part of our society is sexually attracted to children.'

Afterwards, Anita thanked us. 'It's been very illuminating,' she said, shaking our hands.

I couldn't help but agree.

I had no idea at the time but Anita, who was once a schoolteacher, had long been interested in children's charities and had already done a lot of charitable work for orphaned Romanian children. Now she wanted to do something for abused kids in the

UK. Later that year, she launched a major campaign to fight child abuse called Protect the Child, which gave vital support to community organizations that provided services for abused children and their families. She got it exactly right, this was where private money could really make a direct difference to kids' lives. Rob's influence was clear: 'There are no short cuts,' she said, announcing the start of the charity, 'there is no magic formula, no overnight successes to making a lasting and positive change.'

Those children needed all the help they could get.

It was a sad day when Anita died. Her style of campaigning worked wonders and she really made a difference.

CHAPTER FOUR

SOPHIE'S CHOICE

The front reception of Hackney Social Services was not what you'd call an inspiring sight, but for me it was a revelation. About a dozen people were crowded into the small area, half of whom I guessed to be genuine cases while the others were drug or booze-addicted con artists on the hunt for 'emergency payments'.

'My kids need feeding!' one woman yelled, clearly drunk. How could they take that amount of grief from someone and not crack? It was awful. 'What the fuck are you staring at?' she demanded. Although I was fuming inside, I kept quiet; I would've arrested them if they'd behaved like that at the front desk of the police station.

Simon was with me, we were on a grand tour of local social services, something I'd been 'looking forward to' for a while. All Section 47 inquiries were supposed to be joint investigations, so it was a chance to meet the team and to sit in on a case conference.

Here, so I thought, was the source of so many of our problems. Social workers are responsible for enhancing and improving the quality of life for the families they work with and accountable for protecting children at risk. As far as I was concerned, they'd been failing on a grand scale.

Once we made it past the mayhem of the front desk, we stopped by Duty and Assessment where I was introduced to a delightful Irish lady called Brenda who shook my hand warmly. 'New blood, eh? You look far too nice for this line of work. Are you sure you want to be a part of this madness?'

I smiled. 'What on earth do you mean?' I joked. 'Simon told me this was a cushy number.' Brenda laughed and then introduced me to the rest of the team.

'This is Ishwar, he's a multi-linguist, manna from heaven in a borough like Hackney.'

A short, casually dressed Indian man held out his hand and said, 'Pleased to meet you.' At least I thought that was what he said, because his accent was so thick that I couldn't understand a word.

Next was Dev, a short, stocky and very practical guy, full of common sense. I soon learned he wasn't afraid to express his views. Then came Martin, a tough-talking manager, who cared deeply for children.

'Make yourself at home,' Martin said, opening his arms wide and looking round, '*Mi casa es su casa.*'

I raised my eyebrows in pleasant surprise. They seemed enthusiastic, switched on and were happy to let me wander about freely. This was in complete contrast to what I had been expecting, based on my experiences in the neighbouring borough of Haringey. However, I still wasn't won over completely and proceeded with caution.

'Fancy a cuppa?' Dev said. 'We've got five minutes before the case conference.'

Simon and I both nodded. As Dev stirred the sugars into our brew I asked him how things were in Hackney Social Services.

He stopped stirring and looked me in the eye, then across at Simon. 'Is he serious?' he asked. Simon gave a sympathetic nod.

'Harry, you wouldn't believe how bad it is out there at the

moment. I don't even believe it and it's right before my eyes every day. We're seeing children with malnutrition, children who are losing their hair, children who are scavenging in bins. And they're at the bottom of the list. We're snowed under with cases of sexual and physical abuse. Young children battered, shot at, hurled to the wall by drug-addicted parents battling withdrawal. There are children we don't go near, who, in order to survive, have become drug couriers or drug dealers.'

This was something I'd seen often enough when I was on the drugs squad. These were the teenagers who were more likely to kill someone than read a book. Many of them would be stabbed, shot or run over by their employers for messing up a job. No one wanted them back at school. Teachers were only too glad to lose them from the classroom.

'What social worker understands their street language, their criminal network?' Dev asked. 'They terrorize us as they have been terrorized. Our only hope is to get them out before they reach the stage where we simply don't have the strength and resources to manage them. Nobody even believes the stuff that kids are going through out there. Imagine being told by a senior department manager that a teenage girl could not possibly have a £150 to £170 a day drug habit because she didn't get enough pocket money!'

Again, this was something I'd seen with my own eyes, time and time again. Teenage prostitutes addicted to crack raising hundreds of pounds each day by sleeping with multiple clients. They'd often have one baby after another – all of them taken into care. I'd seen stab wounds in their legs after they'd been attacked by clients, pimps and dealers for unpaid debts or refusing to work.

'Try putting a teenage crack addict into a refuge, it's impossible. Refuge workers are simply unable to cope.'

The start of the child protection case conference cut Dev

short, but before we went in, Simon and I agreed that it'd be useful for me to spend the day with him.

During the conference, a fierce debate raged over what should happen to the child in this case. I can't report the details for legal reasons but I can tell you that Simon lost the argument and I came away from the meeting feeling really awed by the compassion and commitment on display. I felt totally reassured by the social worker's determined stance to do what she believed was right in the face of Simon's counter-argument. I was rapidly learning that the majority of social workers were utterly dedicated professionals who deserved respect, even if you didn't agree with them.

I was also learning that all my impressions (and I suspect most of the Met's) were completely wrong. 'You guys have such a bad reputation,' I said to Dev as I joined him at his desk. The police are always moaning about social services, how they never come out, and if they do it takes for ever and then they're only available for five minutes.'

'You need to be in our shoes to understand why,' he told me. 'We're screwed every day of the week for less money, no perks, no benefits and a whole skipful of misery.'

Dev hadn't even warmed up yet. As we drove to his first appointment he fired his next salvo. 'I reckon this is one of the toughest jobs in Britain, if not the toughest. Many of us crumble, some more quickly than others. Others resort to defence mechanisms; a sort of survival whereby they "shut down", numb themselves so they don't "see" what's right in front of them any more. But by doing this they no longer have the will to act, to bring about change. Clients' stories are minimized, or are simply not believed or they ignore them, miss visits and so on.

'Some feel secretly glad when a very difficult client is beaten up. Sometimes they see their management as their client sees their perpetrator and they feel like they're the victims too. But

who watches out for this? Nobody. Nobody but us and we're all
so damn busy it's every man and woman for him or herself until
it hits the fan. Then we all think, well, I could have told you
that was going to happen.'

First stop was William's house. He'd disappeared from school
when he was ten and various letters demanding to know where
he'd gone had been sent to his home. There'd been no response.
No one had actually been sent round to check on William. After
all, it could hardly be called a serious case of abuse, or came close
to being in those categories where the child is in imminent
danger. Then William's brother and sister vanished from school
as well.

'They'd practically turned feral by the time we caught up with
them,' Dev told me as we climbed out of the car and started
walking down the street to the address, a small terraced house on
the edge of a large estate. 'It could have been far, far worse.'

'What happened?'

'Tell you after.' Dev knocked on the door.

It was opened by the mother; she was clearly old before her
time. Her skin was stretched over chicken-thin bones, her deep-
lined face was full of pain, her voice hard and dry.

The kids were all healthy, happy and very, very loud. Mum
was coping having them home through the half-term holidays,
just. After a quick chat and an eagle-eyed appraisal of the house
by Dev, we were off again.

'That,' he said, smiling, 'was a very rare thing.'

'What?'

'A success story. Dad was a violent junkie and small-time
dealer, Mum was a user. Their kids wanted for nothing, every
latest toy was theirs. But alongside that ran a daily stream of
domestic violence. After which came more toys. The kids would
find Dad unconscious and puking on the bathroom floor. Their

job was to help Mum clean up the drug den, full of needles, vomit, bloody tissues and God knows what else. Then they were drug runners for Daddy, delivering the odd little packet, a real door-to-door service.'

Dev paused as he reached the car and spoke to me over the roof. 'I'm a tough bastard, and I know you think you've seen it all already, but when I first went to their place and interviewed the kids I wanted to cry my heart out. Dealer Dad was hanging around outside the room, his foot tapping on the floor, a reminder for them to shut the hell up – a reminder of what happens to grasses. He wasn't worried about the fact that his wife and kids were starving. It was almost as if they hadn't eaten for so long they'd drawn pictures of food on pieces of paper and tried to eat them. That family was saved by the dodgy gear that killed him.'

He got into the car. I stared into space for a few moments before Dev snapped at me. 'Come on! You have no idea what we've got to get through, have you?'

What followed was another home visit to a very well-known sink estate (freshly burned-out car in the street) to check on a vulnerable family of one mother, five kids and several fly-by-night male visitors. Then a meeting with Sarah from our department, part of a joint investigative interview, then back to Dev's desk, where I soon lost count of the phone calls to clients, foster carers, solicitors, other social workers and schools covering evictions, beatings, poverty and missing children. 'And this is a good day,' Dev told me. 'We have to live with the fact that we'll never be on top of things.'

Can it really be this way? Dev had really bowled me over. I had no clue how he coped. He complained a lot to his bosses, which I think helped him psychologically. They told him there was nothing they could do, their hands were tied. Sometimes they passed on his concerns and asked for more funding, and in a few weeks, bureaucrats further up the chain made their decision about people and circumstances they simply couldn't understand. In some way that reassured him. 'I've got used to the word "no",' he told me with a smile. 'The day they say yes, I'll probably have an aneurysm.'

Our system is a mess. How have we let this pass? Kids are not only neglected and abused by their parents, but by the State too. Surely this could be fixed? Surely . . . Otherwise, I thought, I will go mad myself.

'Problem is, Harry, that by doing all that I've generated ridiculous amounts of repetitive paperwork. To be filled out by me. And I do this every day. You think form-filling is bad in the cops, you ain't seen nothing. I have to record those home visits, detailing my concerns and any progress I've made. The joint investigative interview we did with Sarah has to be recorded on a thirty-page child protection report.

'You did the smart thing, Harry. I should have joined the police, too. Yesterday I placed a child in foster care; that's an LAAC (looked-after and accommodated children) set of forms. A real beaut that one, a bureaucrat's wet dream. He also needs a review to set up a care plan and I'll be back tomorrow to make sure everything he needs is in place, make sure he can get to school, fill out some more forms and make a claim so the foster carer will have enough money to provide for him. Then I'll be off to talk to his parents; contact all those involved with him as part of my assessment; arrange and supervise contact with his parents, if appropriate; let the children's reporter know so they can arrange a children's panel, which will require, surprise, surprise, a long and very detailed report at a later date.

'Oh, and did I mention that I had another twenty-something cases, all variations on that theme? I know that the paperwork is supposed to be there to protect the children, but we need extra staff to go with it.

'See, that would be bad enough, but this week I've got four hours' worth of children's meetings, two home visits, two supervised visits between parents and their kids in care plus another ten or so kids I'll have to see out of school hours and about fifty miles worth of driving, plus whatever overriding emergencies we end up with tomorrow.

'Overtime is limited, and we've all reached it. I know we're going to have another disaster soon. And any one of us might get the blame. We're just delaying the inevitable.'

It was with no little relief that I left Dev and his overworked colleagues that day and headed home. I now realized I had stepped into a world of which I knew nothing and had everything still to learn. What I didn't yet know was that before the year was out, Dev would become a victim of his own prediction.

CHAPTER FIVE

EATEN ALIVE

'One of the lessons that came from Victoria Climbié was simply don't mess around,' Rob told me. 'Don't worry about doing nothing because you're worried about allegations. If it's in the child's best interest, bloody well get on with it.' That would be my only rule, I decided, as I snatched a sheet off the antiquated fax.

It said that the local authority had reported that the conditions in the flat were 'bad'. These reports were always difficult to assess as people, especially police officers, often judged others against their own high standards. People can live quite chaotically before we decide to remove a child. Police officers tend to like a certain type of house; Barrett homes on new estates, or small but perfectly formed country cottages. Police officers live insular lives in a world of security; they're never made redundant and only get the boot if they get caught committing a crime. Cops' friends are fellow cops; weddings are like police reunions.

Whenever a beat officer said the conditions were horrendous, I raised my eyes heavenwards knowing that we'd go round and see that yes, there was some mould in the bathroom, some food had been left exposed in the kitchen and yes, there were a few too many cats taking a few too many liberties, but the kids were happy, well-fed and their parents were obviously doing their best. Hardly enough to justify the resources necessary to forcibly remove them from their homes, possibly for ever. I'd once seen an indignant social worker tell off a piqued constable: 'My house is like that on a bad day!'

But of course we checked them all without question. In this case I called up the housing officer who had originally contacted the police. 'It's really bad,' he insisted. 'I've seen everything, or so I thought, this is really something else.' I told him I'd be there in half an hour.

Sarah came with me. Just before we left, Simon came in grinning. He had been to visit our suspected child abuser who had kicked off the riot as part of our strategy of 'monitoring community tensions to ensure public safety'.

'His car's been damaged,' Simon said. 'Someone probably tried to scratch the word "Paedo" along the side, although I'm sure they'd spell it P-e-e-d-o.' No sympathy for him in our office.

Our target was a second-floor flat on a South Hackney estate, a particularly grim-looking place with the look of a Victorian debtors' prison. The intercom was smashed to bits, so I pushed open the heavy fire door and we climbed the concrete stairway. The aroma of dinners from dozens of ethnic backgrounds accompanied us on our ascent and while these wonderful smells would normally have made me very hungry, there were plenty of others to put me off my food. Stains were in every corner of the stairwell. The stink of ammonia made it clear what they were. 'Trisha sucks cock' and other obscenities were scratched on the walls of the urban jungle.

Once on the landing at the target address, I took a look over the side. The concrete balcony afforded little protection from a fall if a fight started up here. As in all council flats in Hackney, the kitchen window was to the right of the brown front door and the bathroom window was to the left. Dirty net curtains blocked my view into the dark kitchen. The bathroom window was frosted. But I could see through the small square windows in the middle of the front door that the hall light was on. My knocking brought no answer.

I knelt down and flipped up the letter box. Like all cops, I did this in a certain way, so that my fingers didn't get trapped if someone kicked or slapped it closed from the other side. I looked in, but from the side. The last thing you need is for a harassed person to shove a broom handle into your face, sick of all the dog faeces and fireworks deposited by local troublemakers.

Tiny specks danced around the naked light bulb in the hall. Flies. Lots of them.

I could just see through the hall and into a bedroom. Suddenly, so quick it made me jump, a kid darted across my field of view. About two-and-a-half; in a top and nappy. This was a relief. Now I could kick the door in if needs be. Twenty years ago, if you were a copper and needed access to a house you simply said you could smell gas and *voilà*, you could apply the skeleton key – the boot.

I coughed. I'd just breathed in and the stench that poured through the open letter box, well, let's just say 'bad' did not do it justice. I let the flap drop and Sarah saw disgust writ large across my face. 'That gross, eh?' she said.

I nodded.

Right. Anger boiled away inside me. I controlled it and put myself in the 'I mean business' mindset. I wanted to kick the door down but I knocked instead, more loudly this time. Still no answer.

The next option was to try out a traditional police ploy. I started to kick the door; not enough for it to actually go in and cause damage, but just enough to get the occupier running to open it as they realize we're not going away. Sometimes the lock is so poor the door just pops open. In this case, however, a male voice shouted and a figure ran to the door, opening it slowly. Sarah and I stepped back, bracing ourselves for a fresh wave of God-knows-what.

The man before us was in his early sixties, wearing a yellowed vest covered in food stains of varying vintages, baggy tracksuit bottoms (also stained) and black socks. Unshaven, his face covered in dozens of tiny scabs, his greasy unwashed white receding hair was swept over a bald spot. I almost laughed. Despite everything he was still vain enough to try to cover his baldness.

I did the introductions and asked if we could come in. 'No,' he replied in a flat voice.

Again, I tried not to laugh. I wanted to tell him: 'You are a dirty, little old man with something to hide and I am six foot four, in my mid-thirties, a member of the biggest gang in London and you have pissed me off. Who is going to win here?' Instead I kept my mouth shut and remained calm, professional and uncompromising. He edged back. I stepped inside. An easy win.

As we entered the hall I clocked the kitchen to my left. Stacks of dirty plates, mouldy food, an overflowing, stinking bin – actually make that overflowing, stinking flat. I couldn't see the kitchen worktop. I didn't want to know about the fridge. Dirty nappies and cat faeces covered the sticky floor.

I was standing there speechless when a young woman, in pretty much the same attire and in the same state as the man, appeared in the hallway. She was holding a child. He was also covered in little scabs; they were on his arms as well as his face.

The young woman's eyes were open wide, frightened. It was obvious why we were there.

My head spinning, I said: 'Show me the child's bedroom.' We were ushered towards the back of the flat where another child of the same age was sat on the bed.

Suddenly I couldn't move. I looked down. My feet were practically glued to the bedroom carpet by . . . well, I still don't know what it could have been. I pulled and my shoe came away with a *schhhlup*. 'What the f—?'

'Oh sorry,' said the man, 'I should have warned you about that.'

Sarah stayed in the hallway, her hand over her mouth; my face must have been the definition of disgust at that moment. With some difficulty, I stepped back in the hallway and, while Sarah spoke to them, I got on the phone and asked for a social worker to attend.

Besides the mysterious gummy substance, the bedroom floor was strewn with old clothes, rubbish and cat shit. There was no chance I'd let the children stay here another minute.

Brenda arrived and we retired to the balcony to come up with a plan of action. I was very surprised to find that we both had very different ideas as to what we should do.

To me, it was obvious. The children had to be placed in foster care, their carers had to be arrested, charged and, once the address was made spotless, after a case conference, then and only maybe then could we consider returning them.

Brenda disagreed. 'It's already early evening,' she told me, looking at her watch. 'Finding foster care tonight would be very difficult. Besides,' she added, 'there are other options. Let's see if there are other family members they could stay with.'

This was a fairly typical disagreement between police and social services. Our job is to solve crimes by protecting the victims and bringing the offender to justice, while social services' job is to try to repair the family unit, to see if they can stick everything back together again.

She argued that this was a borderline case. This may seem like a crazy point of view when you take into account the state of the flat, but it is fairly easy to improve a family's hygiene.

'I'm not going to give in, Harry,' Brenda said. 'I'm not saying you're pressuring me but I always regret the one time I gave in to pressure from a policeman to make a statement against a mother who then lost her children. I'll never let myself be put in that position again.'

I considered the options. Would it be right to split the children from their struggling but loving mother who would be able to cope with the right help? Or had the line been crossed? Was this a case of serious neglect which meant the family must be split, possibly for ever?

Perhaps I didn't know enough about this case yet. Removing the kids from the family really should be the last resort.

'Fair enough,' I said, and went back inside. 'Where's the father?' I asked.

'With his parents,' the man said. 'They live nearby.'

We took the mother and kids with us and drove the short distance to her in-laws. The social worker and I were delighted to discover that it was a modern terraced home – and it was *clean*. The father was also there. We all squeezed into the lounge where I described in no uncertain terms the awful living conditions in which we found their grandchildren. Turning to the father, I didn't try to hide my disgust as I said: 'Your kids are literally living in a rat-hole.' He hung his head in shame; he didn't even try to explain.

Everyone was ready to go, but I just didn't get it. There was something about the lack of shock and outrage from the grandparents and the father that worried me. What possible reason could there be for his kids not staying here? I thought of my experience with the 'cave-man' and asked to see the father's room.

As I ascended the immaculate staircase and reached the landing, I noticed that the father had hung his head even lower. I sensed what was coming. 'Brace yourself,' I said to Brenda. I pulled open the door and stepped into another world. His room was a carbon copy of the mother's flat.

Cigarette butts littered the floor. The armchair, shiny with grease, was covered in ash and cigarette burns. The carpet was utterly rancid, covered in age-old spilled alcohol that had never been mopped up. It was like being in Hackney's worst boozer.

Perhaps this was more of a mental health issue? Could it be that the parents have special needs? 'Oh God, well that's it, they can't stay here,' Brenda said.

'Let's try another relative,' I suggested.

There was an aunt. By the time we got there it was late at night. This time, however, after checking the entire house, we were satisfied that it was a clean and safe enough place to leave the children. Sarah meanwhile had looked up the family and found an old police file on the mother. As a child, she had been subjected to the same sort of neglect. History was obviously repeating itself.

We later cautioned the mother for neglect and a few days later, after meetings with social workers, a specialist cleaning team stormed the flat, took it to bits, scrubbed every last millimetre, let the mother and grandfather back and brought the kids home.

We were soon back to see the same family, though. This time, it was Sarah who took the call. As she rolled up to the estate, she saw fire engines everywhere. To her growing horror she saw that the family's flat was burned black. Showing her badge, she asked a fireman what was up. 'Unbelievable really,' he said, 'I don't think I've ever seen so many fire hazards in one place. The kids were playing with lighters and matches and, well, here we are.'

It only takes a small amount of smoke to kill a child. Is it considered neglect if the parents forget to pick up a lighter off the coffee table? Is that worth calling child services for? Probably not, but lighters left within reach of a toddler were all too common in the homes of drug addicts and alcoholics.

To our relief, the kids were fine but we were frustrated to learn that they'd been in the care of the grandmother at the time and so we had to arrest her, not the mother. Their cycle of neglect would undoubtedly continue.

Problems with hygiene were all too common. A while later, I returned to the same estate with Keira, another former WPC who'd undergone the overnight transformation into a detective. By this time I felt a great deal more confident in the job and was keen to pass on all I'd learned from Rob and Lucy to our newest member, but neither of us could have been prepared for what we were about to encounter.

It was another home visit, this time to an elderly couple who were bringing up their grandchild on their own. We'd received reports they'd been struggling to cope and that the flat was in a bad way.

The grandfather answered the door. He was missing a limb and covered in scabs. 'Do you mind me asking why you have those scabs?' I asked. 'Are you ill?'

He stared back at me blankly for a moment. 'Oh, these!' he said suddenly. 'Nah, that's the bloody rats. They nibble my face at night.'

Good God.

'And what about your . . .?' I said, pointing at the missing limb.

'Yeah, well, that was an infection from the rats; the docs had to lop it off.'

Christ. They were gradually eating him alive.

Once that was cleared up, it was on to my next appointment. From the moment I stepped inside the flat a low vicious growling had come from upstairs. The house was a tip. There was hardly any furniture, rubbish and bin liners containing clothes covered the floor; there were sheets that looked like they hadn't been washed in years draped over a tatty sofa doubling as a bed.

'Tidy this mess up,' was about all I could tell the apathetic, skinny, unshaven, heavily tattooed father. He looked just like Cletus from *The Simpsons*. He grinned as I started to climb the stairs.

I was steadily overpowered by the stink of animal faeces as I climbed. He started to say, 'I wouldn't mate . . .' but it was too late. The foul faecal smell was forgotten in an instant when an enraged pit-bull leaped for my face; its jaws snapped shut just shy of my nose – held by a long chain clamped to the leg of a cot.

I ran back downstairs. I couldn't believe I'd actually seen this. As part of a short child protection course I'd been shown a sad but very effective video on dangerous dogs. It started with a piece of home video footage with a man talking about how his lovely pit bull 'Ricky' loves his two-year-old daughter. The next scene is of police footage two years later, after the beast had torn his daughter to shreds. People who keep pit bulls and toddlers together should go to jail. No question.

Arriving at the bottom of the stairs I explained that the dog had to go now or we'd remove his kids. And I meant it. Unbelievably, the father had to think about this, but I'd already called the dog people and the creature was destroyed. I let him say goodbye to the dog – after all, the animal wasn't to blame for its owner's stupidity.

CHAPTER SIX

YOU'D NEVER KNOW

I sat in front of the computer screen, my heart racing. I'd seen child pornography once before and had not reacted well. It was just one poor-quality image, when I visited the porn squad at New Scotland Yard as part of a training course. It left me feeling nauseous and angry. I didn't need to see it; why had they thought it was necessary? It had taken me quite a few deep breaths to regain my composure and the images stayed etched into my mind for far too long.

I eventually came to understand why this was a good idea. Far better to be introduced to the horrors of child pornography this way, in controlled circumstances, surrounded by professionals, than to have to face it on your own, in the line of duty. Besides, it's important to know whether you can handle it or not.

Sarah and I were in Oxford, visiting the offices of the specialist private company who had examined the hard drive from John's computer. They had a result.

'OK, they're just pictures,' I told myself as we discussed the case and others with the analysts as matter-of-factly as possible. One of the analysts, a young woman, explained how they found the files and where they were hidden on the man's PC. Christ, how can they do this every day and not fall to bits? I wondered.

Asking if we were ready, she opened the file.

The images were of children aged between nine and eleven posing naked. Sarah and I studied the background, looking for clues as to their origin. A small item on a bedroom shelf can determine the county and town where the picture was taken. Most importantly, we were looking to see whether any of these images were taken in John's house. None were.

I felt like I'd been let off the hook. Don't get me wrong, the photographs were indecent and my stomach tightened with anger looking at their innocent faces, but they were not of the nightmare-inducing standard they could have been.

We asked for a disk of sixteen images. We never supply more than this in court as these prove to be more than enough for any jury to bear and everyone gets the point by then.

Then it was time to speak to the suspect.

He'd lost so much weight that I didn't recognize him. He'd aged ten years; his face was haggard and sunken and he walked with a stoop. He said his life had been ruined and he broke down as I interviewed him.

I recalled what Rob said about men discovering sides to them that they never knew existed. My own experiences have led me to believe that because the Internet has made child pornography easily accessible, a number of people have found it 'titillating' to look at mild images. While this is of course hideous, this is the limit of their perversion and they do not go on to actually physically abuse children.

Before this case I would not have believed in the 'curiosity' argument, now I'm not so sure. But he is still a paedophile. I guess even among those who have a sexual interest in children there are still those who pose greater risks than others. But how can you be sure? Of course the first question we always ask in cases like John's is: 'Does he have access to children?' Invariably the answer is yes, but we certainly won't put the child through a traumatic interview, asking them, 'Has your uncle abused you?' Instead, social services will speak to them on a general, non-specific level to find out if anything is wrong; if there is reason to be concerned.

In this case, John admitted the offence and due to the mild nature of the material he was cautioned. He was placed on the sex offenders' register and we informed the relevant people about this. It's a quirk of the law that if we had sent him to court and he had been given a discharge, he wouldn't have gone on the register.

So that was it. Case closed. I felt that he had been punished. As I watched him leave the station I hoped that time would prove me right, that the shock of the investigation had pushed his perverse paedophilic curiosity back to the dark recess from whence it had come.

After that was over it was time for a late breakfast meeting with Rob in Bodrum. This was always an education. He stirred his thick, sweet coffee and laid the spoon on the saucer. 'OK, Harry, I want you to put these cases of child abuse in order of seriousness:

1. Four-year-old Maria is made to do housework, told that she's ugly and given minimum food.
2. Five-year-old Jimmy is forced to give his dad oral sex.
3. Eighteen-month-old Kay cries a lot, and in frustration her angry mother shakes her.'

Like everybody else, I got it wrong and put 2 first. Of course, it's 3 – even mild shaking of a baby can kill.

But I was gradually getting to grips with the job. This was demonstrated after breakfast, when a man accused of paedophilia turned himself in at the front desk. I made a bet with the guys that I could pick him out from the packed reception. I got him straight away: thick glasses, stained shirt and bad teeth.

Of course, it wasn't always that simple. We picked up a 'gentleman' paedophile in his early fifties, perfectly groomed and incredibly polite. As I booked him in a WPC chastised me: 'You meanie – why on earth have you arrested that lovely old man?'

The old, crack-house-busting version of me wanted to say, 'For repeatedly buggering his stepson,' but the new improved version said something more restrained.

Like many paedophiles, he was incredibly devious. Usually, they are so convincing that it's very rare to ever see them become the target of a lynch mob; it was far more common to see the people closest to them leaping to their defence.

They often targeted vulnerable single mothers, especially if they were unattractive and unintelligent and had several kids. They're not used to being given lots of love and attention and this understandably overrides rational thought – instead of thinking, This guy's not good for my kids, she's thinking, What an amazing man, how lucky am I?

One such case involved a fifty-year-old man from Hackney who'd contacted several single mothers via a chat-line. When the man, who was posing as a TV cameraman, was arrested, the officers found a list of twelve children he was grooming for abuse. He was jailed for two years.

Men like this were not uncommon, so much so that after making a thorough risk-assessment, we'd warn vulnerable mothers about certain individuals. On Hackney's sprawling estates were dozens of large, troubled families with five or six kids that everyone seemed to know. Usually several dads were involved, so there was lots of coming and going at home and it was all to easy for a paedophile to worm his way in. When any offence was reported it was often impossible for us to get anywhere because there were too many lovers/fathers/kids involved.

Lucy and I paid a visit to one such vulnerable family in a block of flats in a Hackney estate. Everybody seemed to know everybody else. We'd discovered that a family 'friend' (i.e. the mother's on–off lover) had been previously accused of child sex abuse on more than one occasion and, although he had avoided prosecution, we were very concerned.

These sorts of visits were fraught with danger; we had to trust the mother's discretion. It was always possible that our warning would be telegraphed to the entire community within the hour, with terrible consequences for the suspect.

I knew of one case where a man charged with sexual abuse of a child had hobbled into a police station. 'Thanks to you lot I've been beaten up,' he said, 'now what are you going to do about it? That's what I want to know.' Although his allegation would be investigated, I remember seeing the hapless shrug of the station officer. The community had turned against him and he had a snowball's chance in hell of taking his attackers to court.

Ultimately, our first duty is to the children. If a suspected paedophile has access to a family with young children then it's only right that they're warned. This is one of the principles behind 'Sarah's Law'. Sarah's Law, named after Sarah Payne, who was abducted and murdered by convicted sex offender Roy Whiting in 2000, will allow parents, guardians and carers to ask police whether people who have access to their child have committed child sexual offences. Officers then have the option to reveal the information or take further action if they believe children may be at risk.

Successful trials of Sarah's Law have taken place in Warwickshire, Cleveland, Hampshire and Cambridgeshire. Out of seventy-nine applications for information, ten have led to disclosures – with no vigilantism as a result.[6] A decision is yet to be made as to whether Sarah's Law will be rolled out across the UK. So far, it has proved to be a source of reassurance; parents need to be involved in child protection and have a right to know, as well as the authorities, whether convicted child sex offenders have access to their children.

In this case, the mother was out but her seventeen-year-old daughter, very polite and very pregnant, invited us in. The interior of the flat was typical of others on the estate that Lucy and I had visited. A mountain of dirty plates in the sink, overflowing ashtrays, drawings on the walls and the *pièce de résistance*: a whopping great plasma TV in the lounge.

After the daughter brewed us a surprisingly great cuppa, the mother appeared and Lucy started to explain why we were there.

She barely managed to finish the first couple of sentences before the mother interrupted, 'E'd never touch my kids. I'm telling ya, I'd know.' She drew deeply on her cigarette. 'It's bollocks. Ya know 'e ain't done nuffin', she's a little liar, ya know.'

I couldn't help but think that taxpayers had paid for that cigarette. She puffed on the damn thing as if her life depended on it.

Her body language screamed total denial. The people who can't admit that suspects are paedophiles are the hardest to deal with. For the paedophile, niceness is a means to an end, not a character trait. They're professional liars operating among good-willed amateurs – they paint the picture people want to see. They're churchgoers, they help out locals, the elderly, they're generous with their time. They're more popular than most men their age who pursue more selfish interests in life. By the time the people they've duped are confronted with the unpalatable truth, they've invested so much of themselves in trusting the accused that they refuse to accept that they have indeed been fooled.

In this case, the mother had done nothing wrong but we had

to be absolutely sure that she would take steps to protect her children if the need arose and so I spelled out the possible dangers in no uncertain terms.

Of course, we were deceived all the time by those who promised to do everything we ask. The moment we'd gone they'd phone the suspect, crowing about what the Old Bill had been saying about them.

But what seemed to do the trick in this case was that we recorded the warning. 'Let me make this absolutely clear,' I said, 'if we hear that your man has been doing any babysitting, we'll be back and will leave with your children.'

'What? That ain't fuckin' fair!'

I shrugged. The message clearly received and understood, Lucy and I took our leave.

The effects of long-term abuse in these sorts of conditions were sometimes catastrophic. A couple of Hackney children from single-parent families were so badly abused that they became totally unmanageable and were placed in special secure units outside London. I had encountered one such child when she was brought to the station spitting and kicking like a girl possessed; it was impossible to keep her in a cell unrestrained. She was utterly wild, not quite feral but almost.

Every now and again we'd travel to the secure units to investigate an alleged claim of abuse. These kids lose all normal sense of what sex is because they're so traumatized. It would usually be an outrageous accusation like all of the workers at the institute raped them in full view of the CCTV cameras. But this was precisely the reason why we had to investigate every claim – they made themselves vulnerable by making so many accusations that they were never believed, even when they were telling the truth. These allegations were always born of their history, not from any wrongdoing at the centre, a truly incredible place with workers so dedicated I can't begin to imagine how they manage to do the job they do. Having said that, one girl made so many accusations that we held a special strategy meeting to discuss not investigating any more allegations she made, as her fantasies were taking up so much time and manpower.

When I spoke to the 'gentleman' paedophile, I found it tremendously difficult to get anywhere. I still had so much to learn. 'What nonsense!' he shouted back at me after I put the claims of the mother and child to him. 'How can you believe them over me? Only a sick monster would do such a thing.'

I watched as Rob took him apart in what was an interviewing masterclass. Our suspect ranted against the police and society, as if he were an academic who had made paedophilia his lifelong study – yet of course he was not one himself. This soon went by the wayside as Rob skilfully and sympathetically put the evidence to him.

As the interview progressed, the suspect gradually took up a stance of 'political paedophilia' without even realizing he was doing it. It was a bizarre attempt to portray himself as being of a sexual persuasion that an ignorant society failed to understand. He believed that adults should be allowed to have sex with children, claiming that it was a natural impulse and that kids enjoyed it – and compared paedophiles to gay people, a group that had long been deliberately alienated by society.

He complained that we weren't doing enough to protect him; that his life was in danger from lynch mobs. He recalled the smallest detail of every paedophile case that had made it into the media in recent years. 'We're being witch-hunted,' he raged, 'and you're the tools of a puritanical society. We're not going to go away, you know.'

'Maybe not,' Rob said, 'but we're going to put you in prison for a very, *very* long time indeed.'

CHAPTER SEVEN

GETTING TO THE TRUTH

The two men sat in wait for Bill Malcolm on an icy Thursday night in February 2000. They watched their target shamble up the East London street; a lonely figure, shopping bag in hand. Although forty-six-year-old Malcolm lived in a shabby third-floor flat (so there were neighbours in close proximity), it backed on to a noisy Tube line and was surrounded by woodland. The road was bordered by a triangle made up of the A116, A117 and A118, so there were plenty of getaway routes. It would take the cops for ever to check all the CCTVs and search for witnesses – not that there'd be many who'd come forward.

The men gave Malcolm, who worked as a security guard in the City, enough time to get settled, and, no doubt checking the street was free of passers-by, they left their car and rang the bell at 9.30 p.m.

The moment Malcolm saw them he couldn't have been surprised.

He had first been jailed in 1981, for the abuse of and unlawful intercourse with an eight-year-old girl. Despite being prosecuted for a separate serious sexual offence against a nine-year-old boy at the same time, he was released after only one year. Unbelievably, after he was released, he began raping the same little girl: her worst nightmare had returned. He was jailed again, this time for two and a half years in 1984, after the girl's older sister reported him.

Malcolm was a close friend of Leslie 'Catweazle' Bailey, a notorious paedophile. This relationship meant he was questioned in regards to the murder of a fourteen-year-old boy called Jason Swift, who was garrotted during a paedophilic orgy in a Hackney flat. Bailey, along with others, was part of a gang that may have murdered up to nine children, including Jason. Bailey was jailed for killing Jason and was murdered in prison in 1993. The police failed to find the other members of Bailey's gang. Malcolm was also questioned by police investigating the killings of two other boys – Mark Tildesley and Barry Lewis.

He was released without charge.

Ten years later, in 1994, Malcolm appeared at the Old Bailey on charges of rape, indecent assault and cruelty – a total of thirteen unforgivable crimes were read to the court. A legal technicality meant that Judge Kenneth Richardson, 'with considerable regret', was forced to let him go. Malcolm had no chance of a fair hearing, the judge said, as those allegedly abused included previous victims. That meant his earlier convictions would inevitably be revealed to jurors.

At the time he made his decision, Judge Richardson did not have access to a report written by Dr Jeremy Coid, a psychologist at Hackney Hospital. The report said: '[Malcolm] has marked paedophile tendencies of a strongly sadistic nature. For the foreseeable future, Mr Malcolm must be considered a real and immediate danger to any children to whom he might have access.'

Was that justice?

The men took Malcolm upstairs, knelt him down in his hallway, and shot him once in the head. A real contract killer would have shot two or three times, to make sure – three in the head, you know they're dead. When the amateur killers left, Malcolm was still alive but he had bled to death by the following morning.

The girl Malcolm abused, by then a twenty-seven-year-old mother and alcoholic, told the national press: 'I just wish it was me who had shot him. I'd love to meet the people who did it to say thank you – and buy them the biggest drink in the world. Hearing "The Animal" was dead is the happiest I've ever felt.

'Every day, he would hang around, threatening me, and he would follow me to school . . . He was an animal and he ruined my life. I was receiving psychiatric help for years; I became an alcoholic and it was only recently that I stopped blaming myself . . . when I heard he had been killed, I went out and got drunk. It was the best news I'd had in years.'

No one gave the police any useful information to help catch Malcolm's killers, and no one admitted knowing him. The only people who did speak out simply wanted to thank the killers.

In a local pub, the Blakesley Arms, the landlord said: 'Everyone in here wants to buy them a big drink. They've done a public service. This is the East End of London, where you don't grass on someone who sorts out a child molester.'

One local resident spoke for many when he said: 'It's a relief . . . I have three grandchildren, aged eleven, nine and three, and they used to play on the fields outside his flat. I dread to think what could have happened. If I'd known about him, I'd have kicked his door down and warned him off.'

Malcolm's brother, living in France, said: 'If you have a piece of dirt contaminating the street, you remove it. I loathed my brother and he got what he deserved. Even if I knew who killed him, I wouldn't tell the police. The killers are welcome in my home any time.'

One of his neighbours was the eighteen-year-old older brother of Daniel Handley, who was kidnapped and murdered in 1994 by two paedophiles who met in prison. Handley lived next door to Malcolm for two years without knowing about his criminal past. 'I hope it's the beginning of a long line of executions,' he said.

Retired Detective Chief Superintendent Roger Stoodley, who led the team that arrested Leslie Bailey, said: 'As he is connected with child abuse, then he deserves it. I have no sympathy for him. How many times do we have to convict these people before something drastic happens?'

There was also little sympathy from the Home Office. Not long after the killing, a spokesman was asked where paedophiles might be able to restart their lives in safety: 'Wherever they want,' he said. 'A spent conviction is time served, a debt paid. These people are free citizens.'

A couple of months after the hit, the flat was still empty and the bloodstains were still on the floor. His is a murder no one wants solved.[7]

Now I've got one sitting in front of me.

I'm supposed to interview him. I'm well used to dealing with difficult people. I've lost count of the number of crack addicts, dealers and prostitutes I've interviewed. With these people, though, it can sometimes even be slightly light-hearted – we both know it's a game and most of the time there's no real consequences. They're bailed, maybe we'll see them again, maybe not, maybe they'll clean up, maybe they won't.

But there's a whole different mentality when dealing with the safety of kids. People who are normally quite libertarian, who are against the death penalty, find themselves struggling to justify keeping the bastards alive.

I thought this department needed a kick up the backside to get it moving but by now I realized that this job required skills not contained in any job description. As a police officer, I'm supposed to execute nothing but the letter of the law. But police officers naturally have a 'castrate and hang 'em high' disposition towards child abusers because we see, all too often, every aspect of the damage done.

When we'd arrived at the station with my suspect, I pulled the custody officers to one side. The last thing I wanted written on the white board was 'Cell 3 – Indecent assault on a child' so SAO (Serious Arrestable Offence) went up instead, which covers a wide variety of crimes. At least now the other prisoners wouldn't find out and exact their own form of righteous vengeance, or at the very least kick off in the cells, yelling at my suspect, telling him what's going to happen to him when he gets to prison.

As soon as I'd explained this to the officers, their body language changed. Although they remained professional, they still managed to radiate utter abhorrence at the man in front of them. They tut-tutted, muttered under their breath and avoided eye contact as they booked the man in. They may as well have been chanting 'Scum' over and over.

This all-too-natural reaction had been a constant struggle for me. Throughout my career I had been very much a member of the gung-ho school of policing; I'd signed up for the excitement and impossible challenges and the Met had delivered; I'd raided dozens of drug dens, chased countless fleeing criminals and had been in some legendary rucks. I even got involved when I was on my holidays in Holland and chased a mugger through the streets of Amsterdam, brought him down and delivered him to the local nick. Proactive policing is in my blood and I want criminals to pay for what they've done. But what price can you put on what a child abuser has done? Most people believe that the sentences dished out to paedophiles rarely appear to reflect the seriousness of the crime, which is not surprising really.

The problem was, if we were to have any chance at all of nailing the guy, I had to make him like me. At the moment it was his word against the child's. We needed an admission, something that would save the child from cross-examination. The only way I could get that was via a carefully choreographed interview. Even then it had to be the right kind of admission, one that would guarantee serious jail time, not a lousy suspended sentence.

'Rule number one, Harry,' Rob had told me, leaning over the desk, his huge coffee mug steaming in front of him, 'always shake a paedophile by the hand. Show them warmth. Rule number two: on no account reveal your disgust.'

I wasn't sure I was going to do it. But I had to. Somehow.

The case had started when a three-year-old girl had told her nursery teacher that 'Daddy licked my noo-noo'. To those not having dealt with this type of allegation before it seems obvious what the teacher should do next – call social services. But invariably, this sort of thing comes without warning. Are you one hundred per cent certain you heard and understood correctly? Did the child know what they meant? Could they have been trying to talk about something else, something entirely innocent? Your actions at that moment may very well prove to be the defining moment of that child's life. Very often people won't believe what they've just heard. Those that do will be disgusted and frightened for the child. Sometimes, referrals are not made because the teacher is frightened of recriminations if they're proven to be wrong.

There is conflicting advice for teachers in these circumstances. My advice is unequivocal and dead simple. Don't tell anyone except social services. Don't ask the child any questions except 'What did you say?' or 'What do you mean?' for clarification.

Fortunately, in this case the teacher made the right decision. We gave the child a medical the following day during which she repeated what she told the teacher. We took a swab to ascertain if there was any DNA from her father inside her vagina. The forensics preserved, her underclothes seized, we were ready to interview.

I'd made sure the interview room was tidy and the correct forms were laid out, neat and professional. I smiled and shook his hand, offered him coffee and took a seat opposite. Starting with a few 'welfare' questions, I tried to make the suspect feel cared for. As if he really was a client.

Here we go.

I start with a chat about his family, I'm friendly, caring, boring, putting him and his solicitor into a stupor.

I slowly move towards the incident; taking him through each step; no judgement, just friendship. We reach the crucial part. He is playing with his daughter on the bed.

'There is no way my head was near her.'

Could his head have brushed her groin? We get to 'yes' via 'no' and 'maybe'. Inside I'm taut as a tightrope, but I radiate calm.

'Was she wearing any underwear?' I get the answer I want. I have to keep up the flow, act as if this is normal. Could his lips have accidentally brushed her legs? No disgust, it's all just a laugh.

'Yes.'

Now, could his lips have accidentally touched her vagina?

I sense his pleasure. I could see the thoughts written all over our suspect's face. Paedophiles don't 'harm' children; the kids love it, don't they? He's thinking, It was her fault. She led me on.

I get the reply I need, and shoot a 'Shut the fuck up' look at the solicitor. In any normal criminal case the solicitor would have interrupted and rescued their client. But these cases are different. In one case I had a solicitor storm out of the interview room once he found out his client was clearly guilty of an indecent assault on a child. Former cop, I suspected.

In this case, the solicitor visibly shrinks back. He's given me a free hand. Good man. 'If your lips touched your daughter's vagina, I imagine your mouth was slightly open.'

'Possibly.'

He's back there, remembering. He wants to share. I've already got him to prison and the child will be safe, but I'm not finished. I want years not months. I speak softly, 'So that could mean your tongue went inside?' He's too far now.

'Yes.'

Stay calm. Now for the kill: 'This happened for a while?'

'Yes.' I can hear the slam of the prison door. I want to shout at him but I bottle everything up, maintaining the pretence, and gently draw the interview to a close.

'Good job, Harry,' Rob said outside. I nod. All I can think of is that I need to hit something; release the adrenalin and the anger that's been building up. To immerse yourself in the mind-set of a paedophile and to portray almost support for what he had enjoyed is hard. You need a long time out afterwards. It's very similar to coming out of pitch-blackness into extreme sunlight. If you open your eyes too early, you'll be blinded.

Rob put his hand on my shoulder, 'Now you've got through that, I know you've got what it takes. It's time I really put you to work.'

'Thanks, Rob,' I said, and took off, relieved to be getting away after what had been my toughest day so far.

I didn't know it then but my duties were far from over that night.

CHAPTER EIGHT

FERAL FAMILIES AND CRACK KIDS

As I drove through North London, a Vauxhall swerved danger-ously across oncoming traffic and screeched to a halt outside a pub, about fifty metres ahead of me. Interesting, I thought, and slowed down.

A man opened the passenger door.

He had a handgun.

'Fuck!' I watched, holding my breath as he walked up to the pub door, kicked it open, fired six times and jumped back into the car, where the driver was already revving the engine to a scream. They burned rubber. My heart pumping, I took off after them, weaving in and out of the traffic, dialling 999 on the mobile, trying not to let them spot me. This was extremely difficult to do. (Tip for drivers: sometimes when you're cut up by a lone maniac, it'll be an undercover officer trying to catch up with a suspect he's been following, so try not to beep and do let them get away with it, just in case – thanks.) Normally it would require a team of unmarked cars to follow one suspect across London.

They pulled over in a street in Kentish Town. I double-parked some way back, climbed out of my car and walked towards them.

A third man appeared. By now I was talking to an operator, had described the scene and an ARV (Armed Response Vehicle) was on its way.

As I drew close I pretended to be having a row with my 'girl-friend' on the phone; God knows what the police operator made of my performance as I told her I really loved her and begged her to give her one more chance. A couple laughed at me as they walked past.

The three men split up and so I followed the gunman to the high street where I saw the ARV driving slowly towards us, sirens off. It passed the gunman and neared me. Keeping my right hand low, I signalled that they should pull over and let me in. The driver saw, but, thanks to my haggard appearance, he assumed I was a nutter and didn't slow down. As they drew level I whacked the bottom of my fist hard on the passenger window. That got their attention. They stopped; I explained who I was, jumped in the back and pointed out the target. They pulled out their weapons and made a headline-grabbing 'hard-stop' arrest in the high street.

Officers who had gone to the scene of the shooting found that every one of the hit man's bullets had missed their target. The sound of the gunfire had been covered by punk tunes playing at full volume, and the would-be victims had drunk on unawares. The bullet holes had to be pointed out to them before they believed a shooting had occurred.

Until then I'd been buzzing with what was undeniably a ter-rific collar; I assumed that the shooting was part of an ongoing feud between two high-profile drugs gangs. But I knew from bitter experience from the drugs squad that many drug dealers have wives and children, just like everybody else.

I also knew that stuck to the fridge in the typical-looking kitchen would be pictures painted by a very young child. A family scene: Mum, Dad, kids, smiling sun, blue sky and green garden.

Now that family in the drawing was about to be torn apart. Drugs are at the root of so much misery for kids. If we could eliminate drug addiction (I'm not naive enough to think that this is actually possible) then we'd have enough resources to tackle all the remaining child abuse several times over.

The first time I'd witnessed the effect of drug-dealing parents on children was when I led the drugs squad in Haringey. I raided a crack house in Tottenham at daybreak with four officers and someone from the dog squad. Dawn raids were a rarity (I hated early starts) but the big advantage was that we wouldn't have to spend all night booking criminals in; we would be able to do it within our normal shift. And, as reluctant as I was to start early, I did want to spend some time with my newly pregnant wife and my six-year-old son.

The door flew open on our first swing and we piled in screaming as usual, each running to our pre-allocated rooms, hitting light-switches as we went. When I charged into a bedroom on the first floor I saw someone hiding under the duvet. I threw off the covers.

Two small children huddled together looked at me in terror.

I stood dumbfounded. My first thought was that we had stormed the wrong address. But we found that the garage had been converted into a crack den, a place where users could buy and smoke crack. Inside were two large stinking grey-green sofas covered in burns and worn shiny from age and sweat. Home-made crack pipes were everywhere, along with a bunch of stolen credit cards and other personal documents. Matches, beer cans and newspapers covered the concrete floor. The electricity meter had been 'hotwired', a lethal DIY bodge job of exposed wires that could easily have killed these kids if they'd wandered in and brushed against them.

Amazingly, there is no law stating that kids, of any age, should not be left home alone. Such incidents are judged on a case-by-case basis and a neglect case is often squeezed out of them under the 1933 Children and Young Persons' Act if you can show that there was 'wilful neglect in a manner likely to cause unnecessary suffering or injury to health'. A twelve-year-old who accidently scalds a one-year-old while babysitting is a long way from leaving a four-year-old home alone. They usually get found out when the child has to dial 999 for some reason – after starting a fire or injuring themselves, for example. I'd encountered a few cases of parents going to work, leaving their preschoolers home alone. The worst ones of all are when the mother goes on holiday leaving the children alone and the *News of the World* gets the scoop. In this case the children were clearly in a highly dangerous environment.

'Hi, kids, have you got a mummy or daddy?' I asked. They nodded.

'Do you know where they are?' They shook their heads.

'Do you want to go to school?' They nodded.

They were seven and nine years old. They were lovely kids and, like so many we encountered, they seemed totally unaware as to just how extraordinary their circumstances were.

Bill the dog handler, a six-five, seventeen-stone skinhead, was one of the most terrifying-looking policemen you're ever likely to meet but he soon managed to get the kids smiling and they were giggling as they washed, dressed and fed and played fetch with the police dog while I rang their school and arranged for a teacher to come and pick them up.

It sickened me (and still does) that so many children are in these circumstances. There are thousands of parents with drug problems in Hackney and only a few places where we can send kids; sometimes we were forced to leave children in the care of drug users – it depends on how well they manage their habit.

The worst offenders by far are crack addicts. Crack cocaine is thought to be responsible for sending 20,000 children into care (in 2006 there were 60,000 children in care in the UK, costing the taxpayer £1.6 billion). Researchers at Brunel University found that 34 per cent of childcare cases were drug-related. In another study, out of 186 children taken from 100 families, 67 had one or both parents addicted to crack.

Crack, the cheapest and most addictive drug there is, arrived in the UK at the end of the eighties. By the end of the nineties, use had reached epidemic proportions in our inner cities. It's almost impossible to overstate just how addictive crack is. Some people become hooked within twenty-four hours of trying it for the first time, constantly seeking to recapture that first God-like high.

Drug addicts nearly always put their own selfish needs above those of their children. If the overriding priority is heroin or crack cocaine then all the related utensils are kept close to hand – lighters, pipes, needles, knives. Drug addicts are nearly always heavy smokers, so cigarettes, Rizla papers, lighters, matches and ashtrays are also usually within easy reach. The next need down the chain might be alcohol, so there'll be a ready supply of cans and bottles.

A dirty, hungry child is a big financial barrier and physical inconvenience to scoring drugs. Trying to satisfy their own insatiable cravings takes first priority; the child's care and safety is put on the back burner. A hungry child will pick up and eat drugs that have been left lying around. A bored child, its parents zonked out, will start playing with whatever's close to hand, whether it be a whisky bottle or matches and lighters.

I was always of the mind that if the house was littered in such a way that we should prosecute. It was a clear sign that the needs of the children came after the parents' cravings. Many drug-addicted parents believed that they were able to manage and hide their addictions from their children without putting them at risk. They claimed they were able to make sure their children were fed and adequately clothed before they began their daily drugs rituals but this was usually not the case.

If anything, it was the child who took on the burden of looking after their parent. An addict's child is always in a state of worry, looking out for danger. At the same time they try to become as invisible as possible, in case of physical attack. Living such a stressful life, surrounded by chaos and violence with no one to turn to, ages children prematurely. Enormous bags hang under their eyes, they grow slowly, their hair thins out and they often become ill. Children of addicts sometimes become addicts themselves as a way of becoming closer to their parents. Thousands of teenage girls in the UK have sold their bodies, often having unprotected sex in return for the drug.* As I'd already seen for myself on countless occasions, these girls gave birth to countless numbers of 'crack babies'.

In my experience, crack babies were two a penny. In one of the worst cases of its kind fourteen children born to the same mother were put into care one by one thanks to her crack addiction.**

It's essential to rescue babies from crack addicts for a number of reasons, but most addicts don't realize how much damage smoking crack does to their baby; at the least they will end up with asthma, at the worst they will die from acute cocaine intoxication. I'd heard of a case where a five-month-old baby born to a pair of crack dealers had died in their bed. They claimed they

---

* Studies have shown that up to 95 per cent of street prostitutes are addicted to crack. See www.turning-point.co.uk/NR/rdonlyres/3D5CF3ED-289C-4D3B-B8D5-F60A30D9BCE3/0/TP_CrackReport250705.pdf

** In January 2008, District Judge Nick Crichton, of the Inner London Family Proceedings Court, told newspapers that he had ordered fourteen children by the same mother to be taken into care and said it was 'perfectly usual' for the court to remove four, five or six children from one parent.

had accidentally smothered her but toxicology tests showed that the baby died of acute cocaine intoxication – from the crack smoke. Babies who are breast-fed by mothers with crack addictions also soon become addicts and can die from an overdose.

I saw this phenomenon time and time again here in London and it is impossible to overstate the enormity of the social and financial impact. The majority of these kids were either taken into care, fostered, lived in care homes, or were simply lost in the system and never came to our attention. Apart from the terrible human cost, the bill to taxpayers to look after fourteen children was more than £2 million. It also cost an average of £25,000 to hear each case of care proceedings.

Many of these women were young crack house prostitutes who had had unprotected sex to feed their addiction and kept getting pregnant. Many were under the delusion that this time it would be different, that they would be able to manage their addiction and raise the child. Unfortunately, this is unlikely where crack cocaine is involved.

Some addicted mothers who appear to 'recover' after losing their child, develop something some professionals call 'start again syndrome' where a new pregnancy is seen to present a fresh start, or as a way of filling the emotional vacuum. Incredibly, in some cases this was naively encouraged by poorly trained social workers who thought a new baby would set them on the path to recovery.

In one such case a woman had already lost three children because of neglect brought about by her drug addiction, but her history was ignored when considering her and her partner's ability to care for a new child. Instead, agencies were more focused on getting them to 'start again' – encouraging pregnancies when they should have been urging caution.

Another extreme case included an addict who had her first three children taken away and then went on to have seven more by three different fathers. They were removed one by one until she had lost all ten. Another woman had fifteen children in the care of family and foster homes. Nine children, some of whom were taken directly from the maternity unit, were removed from the care of another woman because of drug and alcohol problems. She had her first child at fifteen.

All too often, the stresses that come with increased family size tended to be ignored or downgraded by social services and escalating difficulties are missed. Very often, parents increased their drug or alcohol intake as the size of their family grew, leading to an escalation in domestic violence and neglect.

Some multiple pregnancies often only came to light during a serious case review, perhaps after a child suffers serious neglect at the hands of the mother or abuse by her deranged partner of the day. One such case featured a very young child whose mother had had more than ten pregnancies, and whose older children were already suffering serious mental problems.

While plenty of research has been undertaken to tell teenage girls that smoking crack while pregnant will harm their baby (who'd've thought?), very few initiatives have delved into what might happen when all these kids become teenagers and young adults.

We know that when children are taken into care beyond the age of eight or nine years, they are likely to suffer from psychological disorders that lead to antisocial behaviour (and further economic cost). There are thousands of children born to crack-addicted parents and who have now reached their teens, or are fast approaching adolescence. They are 'Generation Crack' – the legacy of our failure to stop the rise of drugs.

These were the kids I saw abused and abusing on a daily basis in Haringey and Hackney but were already beyond our help: chewed up and spat out by an inadequate social care and justice system, abandoned and left to rot in our inner cities.

It doesn't take a genius to realize that if they stayed in the environment they were born into there was a very good chance they would suffer extreme emotional damage – traumatic stress disorders that would go undiagnosed and untreated – and be preyed upon by their only role models: the successful eighteen- and nineteen-year-old designer-label-wearing dealers on the estate. These were the only people they could aspire to, the only people who offered them a way out from the unbearable poverty. They were also the people who'd fed their parents' habits and had destroyed their families.

For years ten- and eleven-year-olds have been recruited into perverse 'youth training schemes' and are rapidly absorbed into a whole other system of 'child protection' by dealers. They're prevented from going to school and are threatened at gunpoint if they want 'out'. They're stabbed, robbed and bullied by the dealers who feed their hate and teach them that revenge equals justice.

They start as runners, or 'youngers', a lethal dose of crack and heroin stashed in their cheeks, or as lookouts. Soon, as they make their way up the hierarchy, they're able to take a decent cut of the day's profits – perhaps a few hundred pounds.

'Just don't fuck it up' they're told – otherwise a punishment is due.

I've seen so many members of Generation Crack already; these are the kids who take up most of the police time, the ones who make the headlines with their shocking crimes committed at a supposedly tender age; they show no quarter, take no hostages. When at last they stop coming to school, teachers sigh with relief and time-poor social workers don't look for them too hard. A letter or two will do.

The media and politicians, pushed for column space and interview time, are all too ready to condemn a teenager's capacity for violence. Not many people think to ask *why* they are violent. These kids are simply products of their environment –

an environment where they've suffered every imaginable abuse. When they were small, they were physically unable to defend themselves from abuse. As soon as they become strong enough, they turn to violence to exact revenge. This is where the random stabbings that make the headlines come from.

Abused children can't tolerate boundaries being crossed but at the same time they won't accept the boundaries of others; humiliation is unbearable. An innocent expression may be mistaken for disrespect, and all too often becomes the spark behind a senseless murder.

They've grown up under attack in a world where few are held accountable. It's no wonder they have no respect for the criminal justice system. By the time we get to see them, we don't bring these kids justice, only trouble. So many have been through youth courts and detention centres before being kicked back out on the streets older, stronger and wiser after a harsh education by fellow inmates. Imprisonment is outdated and ineffective as far as Generation Crack is concerned. It simply increases their resentment; there's nothing we can do to them that can frighten them into good behaviour – punishment only works when there's no upper limit, as the drug dealers know only too well.

In the words of Camila Batmanghelidjh, the founder of the children's charity Kids Company (more about this later): 'Too many children are on youth offending registers while too few are on the child protection register.'

A few days after my impromptu involvement in the hit man case, I was stood in another flat on a different estate, gutted to see a handful of used and exposed needles on the coffee table. The mother, in her late twenties, looked about fifty and was on her last legs. This wasn't safe. I explained that she was clearly neglecting her child and I would have to remove Jermaine, her young son, from their home. She snatched my bag and threw it at me. Understandable really.

The father stayed silent as we left. He didn't want our help. Where he came from, accepting help is to admit failure, showing any emotion at all would be an admission of weakness. He avoided eye contact with me. I could feel the stress and rage inside him, waiting to boil over. I wondered whether he had been self-harming, a substitute for tears and an outlet for frustration. Still, we had Jermaine now.

I hated this part, mainly because the building where we had to take teens to wait for a foster home looked like a prison; inside there were holes in the dirty-white walls where kids had punched and kicked them in their fury. The gaps in between were covered in obscene biro-graffiti while the furniture was old and clinical. As Dev the social worker had made clear, the refuge workers were poorly paid, poorly trained and although most tried hard, they had no idea how to cope, so the kids ran wild. They were simply anarchic holding pens.

Kids like Jermaine, who'd already been through enough stress in their lives, didn't need this. I always tried to tell them it wasn't that bad and that it wouldn't be for that long but who was I trying to fool? I had to agree when kids told me it was a shit-hole. Luckily, in Jermaine's case, he had the name, though not the phone number, of an aunt. After a bit of hunting we found her and she checked out, so he was able to stay with her.

I was very relieved but, as I saw for myself, dozens of other kids aren't so 'lucky'. As usual, there wasn't much time for me to reflect. My phone rang. It was Rob.

'There's a job at the Homerton. A baby with a fractured skull in the Starlight Ward; the staff called it in.'

My heart leaped. Everything I had planned was instantly abandoned.

CHAPTER NINE

BABIES DON'T TALK

Rob was entrusting me with a major investigation. I needed to dig deep to gather every last ounce of tact, to control my anger. I was about to throw myself into a family, rip them apart and, after I'd finished, if I thought the child had 'just fallen out of bed', I'd just say, 'Sorry but we needed to investigate to be sure.'

We picked up a great many cases from hospitals; a few were false alarms but we always came out to see anyone the doctors thought had suspicious injuries. Most common were broken bones, especially spiral fractures, which are normally very rare in children – these are caused by sudden, extremely violent twists, arm behind the back, or being picked up by an arm or leg and thrown across a room. Another highly suspicious injury was broken posterior ribs, usually the result of crushing. Any fracture in an infant too young to walk or crawl meant we were called automatically. A skull fracture in a baby was a major red alert. In fact any bone fracture or breakage in young children can raise the alarm as their bones are so soft and their bodies so light. Welts and lacerations that appear to have an implement pattern are obvious causes of concern, as are burns to unusual parts of the body.

The Starlight Ward had excellent security, which I negotiated as discreetly as possible. Any warning tempts the guilty to hide evidence and prepare lies. Every bed was full. As ever there was a shortage – an overworked paediatrician with rings under her eyes told me that one youngster had spent the night in Accident and Emergency and three children had been transferred to make way for new cases, one of which was the baby I was there to see.

Ushered to a side room, the paediatrician and I were joined by the hospital social worker. The paediatrician was one hundred per cent certain and struggled to hide her anger. 'A baby that falls out of bed as the parents are claiming *cannot* end up with a 3-millimetre-wide fracture to the skull.'

Cases where there's still some uncertainty are a nightmare but this time there was no doubt, this was something that had been caused by extreme force. A clear unexplained injury.

'Luckily for her, it looks like she'll recover,' the doctor added, 'but I wouldn't be happy at all to return her to her parents' care.' Damn right.

The family were standing around the cot. My hands were sweating. Nurses, doctors, patients and porters hurried past us in a blur of white coats, scrubs, clipboards, suits and trolleys. Oozing sensitivity, I introduced myself. I looked into the cot: the wide-eyed child stared at her parents – possibly for the last time.

The mother, Suravinda, dressed in a sari, made it clear she didn't speak English. A nurse mouthed 'bollocks' at me over her shoulder. This, along with Suravinda's cold, unemotional gaze, told me I may have found my suspect. The father, Hakim, who spoke English, was tall, slim, polite and in his mid-twenties.

As gently as possible, I used the airbag question: 'Would you mind answering a few questions down at the station?' I explained that we were going to take the baby and their other daughter into police protection before dropping the bomb – they were both under arrest. I awaited the onslaught. None came.

Normally, parents freak out at this point, but who's to say there's a right or wrong reaction in such an extraordinary situation?

We took them back to Stoke Newington and booked them in. We now needed to search their home. We keyed our way into their small and tidy council flat. Everything was photographed. The height the baby was supposed to have fallen from to the carpet was measured. There were no immediate clues that told us what might have happened, although I spotted some knife marks in one of the doors at adult height.

Time to interview the parents. I started with the dad. Even though he spoke good English we brought in an interpreter, a common practice in serious crime. It prevents disagreements over linguistic errors. We also provided different interpreters for each of them; this prevents any bias towards one or the other suspect creeping in on the interpreter's behalf. As usual, the interviews were tape-recorded.

'So, tell us what happened.'

He said: 'I came home from work at the bakery, went straight to the bathroom and heard Salma [their daughter] crying. I went to see what was wrong and our baby was on the bedroom floor.'

I later asked Suravinda the same question, through her interpreter.

'We were in the lounge when I heard Salma crying and ran into the kitchen. She was on the floor. She'd fallen from a chair after having a fight with her sister.'

Here we go, I thought. They didn't have time to prepare their story and already there are discrepancies. I walked out of the room with the interpreter. 'Are you a hundred per cent certain she said kitchen?' I asked. She nodded, 'Yes, of course.'

'Right. Don't translate when I ask her to sign the custody record.' We went back into the interview room with Suravinda. I chatted for a bit and tried my usual method of being very friendly, before boring her senseless with a lengthy list of dull and fairly irrelevant questions.

As the interview progressed, I showed concern and empathy for her situation, the difficulties of motherhood, and family life. When she did open her mouth, I kept quiet until she had finished and then did a little positive reinforcement to try to make her think the interview was going well.

After half an hour, I still hadn't got anywhere. It's extremely unusual not to develop a rapport with a suspect, even during a short interview. But there was nothing, no emotional interaction at all, just flat and cold responses.

Until I asked her the question I'd been leading up to.

It was a common police trick, with a surprisingly high success rate. Keeping my arms folded and my eyes firmly planted on Suravinda I said: 'OK, we're done. Sign the custody record and you can go.'

The translator kept quiet. It worked. Suravinda reached for the pen in front of her.

'You've just proved you speak English,' I said.

I received a murderous stare in return.

I had no problem building up a rapport with the dad. We had a pleasant and, for me, useful second interview where I uncovered several more inconsistencies and filed them away for later use. As I probed away he suddenly admitted that he didn't even have a job. Whatever next? I sidestepped that comment and kept him unbalanced by asking him about the journey to the hospital on the night in question.

'How did you take your daughter to hospital?'

'By minicab.'

'Which firm?'

'I don't remember.'

'I need their number. Which phone did you call them on?'

Silence.

'I need their number. That driver could be an important witness. He may even help you. What kind of car was it? What did he look like?'

'I . . . I don't remember.'

'Why won't you help me find him? And if you don't go to work every night, where are you?'

'I'm confused.'

I went over and over and over everything again and again. By the end of the interview the dad's story was entirely different, except for one detail which he managed to stick to because I think he really believed it: 'She must have fallen off the bed. It was an accident. It was an accident.'

'Must' suggested he was definite on that point but it was no use me pressing him. A few hours more in custody and I'd need to apply for an extension and I was fairly certain I wouldn't get it. They weren't going to flee and their daughter was under police protection in Homerton Hospital, in one of the safest wards in the country.

I bailed them. Hakim said goodbye but there was nothing but disgust and total contempt for me from Suravinda.

I needed to speak to the neighbours, record statements and collect and file medical examination records. It was frustrating; as I progressed the case, I still felt as if I didn't yet have an insight into what had really happened. Normally, in police investigations, the victim of a grievous assault will be able to tell us what happened. Unfortunately, babies don't talk.

I had fifteen days to get to the truth, before the case conference that would decide on the family's fate. Just then, another seemingly innocuous case spiralled into something totally unexpected.

CHAPTER TEN

STOPPING ANOTHER CLIMBIÉ

The caller simply stated that four-year-old Hannah Clarke had missed an eye appointment and her GP was worried. Cases like this can seem quite harmless at first, but underneath often lies a terrible reality. Sadly, there are no statistics that show just how many lives social services have saved, often by a whisker, only the failures like Victoria Climbié and Baby Peter. The case of Hannah Clarke highlights just how difficult it is to identify a serious case before it's too late.

During this particular week only Sarah and I seemed to be around. We were swamped. The call about Hannah came just as eighteen other cases whirred out of the fax in one go after the damn thing jammed. My heart sunk. Everyone was out answering calls and had too many cases to cover. We took nine each and read them through, putting most of them on the 'no' pile, meaning that social services would be able to handle most of them.

I stopped at the note I'd jotted about Hanna, hovering over the 'no' pile. I read it again. Her doctor was concerned that a woman who said she was Hannah's mother was in fact not related to Hannah. Social services rang up the 'mother', Serena, only to find that the child had left that morning on a flight to Jamaica to see her dad.

I discussed the job with Sarah. Normally social services would allocate a social worker who'd undertake an assessment without the help of the police. 'Something's not right about this,' I said, 'but I don't know what exactly, just a hunch I suppose. It shouldn't take too long to find out if there is something wrong.'

Sarah agreed and so I rang the case manager at social services. 'I'm not happy about this one, do you mind if we dig a bit deeper?'

'Sure, no problem,' came the reply. This was just a courtesy call really, no social services manager would ever object if we lightened their caseload.

There was a phone number for Serena. I dialled and introduced myself and asked, 'What's happened to Hannah?'

I was given a tale of woe about the difficulties of getting to medical appointments on time. She admitted she wasn't the mother and that a friend of the mother's, a guy called 'Leon', had collected Hannah that morning and put her on a flight back to her mother in Jamaica.

My cop's bullshit detector had automatically leaped into the red but I played the role of gullible PC Plod and accepted everything she said. She confirmed her address and I thanked her for her time.

I then called the Met's Intel department to get the flight manifests checked for Hannah. An old friend from back when I was a uniformed PC answered the phone. This always helps speed things along and sure enough he bumped me to the top of his list and ran the check while we had a brief reminisce and catch-up.

No Hannah Clarke.

I thanked him and hung up. Of course, she could have been on any flight under any name, but this was reason enough for me to keep trying.

Sarah, meanwhile, had done a background check on Serena. The look on her face told me we were going to have to move fast. 'Drop everything, Harry,' she said. 'A few months ago Serena was charged and acquitted of being a getaway driver in a Yardie murder. Her trial was at the Old Bailey. The murderer was done and he was a close associate of hers.'

'Let's go!' We raced downstairs, jumped into the Peugeot and bombed round to Serena's address; there was no sign of Hannah. Again, as we spoke to Serena, we played it calm and gullible.

I'd checked her house for any sign of a landline and there was none. I asked to have a look at her mobile and she agreed.

'We just want to know who Leon is,' Sarah said quietly.

'I don't know,' she replied, avoiding our eyes, 'he's a friend of the mother.'

'Did you speak to him today?' I asked.

'Yes.'

Ah-ha.

With a bit of luck the number would still be on her mobile. As I flicked through the numbers, Serena started to radiate tension. She'd been busy. She'd called lots of numbers that morning, but there were no names attached to them. I was now really worried. Why wasn't Serena being more helpful? Where was this child?

Time to shed the gullible cloak. I changed my tone and, raising my voice a good few decibels, I demanded: 'Where is Hannah? Where is she?' Pressure, pressure, pressure. Serena started to panic. Suddenly we were no longer naive, over-polite police officers.

Sensing Hannah was in danger, with no time to waste, I called for prisoner transport, the implication being that I was about to arrest Serena. Sarah cast me a sideways glance. This was a high-risk strategy; if Serena stayed silent and demanded a brief, then we were screwed as we didn't have proof that she'd done anything wrong. We had absolutely zero proof that the child was even at risk. Then I'd have to call all the numbers on her phone hoping that one of them would yield crucial information – this was at best a long shot.

I kept the pressure up. After thirty minutes, a crack appeared.

'She might be in Lincoln,' she mumbled.

'What?'

'With her dad. She might be in Lincoln with her dad.'

I called directory enquiries and got them to put me through to Lincoln A&E. Trying to remain calm, I asked if they had a child called Hannah there.

'No, sorry, there's no child by that name.' Sarah looked at me questioningly. I shook my head. Damn. There was a pause on the line. 'Did you say you were from Child Protection?'

'Yes.'

'That's funny, there's a doctor here who's just asked to speak to you, hang on.'

The doctor came on. 'Yes, I'm treating a four-year-old black girl for a number of non-accidental injuries.'

'What's her name?' I asked, walking into the kitchen for privacy.

'Helen Charles. A Jamaican girl. She has a badly broken wrist, various scalds and cigarette burns, a slash mark on her chest and there's something wrong with her eyesight – she keeps walking into things.'

Got her! They'd chosen a poorly faked name. My grip tightened on the plastic phone. It cracked as waves of anger broke over me; there were so many injuries.

'Right,' I told the doctor, 'as of this moment she is in police protection, do not release her into the care of anyone until the Child Protection officers show up. This is now a criminal investigation.'

I'm so grateful for the power that comes with this job; we now had total control over the child; she was safe. I walked outside the flat and called Rob.

'Don't arrest Serena yet, Harry,' he said, 'she's still not admitted anything; you've no evidence yet; it'll be a waste of time.'

'Got it. I'll turn over the flat and then we're off to Lincoln.' It was getting dark so we worked quickly and, as far as I could tell, it was clean. I hoped that even though she was only four, Hannah would be able to describe who had hurt her.

Sarah and I were just walking out the front door when a woman, who we soon discovered was Serena's mother, appeared on the pathway with two of Serena's kids, Alex, aged ten, and Natasha, aged three.

Remembering Rob's words: 'If it's in the child's best interests, get on with it,' I plucked Natasha up before she got to Serena; she winced. A nasty untreated burn marked the palm of her hand.

'What's this?' I said, looking at Serena.

'It was an accident. I ran it under the cold water tap.'

Not good enough. I tried to hide my anger as I told Serena that both children were in our protection as of that moment and that she should pack their belongings. She glared at me but stayed calm, more annoyed with me than the fact we were taking her kids away.

I called the manager at Hackney Social Services. Her voice trembled with emotion as I described Hannah's injuries; by the time I'd finished she was in tears. I defy anyone to tell me that social workers don't care. They care all right, perhaps more than anyone else because their passion drives them to stay in a job very few people are brave enough or able enough to do at all, let alone do well. They're let down by a tiny few.

The next step was to head back to the office to plan the investigation. We needed to agree strategies with other agencies, have the kids examined by a doctor, interviewed and homed, find and speak to possible witnesses and arrest Serena. As it was getting very late, I called Lincoln's Child Protection Team and they immediately sent someone over to check on Hannah. They also sat in on the official medical examination and interviewed Hannah over the next few days.

The official examination is very thorough and takes up to an hour to complete. The doctor described Hannah's injuries from the feet up. As he did so, the reality of what Hannah had endured suddenly hit me; I thought about her agony for far too long and I soon felt sick with anger. Hannah's wounds covered her entire body, it seemed as though no part of her had been spared. In fact, her injuries reminded me of those suffered by Victoria Climié, whose medical report I had seen when I was sent on attachment with Haringey Child Protection.

The next week, I travelled up to the hospital in Lincoln. As I entered the ward, a little girl with a pink plaster cast on her arm was entertaining about twenty nurses with a dance routine.

It was Hannah.

I was overjoyed to see her so happy and bright, so full of life. The hospital staff had done an amazing job of patching her up – physically and mentally.

The job was only just beginning. I needed to jail the people that did this and that meant a difficult investigation was on the cards. I had little time to think about that before my phone rang. It was Rob. 'Get back to London, Harry, we're swamped; I need you to deal with a six-year-old boy who's allegedly been pushed out of a window from the sixth floor of a tower block.'

CHAPTER ELEVEN

THE JAMAICAN JOB

I stood below the grim-looking tower block, deep in a Hackney council estate, looked up and scratched my head. The kid had not only survived a six-storey fall – he'd walked away.

There were witnesses who told me they'd seen the boy fall, land in some bushes, bounce and get up, a little unsteadily, before sitting down again in a daze. The paramedics put him on a backboard with a head brace. But when the doctors checked him over, they thought they had the wrong child. Not a single bone was broken. I'd checked the bushes and they weren't likely to offer much of a cushion.

'I had opened the window as it was such a nice day, to let some air in, but I won't be doing that again,' said his shaking mother, biting her nails, still in shock. 'One moment he was there . . . he was bouncing around the house, then he was gone. I screamed and reached for him but he was gone. I thought he was dead. It was the most frightening thing I've ever experienced. God saved him.'

I was hardly in a position to disagree as I looked out of the window, down on the bushes that surrounded the concrete car park six floors below.

'So, how are you feeling?' I asked the boy at the hospital.

'I fell out the window but I'm OK – my back is still a bit red.' He turned round and raised his shirt to show me, with some pride.

'Since then he's been a lot quieter,' his mum said. 'No more leaning out of windows.'

There was absolutely no suggestion that he could have been pushed, and apart from the bruise on his back he was a perfectly healthy and happy little boy. I could only conclude it was accidental – and that kids bounce.

In the case of baby Salma, who had a fractured skull, we'd found out that her mother, Suravinda, had fled domestic violence as a child, while her husband had been treated for anger management. Slowly we started to unravel various lies and inconsistencies in their story but we still didn't have enough for a conviction. The only thing we had was that the doctors at Homerton Hospital were adamant that a baby falling off a bed onto a carpet will not end up with a 3-millimetre-wide skull fracture. This should have been enough material but it wasn't.

Rob suggested we find some more authoritative expert opinion. After a bit of research I found that one of the world's leading radiologists happened to be in Birmingham, so that evening Simon and I hacked up the M1 on what was known as an OMPD mission (Outside the Metropolitan Police District). When we arrived the city was a mess, everybody was out on the streets and drunk. 'Bloody hell,' said Simon, 'it's a bit early.' Everything was green, green faces, green beer, green burgers, green buildings, green vomit. The penny dropped – St Patrick's Day. We tried to retire quietly to our city centre hotel, we really did, but the noise was too much. Simon suggested a quick drink in the bar.

'Why not?' I replied, 'one pint of Guinness won't hurt.'

The following morning, our heads pounding, we handed over our X-rays to the specialist. He examined them and provided a statement citing a non-accidental injury as the most likely cause.

I turned the case over and over in my mind on the drive back to London. The parents weren't telling us the truth. We didn't have enough evidence. What now? Go back and research the background of the parents again? I'd already found some clues in their history. There must be something else in their past, I thought, something that will get them to talk.

Once back in London I had to crack on with the Hannah Clarke case. Serena claimed that Hannah's injuries had happened in Jamaica while in her mother's care. She assumed that we'd never go to Jamaica and would have to take her word for it. She was wrong.

I filled out the paperwork and called the staff officer of the commander (he had to authorize all trips abroad). The staff officer told me that as it was an urgent investigation I could go ahead and book the flight and he'd get it signed off on the morning I was due to fly.

'But he normally requires ten days' notice,' I said, pleasantly surprised.

'No, it'll be fine,' he explained, 'my boss is always in at 7 a.m. without fail so come down as early as you like.'

So as instructed, Sarah and I arrived at New Scotland Yard at 7 a.m. on the day of the flight with the paperwork, all ready to be signed. And guess what, there was no sign of the commander. Nine o'clock came and went and there was still no sign.

We were cutting it fine so I left the paperwork with another staff officer and we drove to the airport.

At the check-in, my phone rang. 'Here we go,' I said to Sarah, raising my eyebrows, 'stand by for the fireworks.' It was a detective chief inspector, the commander wasn't happy about the short notice! After a short bollocking he rang off. Sarah and I sat and waited, clockwatching as the gate closure drew near. My phone rang.

It was the DCI again. 'Why on earth are you flying business class?'

I explained, as patiently as possible, that this was normal police procedure to avoid travelling alongside drug mules,* as there are so many on every flight to and from Jamaica. The question was fair enough but I had already explained this in the paperwork, and the gate was closing.

'OK,' he huffed, 'just get on the plane.'

I shouted 'Go, go, go, go!' and we scraped through the closing gate. I was pretty pissed off, all this kerfuffle had drawn unnecessary attention to us, as we were the last to board the flight. As we settled down I was surprised to spot a familiar face. We weren't the only cops on the plane on a mission.

With ten hours to kill, Sarah and I got to know each other quite well. I asked her the inevitable question: What made her join Child Protection?

'I worked for the Domestic Violence Unit, so of course I'd see loads of griefy domestics,' she said. 'I always thought that the wives and mothers who were victims had a choice: stay in the abusive relationship or leave, if they could summon the strength. The kids, however, don't have a choice. Our intervention gives these kids a chance to express themselves, to say what they want – we give them the option of escape.

'The thing I find hardest to deal with is that some women choose their partners over their children. Sometimes, when I

---

* In a surprise sweep at Heathrow airport in December 2003, a planeload of passengers from Jamaica were X-rayed. Twenty-three drugs mules were arrested, including two children (one sixteen-year-old eventually passed fifty-three latex lozenges and a twelve-year-old passed eighty-four). One week later a further nineteen were caught on a BA flight from Jamaica to Gatwick. The flights were not targeted because of a tip-off, but were chosen at random.

told them that their partner would have to leave the family home while their case was being investigated, they told me that they'd prefer it if the child was removed instead of their partner. They sometimes even blamed the kids after I told them that their partner was suspected of abuse.'

There was a hint of anger in Sarah's voice as she continued. 'They need to at least give the allegations against their partner a fair hearing, they need to listen with an open mind, reserve judgement and set aside personal feelings. The needs of their children, their own flesh and blood, have to come first. I've watched abusers walk back with their partners into the family home grinning in the belief that they've got away with it.'

'But what can we say to convince these women?' I asked her.

'I think that with women it all comes down to instinct. If you have a gut feeling or see something that doesn't look right, act upon it, don't dismiss it, be vigilant and don't leave anything to chance. Look for the signs and don't bury your head in the sand. After we ended up arresting their partner/husband, the mother would say something like: "Looking back on it now, I knew something was wrong." They just stayed in denial until it was too late.'

'How are you coping with the work?'

'Even though I have dealt with some very disturbing events, including post-mortems, I was never so affected that my work intruded into my personal life. Specializing in the field of child protection was a choice, not a deployment. I don't have nightmares. Not yet, anyway.'

Shortly after we got off the plane my name was called over the tannoy.

'Oh, Christ, what now?' I said to Sarah, thinking we might be recalled to the UK by the grumpy commander.

I marched up to the flight attendant. 'Yes, I'm Harry Keeble, what is it?'

'Mr Keeble, I'm very sorry but your luggage is still in London.'

Fucking hell! I had nothing on me except for the case papers, not so much as a toothbrush. I fumed quietly while the clerk explained they'd get my bag on the next flight and would deliver it directly to my hotel. Oh well, at least we hadn't been recalled.

We were met by a man who held the rank of a detective inspector called Harrison. I had no idea if it was his first or last name. Harrison was a broad muscular man who came up to my shoulder. He beamed at us, said hello and asked, 'Where's your luggage?'

I explained and suggested we stop by a local department store to buy some more. He laughed and, in an avuncular manner, said, 'Not after dark, not without an armed bodyguard, my friend.' Damn. However, I spotted the other police officer who was on the plane and after I explained my predicament he kindly lent me some clothes. We weren't exactly the same size but I was hardly in a position to refuse.

Harrison dropped us off at the hotel. Not needing to unpack I headed straight for the bar and grabbed a cold beer. Sarah soon joined me. 'Cheer up, Harry,' she said, 'at least you're in Jamaica, let's relax a little.'

Just as she said that I heard a distant rat-tat-tat. It was a sound I'd heard before in Hackney. 'Was that gunfire?'

I called the barman over and nodded towards the distant rat-tat-tat. 'What's going on?' He just shrugged. Gunfire, that's all.[8]

Not long before our visit a taxi driver and a newspaper seller had been shot dead by police. They'd mistaken them for armed robbers. This had led to a full-on riot of about two thousand people; buses were torched and a battle was now raging between a hundred cops and a small army of outlaws led by criminal strongmen with a large arsenal.[9]

And this, apparently, wasn't unusual. I didn't know it at the time but there were around 1,000 killings each year on Jamaica,

CHAPTER TWELVE

PAGANS AND TUGS OF WAR

This couldn't be right. I checked and re-checked the address. The brand-new swanky town house belonged to a prominent politician. I looked at Ashia, the social worker who'd picked up the referral and had taken me up on the offer of a lift. Unlike the police, social services don't have cars or mileage expenses.

'I used to work for a much wealthier borough,' Ashia said. 'Rich parents abuse their kids, too, you know. I've seen children who've cut up works of art and smeared faeces on fabric wallpaper. Little boys who hurt themselves because they were pushed too hard and who didn't smile when they brought home ten A-grade GCSEs from school. The abuse might not involve knives, guns and drugs but it was there. Of course, no one guessed they were being battered with belts and locked up because they went to a posh private school in immaculate uniforms.'

I nodded. 'Good point,' I said.

I loved the fact that I never quite knew what was waiting for me during my working day but this really took the biscuit. I hoped this was just a case of mistaken identity, or a vindictive neighbour. Our referral said that children had been seen dancing round a fire in the garden 'chanting satanic spells'.

'Still, this could be one hell of a hot potato,' I added.

'No, really?' Ashia answered with amused sarcasm. 'Jesus, if the papers get hold of it . . .'

I rang the bell and knocked loudly. There was no answer, so after a brief conflab, we decided to pop a note through the letter box, asking them to call us. I then rang the Diplomatic Protection Group, just in case the politician was being stalked by a nutter.

Once I returned to the office I uncovered the error. Somewhere along the line between receiving the referral and sending the fax someone had transposed the street numbers. Damn! Before I could get my arse back down there, Lucy came over with an urgent referral.

It had come from a school. One of the teachers had noticed five-year-old Michael's facial injuries. 'Daddy hits me with a belt when I'm naughty,' he told her, 'he hit me in the head last night.'

It was 2.30 p.m. on a Friday. If we were going to do this we needed to see Michael fast, before his parents picked him up. Lucy offered to come with me. I agreed, grabbed a radio, an asp (an extendable truncheon, just in case we collided with a violent dad) and spun the wheels of my tiny Peugeot as we hauled our way through the beginnings of the school-run traffic. Ignoring the parking signs, I plonked the car right at the front entrance, in case we needed a fast getaway.

We were shown through to the head's office. I spotted Michael waiting outside straight away. Head down, legs crossed, no eye contact. Realizing the time pressure, the head quickly gave us the lowdown: 'Michael hasn't been in the UK very long; his family moved here from Jamaica two years ago. He can be pretty difficult in class and his teacher's quite nervous of having anything to do with his dad.'

It wasn't looking good for the dad. We needed to talk to Michael. Lucy spoke first and did the introductions. There was a bruise on the side of his temple; there were also some grazes on his face.

It's always vital not to plant any ideas in a child's head as they often try to give you the answer they think you want. So you don't ask 'Did someone hit you?' or 'Where did Daddy hurt you?' You don't lead the child, you follow. Lucy expertly showed me how it was done.

The poor kid was really scared but Lucy kept him calm and he seemed to relax a little, although it was clear he was in some physical pain. Before Victoria Climbié, officers would have been wary of asking a child to remove any clothing, but Rob's words rang clear and true in my head: 'If it's in the child's best interests, get on with it.' Michael could have a broken rib and internal bleeding or other serious injury that needed urgent hospital treatment. I asked him to lift up his top. He did so slowly, wincing. His ribs were bruised, nothing looked broken, but a medical examination would be needed.

'Who normally picks him up?' I asked the head.

He shrugged, unknowing.

Decision time. Michael's parents were due to arrive any moment. He was scared and his injuries were way above moderate correction, the result of a powerful adult out of control. He had to stay somewhere else tonight. Normally we'd leave the child in another room while we discussed the situation with the parents and set their boundaries, but I felt Michael and his parents shouldn't be in the same building when we spoke to them in case it all kicked off.

Problem was, Michael didn't want to come with us. I wasn't surprised. This kid had been through enough without us pushing him down a path he didn't want to take. I was always in awe of the courage of those kids who fought all their fears to come with us. The child's view is very often the deciding factor in less serious cases, but not this one.

'I don't know, Harry,' she said, uncertain. 'I know he really doesn't want to come but he is at serious risk.'

'You're right. He's had a proper beating,' I replied. 'We have to make sure he's safe before we talk to the parents.'

A small voice came from across the room: 'I don't want to come.'

Damn. I needed to get him out of here, and fast.

I'd had problems before when I'd left a child in school under 'police protection' and didn't want to repeat them. If I suspected a child was the victim of abuse and time was short, I had the power to place them in the school's care, so they could legally refuse to hand him over to the parents.

I was alerted to one case first thing in the morning, so all I had to do was call the head and place the child in the school's care, leaving me the rest of the day, at least until 3 p.m., to have strategy meetings, launch the investigation and hopefully arrest the suspect. While I was doing this, the child was just going through their normal school routine, oblivious. This method was clearly in their best interests.

An hour later I got a call from the school. The kid had been sprung. His mother had showed up at the gates and had been refused entry. She'd then climbed the perimeter fence (the school gate was locked and covered by a security camera), walked through an open fire door into the building, grabbed the child straight from the classroom, right under the teacher's nose, and legged it.

Suddenly the case had turned into child abduction. Everyone dropped everything and hunted for the child in a street-by-street search. I got a call from Downham Road Social Services – mother and child had just left their offices. I hacked it down to Downham Road in the Peugeot, alerting uniform officers on the ground.

'That's them!' I yelled, spotting mother and son in the street.

Seeing me approach, the mother screamed: 'Don't you dare touch him!' She pushed the poor kid behind her and raised her fists. Leaving the car in the street, I marched confidently up to her. She crumbled; I grabbed the boy, who had stayed quiet, popped him in the back of the car and drove off, leaving a screaming mother in the street.

I'm sure that cops reading this will ask: 'Why didn't you arrest her?' That's not our primary concern. We have to put the child's safety first and, besides, I didn't want the boy to see me arrest the mother, who was very likely to resist. I'd got her son, and I was able to prove he'd been the victim of abuse, so she'd already lost. I didn't need to hand out a £50 fine to the mother and fill out a mountain of paperwork to reinforce that.

With Michael we were under time pressure. Lucy and I were now convinced that we needed to get him out of the school before his parents arrived to collect him, and she started trying to talk him round. The last thing I wanted was to drag off an injured child, kicking and screaming, just as school finished, with all the parents arriving to collect their children.

Eventually, he accepted his fate and Lucy persuaded him to walk to the door. I went ahead, looking out for any parents. As we reached the stairs Michael slowed down. 'I've changed my mind. I don't want to come.'

We gently started to guide him onwards. I scouted ahead, wary of any parents. Oh crap, I thought as we turned a corner into a load of kids just released from the classrooms, that's all we need. Everyone stopped talking as we went past; they knew something was up. A few seconds later we were out of the building; thank the stars I had parked near the gates. I ran ahead to check the route. Just a smattering of parents so far. I wasn't worried about fighting the father, but I didn't want to end up playing a violent tug of war with Michael.

He stopped again. Lucy used every ounce of her skill to get him moving. Once in the car, the mood began to lighten. He was a bright boy. We talked about football and Jamaica; he really perked up when I told him about my trip to Kingston. I was so relieved we'd got him safe and sound.

Once the mother arrived at the school I spoke to her on the phone and she agreed that Michael could stay the night with a foster family. As ever I worked to get the trust of the parents and, in an interview, the father admitted he was simply repeating what his father had done to him. The old 'it never did me any harm and I turned out all right, didn't I?' approach to parenting.

We arrested and cautioned him and I spoke to them both, emphasizing that their cooperation would go a long way. 'If we can trust each other, then you and Michael will get all the help you need,' I said. 'If we can't be sure that Michael will be safe, then we'll have to make some tough decisions.' They got the message and did everything asked of them. Within forty-eight hours, after a medical and a memorandum (video-recorded) interview, a happy Michael was back with his parents, without court proceedings and under the watchful eye of Brenda, one of the best social workers I ever had the pleasure of meeting. She would report back to the Child Protection case conference group. A good case. One child's life successfully transformed from hell to recovery, and not a poxy statistic in sight.

After Michael had been placed into foster care that night, I returned to the office. Simon came over to my desk. 'Moving in high political circles, are we?' he said enigmatically.

'What are you talking about?'

'That politician called for you, wanted to speak to you personally. Here's the number.'

Luckily, the politician was very understanding about the mix-up.

But there was still the matter of the dancing devil worshippers to be dealt with. So I zipped back to the street I'd been to that morning with Ashia. I knocked on the door of a Victorian town house that had been converted into flats, further up the street. Who would it be this time? Once again, I was in for a surprise. The door was answered by an attractive thirty-something woman with long brown hair. The surprising part was that she was wearing nothing but her knickers and a see-through string vest. She invited me in.

Red-faced and trying to look anywhere but below her neck, I awkwardly explained the allegations that had been made, prefixing them with the phrase 'This is probably a load of old rubbish, but . . .' My eyes roved around the house and noted the 'green' festival posters hung on the walls. These, along with pamphlets on the hall table, the ethnic-style furniture covered in African-style drapes, were all suggestive of a fairly alternative lifestyle.

My embarrassment was immediately forgotten when she said: 'It's true.'

'Excuse me?' I said, unable to believe my ears.

'Well, except for the part about devil worship,' she said, leading me through to the living room. 'We're pagans.'

We had reached the living room and it seemed pretty much like any other living room, except for the fact it looked, well, a little more 'ethnic'. There were a few totems, wooden carvings and portraits of what I assumed were pagan gods. Knowing I was out of my depth in very murky waters, I proceeded with caution.

'So, you were dancing naked in the garden with your children?'

'Oh no! We were dancing, all right, celebrating the summer solstice, but the kids were dressed up for the occasion.'

The kids were home, were perfectly happy and showed me their costumes, so I quickly concluded, with no little relief, that there was no need to take this further. I was impressed to see that

CHAPTER THIRTEEN

WITCHCRAFT

Once again my Peugeot raced through the cold damp streets of East London in the pre-dawn darkness. As Rob was on leave for the night, he'd made me the acting on-call detective inspector and that meant I had to attend any child protection case that came up for the whole of East London.

I'd been woken at 4 a.m. A witness had seen a parent trying to drown their daughter in the River Rom. Police had the suspect in custody. Adrenalin pumped all my weariness away. My mind raced as I went through checklists for forensics, witnesses, interviews and investigation. I needed to get to and evaluate the scene pronto so I could start calling in all the necessary resources and get everyone working hard on what would be a fast-moving case. I also wanted to speak to the witnesses while their memories were still fresh.

'The witness said she saw it happen over there,' a uniformed constable told me, swallowing a yawn and pointing out into a wide section of the river. I knew the River Rom all too well, from my early days as a PC in Romford when, after a drink-fuelled curry, I leaped from a bridge straight into it. But that was much further upriver. It looked quite different here.

I strolled down to the water's edge. The orange city-lit clouds were fading into grey above what was a very bleak scene. Kneeling down, I looked into the water. Then I walked up and down the river for a hundred yards in each direction – and then across it.

I went back to the officer. 'It's one-inch deep,' I said. 'I'd struggle to drown a hamster in that.' The officer looked surprised and shrugged his shoulders.

I rang one of the constables who was with the prisoner. 'The river's one-inch deep,' I said, 'so where's the scene?' Nobody knew.

Damn, that meant I had to wake the witness. This spirited member of the public had probably gone back to bed after the night's excitement. Now I was about to test their patience but I had no choice. I couldn't just ask the child where it happened; that had to wait for the memorandum interview, which would-n't take place until much later that morning. The suspect couldn't be asked either, that also had to be done in an official interview.

If the witness could point out an accurate location for the 'attempted drowning', then it was possible I would find finger and face marks somewhere in the mud at the water's edge – before they were washed away.

I knocked on the door with no little dread but I needn't have worried. Although I got the whole family up, they told me every-thing they could over a cup of tea while in their dressing gowns. They were typical of mainstream British society, willing to help us in any way they could. Once I'd confirmed that I'd been in the right place all along and after I'd checked that the river levels hadn't changed dramatically over the last few hours, I decided that whatever had taken place here was not a major inquiry. I handed it over to the local child protection team, and carried on into work, my feathers slightly ruffled.

*

James, a quiet yet determined detective constable, picked up the referral later that morning. It had come from a foster carer. The eight-year-old child she had been looking after had disclosed something new and highly disturbing about her past.

I looked at her file in horror. A body map of her injuries when she was rescued had been included. It was covered in pen-marks, there was hardly a clean space of white on the entire page. They had been fortunate to catch her in time. She had multiple scars and cuts on her face, and old and fresh stab marks on her leg. She was malnourished; could've easily been another Victoria Climbié, I thought.

The child, Tundé (not her real name), was already on social services' radar. Three months earlier, on a freezing November morning, two street wardens had found her, sitting barefoot, weeping on the steps outside her aunt's flat on the Woodberry Down Estate, the grim, run-down prison-like blocks of flats, many of which were boarded up, that mark the division between Stamford Hill and Manor House.

Tundé told them she had been surviving on tea and bread. The street warden noted her swollen eyes and cuts on her face and told social workers she was 'freezing cold and terrified'. She then lived within Haringey so was handed over to Haringey Social Services. As Tundé didn't tell them about any abuse, they released her back into her aunt's care on Christmas Eve.

Once again, because social services were overloaded with a stupefying amount of urgent cases, a child hadn't received the attention she deserved. Tundé had endured nearly another three months of terror and torture before her school's headmistress became seriously concerned about her. Her attendance had been highly sporadic – never a good sign – and she spotted some suspicious injuries. She was placed in the care of a foster family but had only started to disclose what had happened to her some weeks later.

This is quite common when abuse has taken place over a number of years. There's no way you could expect an eight-year-old to recall everything that had happened to them in chronological order during an official interview. Very often they won't say anything to the police because they think they've done something naughty. They need time to recover.

Of course, that's not how the police usually operate – bailing a suspect for three months while giving a witness a chance to recover is never an option. Once again Child Protection was the police's little random variable.

James was a tenacious investigator. He didn't always do all the paperwork on time, but once he had a case he would never let it go. He was a highly experienced detective with a major investigation background and had hunted serial sex attackers in the past. He could have joined any snazzy department that he wished. But he didn't, he chose the Cardigan Squad because he knew that's where he could be most effective.

The interview was one of the most difficult and delicate we ever had to do. The last thing we wanted was to traumatize Tundé by making her relive her nightmares and face medical examinations for which she was not prepared.

Rob had told me about interviews he'd witnessed where the interviewer had used words the child didn't understand before eventually deciding that she wouldn't make a suitable witness. 'They thought they were doing the right thing by sparing her a courtroom ordeal,' Rob told me, 'but they also failed to honour their promise to protect her and bring her abusers to justice.'

Mistakes like that simply shouldn't happen during memorandum interviews, they're just too important. Having said that, interviewing traumatized children is an incredible skill that few possess. Abuse often leaves children withdrawn and emotionally numb, which makes them come across as cold and unloving. Sometimes this is unintentionally reinforced by the police and social services; few people feel able to hug, compliment or hold the hand of an unemotional child and tell them how cute they are and how good they've been. Violated children cannot tolerate boundaries and if they feel someone has overstepped a physical or mental boundary they may suddenly explode. It then takes them much longer than a 'normal' child to come down from such an outburst. If this happens, then interviews have to be abandoned.

I sat in the tiny control room with a social worker, our eyes fixed firmly on the monitor as James started with a few gentle questions about where Tundé was from originally – Angola – and who was looking after her – her aunt, Sita Kisanga, along with Sita's brother and another aunt, who lived at another address.

We soon got on to the abusive side of her carer's relationship. 'She [Sita] told me to take my jumper and vest off, she pulled a knife and she did little marks. I was bleeding. They stood round me in a circle, hitting me and laughing . . . my aunt said that my mum [whom Tundé believed was dead] and me have got witchcraft.'

The social worker and I exchanged glances. 'Did she say witchcraft?' She gave a grim little nod. The only other two cases we knew of relating to witchcraft were Victoria Climbié and the 'Adam' case, when a child's torso was recovered from the Thames in 2001, thought to have been dismembered as part of a sick ritual used to combat 'evil spirits'.

'In my mind, I will never forget what happened,' the girl said. 'One kicked me, one slapped me and one pushed me. I asked myself "What have I done?" . . . My aunt beat me with a shoe.'

I marvelled at Tundé's quiet but clear voice. She was one tough kid. If she hadn't been so strong, she may not have survived.

'She laughs when she hits me. She says if I tell anybody she hits me, she will take a knife and stab me.'

Tundé had been beaten with a belt buckle and stabbed with a stiletto shoe, was sliced with a kitchen knife and had chilli peppers rubbed into her eyes. She was also starved for days at a time.

'I have nightmares about bad people trying to kill me.'

She had good reason. As the interview progressed, James unravelled the abuse, which culminated in attempted murder. Sita had made Tundé strip and said to her other aunt: 'Why don't we throw her away?'

Sita then laughed: 'Oh, you've got it now,' and took out a laundry sack. Beaten with a bat, slashed with a knife, barely able to see thanks to the chilli peppers that her aunts had yet again rubbed into her eyes, Tundé was stuffed naked into the sack and told: 'We're going to throw you in the river!'

They zipped up the bag, intending to make the short journey from Woodberry Down Estate to the nearby New River Canal, which runs alongside the enormous East and West Reservoirs, ready to drown the orphan child.

As they were about to leave, Sita's brother Sebastian Pinto arrived. He told them to stop, not out of any wish to save Tundé, only out of fear: 'You can't do this, you'll go to prison!'

He then joined in the abuse. Tundé wasn't allowed to sleep in her bed that night because she was covered in blood from knife wounds.

After the interviews were over, it was time for the medical examination, which only served to confirm the horrific extent of Tundé's injuries. The new body map was soon covered in even more pen strokes. She had scar tissue three centimetres long from one cut to her face. Whip scars and stab marks covered her back and legs. There were at least twenty marks made by a knife. She was extremely malnourished and was tiny for her age.

As soon as James had collated all the evidence, it was time to strike. We raided her aunt's flat and turned it over. Tundé seemed to be right about everything she'd told us. There was a large laundry bag and I opened the freezer to find a bag stuffed full of red chilli peppers. We also confiscated all the kitchen knives we could find for analysis. We arrested Sita, her brother Sebastian Pinto and her other aunt who lived at a separate address.

We also recovered a diary. Studying it with a translator before the interview, I could tell that Sita Kisanga clearly believed in evil spirits. There were entries, in her handwriting, about sorcery, witchcraft, the devil, shape-shifting and possession. She wrote about a dream in which she met the 'Holy Spirit' and referred to a girl with a snake in her stomach.

Even though I was gradually becoming used to interviewing all sorts of child abusers, this was a real first. Sita looked uncomfortable and confused as we started. I asked her why she abused Tundé.

'She is a witch,' she said.

'How do you know this?'

'My son had a dream. He said she [Tundé] went out at night to curse and kill people. In the dream she hit him in the back of the head with a big stick. She is having witchcraft. I woke her and she told me: "Yes, I hit him with the stick. I want to sacrifice him for the New Year." That means that she really is Kindoki.'

'Kindoki?'

'A witch!'

'So you took this to be true from your eight-year-old son?'

'A priest told me as well.'

'What priest?'

'From the Church of Spiritual Warfare. He confirmed she was a witch.'

I'd never heard of it.

'A church here? In London, in the UK?'

'Yes. I went with my son every week.'*

Neither Rob nor I knew anything about witchcraft, let alone African witchcraft, which made the interview quite tricky; it was hard to think of questions. I focused on the type of 'cures' that Sita and her brother employed to 'cleanse' Tundé's spirit. I started by asking Sita to define Kindoki to me.

'In our community Kindoki happens. It is killing people. It is doing bad things. In our community it is a serious matter. Kindoki is something that you have to be scared of because, in our culture, Kindoki can kill you and destroy your life completely. Kindoki can make you barren; sometimes Kindoki can ruin your chances of staying here.'

For two hours I questioned Sita about the abuse, or 'cures' she'd meted out to Tundé. She clearly understood that it was against the law and that it was wrong to hit a child in this country and claimed that she didn't do anything physical. It was the other aunt, she said, who was new to the country and didn't understand the law.

Clearly, Sita didn't see hitting a child as a moral issue, just a legal one.

'If you had been in Angola, would you have hit this child?'

'African children are treated differently. You won't understand. You are from a different culture.'

This was true of course. On a later investigation I would see African children being hit by their schoolteachers for misbehaving. Kids still got the cane in the UK when I was a kid. But beaten for being a witch?

---

* We later found that this was true. The church, Combat Spirituel, originally from the Congo, and with a base in Dalston, is a fundamentalist wing of Christianity. I would like to make it clear that the pastor never sanctioned any abuse whatsoever of Tundé. The president of Combat Spirituel, based in Kinshasa, believes that witchcraft is clearly mentioned in the Bible, but he insists that it is completely against the doctrine of the church to harm children in any way or to force them to undergo 'deliverance' ceremonies (more about these later).

Sita looked at me like I was mad when I questioned whether Kindoki really existed.

'Of course! Everybody in my community believes in Kindoki!'

During the investigation, some of the team thought that this belief in possession was a smoke screen for the abuse. After interviewing Sita, I really don't think it was. She believed it with a hundred per cent certainty.

Of course, this didn't excuse her actions for one second. This is not a cultural issue. All too often, when police or social services are confronted by a crime with cultural connotations they run for the hills. A journalist once said it must be difficult dealing with witchcraft issues as they were part of a religious belief – and the police had to respect religious and cultural differences.

While I understood where he was coming from, it was of course a totally ridiculous view. If a child is being beaten, it's child cruelty whatever religious or cultural excuse the abuser gives, whether Muslim or Christian, Hindu or Sikh.

Steadily, we built up Tundé's story. Her aunt, who was thirty-eight, arrived in Britain in August 2002, saying she was the girl's mother and that they were from the Angolan province of Cabinda. She claimed political asylum and told the authorities that the girl's father was a member of a political movement, the Flec-FAC, which was seeking to 'liberate' Cabinda from Angolan control and that he had been murdered.

She claimed that she fled to Britain with the child when soldiers started looking for her. She settled in Tottenham, North London, and joined the Cabinda Community Association. It was here that she met and ended up living with Sita Kisanga in Hackney. Kisanga was also from Cabinda and spoke the same Lingala language. When we ran DNA tests, they confirmed that Kisanga, Pinto, Tundé and the aunt were all related – although exactly how was never established with a hundred per cent certainty.

I wondered if Tundé's real mother was still alive, whether she perhaps had been living in overwhelming poverty, in a mud hut with no running water, fortified by corrugated iron sheets, surrounded by street sewers. Perhaps she thought if Tundé could make it to the UK then she'd have a better life, a chance of happiness, success and comfort.

How many other parents have thought the same?

'How many other children like Tundé are there?' I wondered aloud to Rob.

'I think we've just touched the surface, Harry,' he replied, 'just touched the surface.'

Neither of us then had any idea just how spot on he was with that statement. With the awareness that Tundé's case brought, more and more cases started to crop up. It soon became clear we'd opened a can of occult worms. Dangerous and primitive beliefs were alive and thriving in twenty-first-century London, culminating in a case where a 'possessed' child was abducted off the city streets and sent to the Congo for sacrifice. It would be up to us to find her and bring her back before it was too late.

CHAPTER FOURTEEN

OCCULT EPIDEMIC

No one passing by would have given the red-brick church hall in Hackney a second glance. But inside was a scene so extraordinary that most people would have a hard time trying to accept that it was actually happening, let alone in our capital city.

An eight-year-old boy was lying on the floor, surrounded by adults gripped in a fever of chanting. Suddenly a 'priest' launched himself forwards and spat on the terrified child. He smeared ointment over his chest and stomach before shaking him and kneading his belly.

This church hall had been hired by a so-called 'Frankenstein' religion (not Combat Spirituel), a bizarre marriage of voodoo, fetishism and Christianity. It was hard to comprehend that grown adults actually took these 'priests' seriously. 'If the child is not exorcized then it will grow up to be horrible. I get results,' one seventy-five-year-old mystic told a Hackney journalist.

Unfortunately, the mystic was only one of dozens performing rituals in London church halls and back rooms in return for cash. For example, 'deliverances' are common and do not come cheap – prices start from around £50.

The number of breakaway churches in the UK has shot up in

recent years; current estimates put the number at three hundred and most of these are in London. They have thousands of devoted followers; many pay a subscription of up to 10 per cent of their income for the right to attend a weekly service. Their rise has been fuelled by the legal arrival of more than 1 million Africans in Britain between 1993 and 2003, most of them from Nigeria and South Africa as well as the war-torn nations of Angola and the Democratic Republic of Congo – the nations where belief in witchcraft is rife.[12]

Most of these breakaway churches host harmless ceremonies. In one Hackney church, a pastor simply placed his hands on those who believed they'd been 'infected'; some of them wept as he whispered prayers to them. We soon discovered, however, that a significant minority were behind the sudden leap in witchcraft cases. All of us had thought cases like that of Tundé and Victoria Climbié were exceptional but this was not the case.

Now we knew it existed it seemed so obvious, it was everywhere we looked. In *Loot* that week, for example, a free ads paper published in London, an entire page had been given over to spiritual healers. All of them offered their services to the afflicted, dealing with black magic and evil spirits as well as more conventional complaints. 'I will,' promised one 'professor' in his advert, 'protect you from EVIL forces (Black Magic) and from Jealous enemies.'

In Ridley Road market in Dalston, Hackney, it was possible to buy home-made 'deliverance' videos for £5; most were filmed in Africa but, much to my horror, some were recorded in the UK. In one scene, a boy, who could not have been more than five years old, was beaten by a 'priest' using a thick stick, while the congregation murmured their approval.

Believers in Kindoki state that the devil enters the weak to bring a curse or bad luck on other people's lives, even to kill them. Kindoki is said to target children while they're in the womb or in early childhood through a piece of food infected with the evil spirit. What was clear to me was that 99 per cent of people who attended those ceremonies believed in witchcraft without question.

The power of their belief cannot be overstated. Congregations take the pastor's word as the 'Word of God' and so if the child is declared as possessed they accept whatever treatment is suggested. The problem is that behind closed doors, acting out of fear, friends and relatives all too often literally try to beat the devil out of the child. Even more worryingly, every now and again these children are taken back to their home countries for more extreme deliverance ceremonies.

These insights came to us largely thanks to the work of Dr Richard Hoskins from King's College London, who later appeared as our expert witness in Tundé's trial. Dr Hoskins was a renowned authority on African religion and he travelled to Kinshasa in the Democratic Republic of Congo in search of the source of witchcraft in London. Dr Hoskins wrote later in an article for the *Sunday Times*:

I went from church centre to church centre. I saw children cut with razors, stamped on, beaten, shouted at and forced to drink pigeons' blood. Chillingly, I was often given open and unfettered access to these scenes by pastors and practitioners who plainly believed that what they were doing was in the name of God and thus could do no harm to the children. I saw children starved for days – the churches call it fasting – intimidated, shaken and shouted at by pastors. I heard rumours of much, much worse – of children from Europe ending up on the streets and others beaten to death. I know of at least one case where the child was snatched off a London street and taken unwillingly.

By way of illustration, Dr Hoskins described the case of Londres, a twelve-year-old boy:

> He lived in Tottenham with his mother, a single parent. He was passionate about football. One of his most prized possessions was his red Man U shirt. He was cheeky and streetwise. He got into trouble and messed up at school a bit. He could sometimes be a trial to his mother.
>
> He was also a witch. At least, that was what his mother decided. So she told Londres that she was taking him on a special holiday. He thought that he was going to the Swiss Alps – he had never seen real fairyland snow. But the flight did not go to Switzerland. Instead it ended at Kinshasa, capital of the Democratic Republic of Congo, where his mother's family still lived.[13]

Among the biggest and most influential of these revivalist churches, with about 50,000 believers in Kinshasa alone, is Combat Spirituel, which caters for Angolans and Congolese and which Tundé and her family had attended in London. Londres's mother had also attended Combat Spirituel, and it was to the church centre in Kinshasa that Dr Hoskins said the boy had been taken.

While in Kinshasa, Dr Hoskins visited the church of a prominent government-registered traditional healer. He said he had the power to deliver people from the influence of 'bad spirits'.

The 'clinic' was more like Bedlam, the barbaric mental asylum of eighteenth-century London. Many of the very young 'patients' were chained to the walls and floor. He came across an eight-year-old girl who'd been shaven, starved and had peppers rubbed into her eyes – all part of a four-day ritual to remove evil spirits. In a report broadcast on BBC Radio 4's *Today* programme, Dr Hoskins said:

What we see next is even more appalling. Lying on the floor of the main hall – the healer's throne room – is the limp, bloated body of an eight-year-old boy, Domingo Jose, who is barely conscious. His face, belly, arms, legs – even his fingers – are gorged and inflamed. He is barely alive. The healer approaches. He takes a large swig from a glass bottle and spits water into Jose's face. The child winces, too weak to cry out. I challenged the healer. But he insisted the boy would respond to his traditional medicine: 'That child isn't going to die. If the child dies it means the child is evil.' As we left, the healer earnestly asked if we might know anybody who would sponsor him to open a clinic in Britain.

Dr Hoskins went straight to the authorities and demanded help for the boy. It took four days for anyone to visit Domingo Jose. By then he was dead.

A huge part of the problem is poverty. Countries like Angola and the DRC have been wracked by nearly thirty years of civil war. There are many thousands of orphaned children whose extended families cannot afford to look after them and while it is unacceptable to push a child out because of poverty, if they're possessed, well, then it's different.

According to Congo's social affairs minister, Bernard Ndjunga, there are about 50,000 homeless children on the streets of Kinshasa, stealing, begging, selling anything they can find.

Still more children are not on the streets but are held virtual prisoner in church compounds, apparently awaiting exorcism. For most people in Western society, understanding how anyone can believe a child is a witch and then beat them is, thankfully, near impossible. But old religions run deep in some communities.

'Superstition and ignorance are part of being human,' Rob told me before reminding me of our own history. 'Remember, we hanged our last "witch" in the UK in the eighteenth century; it's not that long ago. I had a look on the Net; did you know that in 1944 a medium called Helen Duncan was imprisoned under the Witchcraft Act of 1735, which was only repealed in 1951?'

'Bloody hell,' I said, 'it sounds like we could use an Act like that right now.' Yet prosecuting those people we consider responsible for occult abuse is almost impossible. In 2006 Dr Dieudonne Tukala of the Church of Christ in Mission in Tottenham, North London, was arrested and questioned about allegations that he had ill-treated children during deliverance ceremonies, which he denied.

Parents came forward who said Tukala told them to send their children back to Africa and he would pray for them to die. The BBC obtained stills and photographs taken from a video of one of his services showing him boasting about how he had sent a 'possessed' child back to Kinshasa. In the film, Tukala waved a tangle of electrical flexes in front of the audience and described them as 'satanic tools' the boy was using to kill an unborn child. No charges were ever brought against Tukala. It is not against the law to accuse a child of witchcraft – neither is praying for a child to die.[14] Our hands were tied. While I understand the need for freedom of speech, there is a clear argument that the law needs to be changed so that pastors who hold tremendous sway over their congregation can be called to account if they incite any member of their congregation to commit child abuse. One thing is certain: as long as things continue as they are, this problem will continue to grow in the UK, leaving more and more children in danger.

Understanding the motivation of some healers and pastors is comparatively easy. It's all about greed and power. In a bid to line their pockets they are guilty of distorting people's beliefs and preying on the vulnerable and needy. It seems too incredible to believe, but they're getting away with it here in London.

Altogether, we dealt with more than thirty instances of 'possessed' youngsters being named as witches by their families in a matter of months. Some details were later published as part of the Met's own ten-month London-wide study into African witchcraft.[15] Examples include a ten-year-old boy, who was burned with matches, lighters, irons and scalding water by his parents, who were convinced he was possessed.

Nine couples asked social workers to take their child into care, glad to get rid of their 'demon'. Other related cases included ritual abuse, beating, starvation (one boy was starved for three days; another child lost half her bodyweight), stabbing, burning, semi-strangulation and abandonment.

Another boy of nine was beaten and burned after a pastor told his family he was a witch. The terrified child leaped from a first-floor window of his home to escape. A teenage girl was tortured by her relatives, who claimed she was possessed by demons. They were planning to have her exorcized in a London church.

Several children were not allowed to eat meals with the family and suffered from malnutrition, while others were starved for several days. In four cases children were stabbed – the explanation being 'to create a way out for the evil'. In one case, a family was so scared of their child they only touched them with a stick.

Eighteen children who had been abused following an accusation of 'witchcraft' or 'possession' were placed in long-term foster care. Two were placed in secure care. A further twenty-three of their brothers and sisters were also placed in foster care, even though they had not been abused. Seven were eventually returned home and placed on the child protection register. Ten vanished overseas.

Many kids suffered severe psychological trauma as a result of these accusations and came to actually believe they were possessed – how could they not, when their parents, whom they loved most and who knew best, had drummed it into them? Some displayed symptoms of 'possession', including fits, rolling their eyes and talking in tongues, psychological disorders born out of terror, which frustratingly only served to reinforce their parents' beliefs. Most kids who were accused of being witches were actually born in the UK – suggesting perhaps their parents found it difficult to cope with their Westernization.

The research also revealed that many mistakes had been made, thanks in part to a lack of knowledge about this type of abuse. Before Tundé's case came to be widely known, one social worker left a 'possessed' girl who'd been displaying 'symptoms of possession' alone with her father while she was awaiting a medical examination for a suspected physical assault. When the social worker returned with the doctor, the child refused the examination and withdrew all allegations. Not speaking to a child alone remains an all-too-common mistake.

Another child had been sent home for family counselling, even though the carer had already asked for the child to be taken into care. In a separate case, a social worker failed to visit a child even though she'd been taken to various churches for a 'cure' and her family had threatened to send her to Africa.

Previously, while teachers were able to identify children at risk (who were later found to be accused of possession) at an early stage, the level of abuse did not usually reach social care 'threshold criteria' so social services had not been contacted. For example, some of these children had arrived at school hungry and had no packed lunch or money for the canteen. Others were wearing dirty, unlaundered clothes. Once again, a lack of time and resources endangered children and they were left with their families with no further action.

Fortunately, as the knowledge about witchcraft grew, most referrals came from teachers – they practically became our front-line workers, bringing twenty cases to our attention. Some children were referred because of suspicious injuries. Two 'possessed' children were excluded from school for their aggression and two came to a teacher's attention after truanting. Sometimes, as soon as a teacher referred a child, they vanished, turning it into a race against time to find them before they were smuggled abroad.

Once again, the job had taken me to a place I never thought I'd go. It was 6.30 a.m. and I was sitting in the office listening to the *Today* programme on BBC Radio 4. As part of an investigation into the influence of witchcraft in London, the BBC had uncovered evidence that a child in Hackney had been taken out of the UK to be killed for being a witch. My boss was away at the time and I was 'acting up', so I headed this investigation.

The first thing had been to set up the Gold Group. This approach was used for complex and sensitive investigations, which were likely to involve several different agencies. The group is made up of representatives from several agencies and the local community who work together to ensure everything that can be done is done. In this case the BBC also formed part of the group.

Although the BBC had warned us of the report's general content, they hadn't handed over a full transcript. As a precaution, I'd put a team together just in case there was any evidence that identified more children at risk. If it did we needed to be in a position to quickly double-check the facts and interview the journalists before springing into action.

'I hope they do our story first,' I said to Simon, who was listening with me.

'Too right,' he said, stifling a yawn, 'I want to make the most of this ridiculously early start.'

But the broadcast yielded nothing more than what we already knew, so it was time to go after the child in the Congo. This meant another meeting of the Gold Group. I wanted it over with quickly. We had a child abducted to the Democratic Republic of

Congo for possible execution, so we needed to go and bring her back before it was too late.

Now, even I knew that the UK did not have the best of relations with the Congolese government and so we couldn't be sure if they were going to cooperate. I also knew that the higher-ups in the Met would take issue with me jetting off to the Congo, not the safest of destinations.

In preparation I'd called up a friend who'd done some business in Kinshasha and had travelled there several times. Although he said there were risks, it was no more dangerous than your average Friday night in Hackney and many Western companies, such as Shell, had large offices there which were full of European workers.

Right. I entered the meeting ready to do battle. My stance was quite simple: we go and get her back, no messing. I admitted that my style of policing had needed serious adjustment since joining Child Protection but I remained adamant that this was clearly the best course of action.

Previously, PC Karen Jones decided not to interview Victoria Climbié in her home because she was afraid of catching scabies.[16] This to me was unacceptable. If you're worried about going into a child's home, then you find the resources to deal with it. If you just leave the child because you're too worried about yourself, then you shouldn't be a cop, simple as. Taking risks is part of the job. Go in, get the child and then go to the doctor if you're worried about infection. Children are precious, clean or dirty, rich or poor; if they need to be taken from their family or wherever to make them safe, then I will get them, whatever it takes, come hell or high water.

Unfortunately, my adoption of the bullish drug-squad approach of yore did not go down as well as I'd hoped. I was politely commended for my desire to rescue the child before it was pointed out to me that she was in fact a citizen of the DRC, not of the UK. She may well be a 'Hackney Child' in the eyes of the UK law but I couldn't just go to another country and remove one of its citizens because she might be in danger. That would technically be kidnap and would cause a diplomatic incident.

A senior cop added: 'Besides, what country in the world would let a foreign police force in to take one of their own children in circumstances that could embarrass them? Even if we let you go, they'd make the paperwork go on for ever. Once they learn what you want to do in the DRC, they'll probably deny you entry anyway.'

'This is unfortunately a domestic issue for the DRC,' a social work manager stated. 'Witchcraft in the DRC is not seen as the barmy preying on the vulnerable. It's taken as seriously as Christianity is here, by millions of Africans. You won't get her out.'

'Well, if we can't get her out,' I said, trying to hide my exasperation, 'how on earth do we protect her?'

This was met with an uncomfortable silence. Finally, the social worker came up with an idea.

'It may not be the fastest method, but there is International Social Services (ISS). We have liaisons in Africa and they may be able to help.'

And that was it, the decision was made.

Amazingly, they did it. The ISS did indeed find the child. She was safe in an orphanage in Kinshasha. Somehow in the DRC, something had worked to protect her.

She will never know about the Gold Group, the Radio 4 broadcast that told her story to hundreds of thousands of people, and how the BBC, social services, the community and the Met got together to do everything they could think of to save her.

Although we didn't actually do anything to save the child, we had shown that we had a working system in place. Any threat to any child would be followed up with all the resources available to us until the case was over, for good or for bad.

It typified the sort of thing that went on every day in Hackney as part of our effort to do all we could to make life safer for children. In this case we undertook a number of actions that (with hindsight) proved unnecessary. But what we did do was care.

Once again my eyes had been opened to a whole other side of policing; these cases were changing me, as a policeman and a person. Perhaps nothing changed me more, however, than the next case, which took me to the other side of the world. It would show me that even when things didn't go to plan, our efforts could still totally transform someone's life for the better.

CHAPTER FIFTEEN

PREDATOR

Protestors swamped the Strand, meandering noisily as they chanted their way to Trafalgar Square. I punched the inside of the car door in frustration. Rob was driving; we were on our way to the Royal Courts of Justice and in an effort to get there early we'd made the mistake of driving. This demo was going to ensure a child abuser walked free.

There was no way I was going to let that happen.

Rob came to the same conclusion. 'You'd better run for it.' Abandoning the car, I sprinted down the Strand, waved my badge at a startled security guard as I piled through the huge arched entrance of the Royal Courts of Justice and skidded to a halt at the court listings hanging on the wall. I found the location of the relevant case and took off again, my running steps echoing through the huge main hall until I skidded on the stone and burst into a full courtroom. All heads turned.

The barrister, who'd been stalling, said '. . . and here is the officer now.' I received a proper telling-off while I fought to get my breath back, but at least the hearing could go ahead. This was the last chance for my suspect's pre-trial freedom and if he'd got bail I was certain he would've fled straight to Africa.

Just seven days earlier, Jimmy, an old mate of mine from Stokie, had phoned with a terrible case. Two sixteen-year-old sisters, Sylvia and Alison, had been raped more than 150 times by their father. Sylvia had finally called the police after he beat her following a church meeting and told her that they were going back to Africa. Alison, meanwhile, had gone on the run and was still missing.

'Can you deal with Sylvia, Harry?' Jimmy asked. 'She's a bit older than most kids you work with but it might be in your remit.'

I told him no problem, leaving Jimmy free to concentrate on the desperate hunt for Alison. Sylvia had told him her twin may have already been found and smuggled abroad by her father.

My pulse always takes off at the start of a case; I can see it panning out in front of me: get the sisters safe, interviewed, then the hunt for the criminal, the prosecution and a big fat jail sentence at the end of it all. I want to get there as fast as possible.

After talking to Rob, I grabbed Sarah. 'We have a job on,' I said. I love this quiet understatement. Sarah got my meaning straight away, cancelled appointments, rang home to say something important had come up and she didn't know when she'd be back. I did the same; a pang of guilt rippled through me. My wife and kids would be deprived of a husband and father once again. And they couldn't even complain – they knew it was for a good reason: I was hunting evil and protecting the innocent. But that didn't make it fair on them, of course.

That done, I refocused and called a council of war with Rob where we officially launched the inquiry and decided on a strategy. The first step was to gather the immediate evidence. That meant we had to get hold of both daughters and interview them as fast as possible.

Once Sylvia had arrived at the suite and had been given a

thorough medical, Sarah conducted the interview. There was no social worker because, being sixteen, they no longer considered her a child, but she was still a child in relation to the law. Her main concern was for her sister. 'Alison is quiet and shy,' she said, 'I'm really worried about her.'

Gradually, Sarah steered Sylvia through the difficult process of telling her traumatic story. They'd arrived in the UK from Ghana just a year ago. As soon as they were alone with their father, he'd raped them repeatedly – always starting with Sylvia, the stronger of the two sisters. He took them to seedy hotels or simply raped them in the back of his car in quiet industrial estates, railway yards and parks. Sexual predators recognize these ordinary, anonymous areas as places where they will be virtually invisible to people passing through and, mindful that using the same place too often might possibly attract attention, they tend to use several different locations, just to be sure.

I used to find it funny when the dazzling headlights of a marked police car swept a car park late at night, illuminating the silhouettes of men having sex with their girlfriends, wives or prostitutes. There typically would be a frantic attempt to regain decency in record time.

Some guys have really weird reactions about being caught with their pants down. Some seem almost pleased to have been caught. Others are quite aggressive, as if we've intruded on their right to have sex in public.

Most men stare back at the beam of an officer's torch and say 'What?' in a very aggrieved manner. What they actually mean, of course, is, 'Get the hell out of here!'

The problem is that women are sometimes abducted by men in cars, and are often raped in them. There are many, many cases of illegal minicab drivers preying on women who travel alone late at night. It's all too easy for a young woman to step into a car after a night out, thinking it's a taxi, that this is their safest option to get home, only to realize too late that they've just stepped into their worst nightmare.

This is why cops disturb couples in cars (not just because we're having fun or are perverts), just in case someone is being held against their will. Now and then, we find children.

With teenagers it instantly becomes more complicated. Officers wouldn't necessarily know that man was their father, and the sixteen- or seventeen-year-old daughter may be too scared to cry for help. This situation is typical of that suffered by children in trouble time and time again. The safety of the police and social workers is so close they can touch it, but the words won't come out, for fear of what their father will do to them, or in case we don't believe them.

I made a note of all the locations where they were attacked. We would check these sites for forensic evidence. No stone would be left unturned – literally. There were, however, tremendous difficulties in collecting forensic evidence in these cases. A father might say: 'Of course my DNA was on my daughter's trousers; I'd had sex with my wife on the sofa the night before last.' In cases of rape by a stranger, it's different as criminals are pretty much convicted when presented with that type of evidence.

Sylvia told us that her father started by raping her first before moving on to Alison. I had expected it to be the other way round, that he would start with the weaker, quieter one first. 'He raped us separately at first, then together,' she said quietly.

He was a deeply religious man, she told me, and said he often referred to a passage in the Bible about a prophet 'laying down with his daughters'. Another insight into the mind of the abuser – in this case he was looking for religious justification for his actions.

The interview was interrupted when news came in that Omari, Sylvia's father, was downstairs. This was bad. We were allowed to hold him for thirty-six hours; it would take almost that long to finish interviewing the daughters – assuming we found Alison – before we could even consider starting on the father.

Even then, once we had him in the interview room, those precious thirty-six hours would fly by (and at least eight of these hours are put aside to allow the suspect to sleep). Time is vital in interviews of this nature, where we were using the information from the highly detailed interviews with his daughters to catch him out and to persuade him to make admissions. This, of course, would be all conducted under the watchful eye of a solicitor – who would make sure his client got plenty of rest.

I spoke to Rob and we quickly agreed to send him packing. This is often the case in serious crimes, where news reports say: 'The suspect has been bailed pending further inquiries.' It's to make sure we don't use up those precious thirty-six hours of interview time. There was a chance he'd flee the country while we interviewed his daughters but I banked on the father being too confident of getting away with it.

As soon as he was bailed, I returned to the interview suite to finish talking to Sylvia. A few minutes later, Rob came marching over to us, smiling. 'Alison's been found,' he said, 'she's fine and will be with us shortly. She'd been sleeping rough.' Jimmy had done a great job, finding her on the streets of London so quickly. Now we could really motor on with the investigation. The sisters were delighted to be reunited but as they hugged, crying tears of joy, I had to apologize and drag Alison off to be interviewed.

When we had the full story, totalling over eight hours, we checked that all the details in their stories had matched (which they did) and decided on our arrest strategy. In these sorts of cases, there is no 'bloodstained knife' but I called the forensics team and gave them a very specific shopping list of items to examine, including everything from a mop used to assault the sisters to both of his cars. I then scooped up the suspect while a POLSA (Police Search Advisor) team and forensics took the house apart.

While this was going on, other officers were already questioning people from the suspect's church group and hunting for DNA and CCTV evidence at every location the girls had told us about.

I arranged for his brief and as he was booked in by the custody sergeant, I set about trying to build a rapport, in an effort to get him talking, but he stayed silent. Either he thought that he was in deep shit or that we had nothing on him. I couldn't tell.

I started playing a little strategic game where we disclosed the evidence we had against him. We don't actually have to supply a thing at this stage but the trick is to supply the basic facts, while withholding a few vital pieces of evidence. This way the suspect thinks we don't know about certain aspects of his crime and will lie, effectively stitching himself up. We leave this part to the end as solicitors sometimes kick off and demand consultations and act as if they were entitled to know about them beforehand. Of course, an innocent person doesn't need disclosure at all because they can just tell the truth.

Day one of interviews was handled gently; I gave him plenty of time to emphatically deny every single allegation. This is a good way of building rapport; standing back, giving the interviewee time and space to speak how they choose, to carefully deconstruct the accusations at their own pace. I'll nod sagely all the while, as if I'm taking their nonsense seriously.

Towards the end of the day, I took a photocopied sheet out of my file and read: "'And they made their father drink wine that night: and the firstborn went in, and lay with her father; and he perceived not when she lay down, nor when she arose.'

"'And it came to pass on the morrow, that the firstborn said unto the younger, Behold, I lay yesternight with my father: let us make him drink wine this night also; and go thou in, and lie with him, that we may preserve seed of our father."

"'And they made their father drink wine that night also: and the younger arose, and lay with him; and he perceived not when she lay down, nor when she arose."

"'Thus were both the daughters of Lot with child by their father.'"

This was the passage he had quoted to his daughters. For a few moments, it was so quiet I could hear the spools on the cassette tape turning. I could see his discomfort; he broke eye contact, fidgeted. To me, it's obvious he's as guilty as hell. To a jury listening to the tape, however, this is simply a silent pause.

I broke the silence. 'Did you quote this to your daughters?'

No answer.

'But you are familiar with the passage, are you not?'

No answer.

Our time was up for day one. The following morning kicked off with a series of 'no comments'. Now, if anyone thinks we hear 'no comment', and give up, then they're very, very wrong.

I started from where we left off, this time speaking as if I was in the courtroom: 'All I'm asking is whether you are familiar with that passage from the Bible . . . Come on, Omari, an innocent man would surely answer this . . . the jury will wonder why you didn't want to answer that.'

I kept the pressure turned up high, looking for cracks. Once again, I saw the emotional leakage in his expression, body language and sweat – sadly something the jury would never be able to take into account.

'Come on, Omari,' I said, 'you know this is serious stuff you're accused of. If you're innocent, you can talk to me. Hell, I'm the only one who will listen to you now and take you seriously. You know what people are saying about you now? You of all people know that confession is good for the soul. Truth is the only relief.'

Still getting nowhere, I showed some concern, tried to empathize, told him he was someone special, hinted that I might even share his views. On the rare occasions he did speak, I responded positively, 'I hear you, Omari, I hear you.'

I always keep going throughout a no-comment interview. It's important for the jury to understand that he has had every chance to explain himself, every opportunity to present us with an alternative story.

But by lunch, we were running out of time. I met with the solicitors from the Crown Prosecution Service. 'We need to get him banged up,' I told them, 'he has to be remanded or he'll do a runner. We need more time to examine scenes and take statements.'

They agreed. That meant we could hold him overnight, haul him up before a judge in the morning for a pre-trial hearing where a decision would be made whether to keep him in jail until his trial date.

The problem was that the CPS solicitor may have twenty cases to process that morning and will not be on the ball on all of them. I needed to be there to make sure I was on hand to answer any crucial questions that arose.

And arise they did. Although we got him remanded, we soon had a nasty setback when Omari's legal team dropped a proper bombshell. The mother of the girls had sent in a fax from Africa that stated she did not believe them. We asked for time to consider this development. I grabbed the fax and saw it was typed in excellent English and signed. The brief read over my shoulder. 'A mother supplying evidence against her own children; now *that's* a serious obstacle,' he said.

We were seriously fucked. The guy was going to get bail and hop on a plane back to Africa.

'I can't let that happen,' I told our brief. 'What have I got to do to put him away?'

At that point, Rob rolled up, saw my gloomy expression and asked what had happened. He wasn't fazed. 'What do you do, Detective, when you receive a statement like this?'

'Well, find out if it's true,' I supposed, 'but . . .'

'Exactly. Check it out. Get hold of the mum.'

Now I like a challenge but trying to get through to an almost phoneless small town in a Third World country is not as easy as it sounds. There's no 118118 in Ghana. But, miraculously, I rang a number in the right town in Ghana and the person who answered handed me over to someone who spoke English. 'Oh yes, I know the woman you want.'

'Can you get her to come to the phone?'

'I can but you'll have to wait.'

'It's urgent!' I yelled through the static, causing heads to turn. Not wanting to lose the connection, I also yelled, 'I'll hold!'

Unfortunately the line went dead. After a few more false starts, we finally got the mother on the phone. The first thing I noted was that she didn't speak English (so how could she have put her name to that statement?) and it's only after a translator joined her that we started to get to the heart of the matter. 'She say she sign fax,' the translator said, 'but she thought it something so her children could go school.'

'I see. I'll call back.' After a quick conflab with Rob, the next part of the inquiry was soon made clear. We had to get to Ghana to find and interview the mother, before Omari's team arranged a new bail hearing.

'I'd better get my passport,' I said to Rob, and then, more to myself, 'I wonder how the missus is going to take this bit of news?'

'Just don't kick off any wars, Harry!' Rob replied, only half-jokingly.

CHAPTER SIXTEEN

BIG GAME

If you'd told me six months ago I'd be on a plane bound for a tiny West African country to take a witness statement I would have laughed my head off. Instead, I was holding my breath as we descended towards Ghana's international airport – a fellow passenger had tapped me on the arm to tell me (with a grin) that we were lucky – the runway had just reopened after a Boeing, just like this one, carrying delegates to Liberia's peace talks, collapsed on its wheels during take-off.

Luckily this sort of thing just added to my excitement. I always enjoyed a challenge, and this was about as challenging as it got. Besides, I was damned if a few thousand miles of ocean and desert were going to stop me from convicting Omari.

The Republic of Ghana is a small country about the size of the UK, which sits on the Gold Coast between the Côte d'Ivoire and Togo and faces the Gulf of Guinea. Its coast is lined with colonial ports, built by the French, English and Portuguese, who all mined the little country dry of gold. Now they're after the estimated 3 billion barrels of oil hidden below the dusty earth.

Sarah was with me. We stumbled our way out of the plane, through the chaotic airport into a gusty evening heat – it was like being slapped with freshly boiled towels. Outside, a makeshift bus station was packed with overloaded minivans coming and going, disgorging dozens of passengers. Nearby was a ramshackle market where women squatted behind tiny tables stacked high with bowls of rice, salted fish, as well as dozens of baskets of fruit and vegetables. They shouted out their prices to passing shoppers. Another sauntered across a dusty, cracked football pitch, a large tub balanced effortlessly on her head, oblivious to the game under way – kids shouted for her to get a move on.

We were met by Ray, our very smartly turned out official unarmed police escort. 'Hi, Mr Keeble,' he said, throwing out his hand with enthusiasm. 'We'll drop your things off at the hotel before going to the police station.'

He led us to the 4×4 we'd hired, along with a driver (who had cost less than the fuel). We needed it because our witness lived 'up-country'; in other words, it was a bloody long drive.

As we loaded our equipment, a screaming voice suddenly erupted from behind me. I span round to see Ray rummaging frantically through his trouser pockets. This continued until Ray retrieved his phone. 'That's my boss,' he grinned apologetically, 'I recorded him telling me off.' I took an instant liking to Ray; he seemed like a man to trust.

Having said that, when we reached the hotel, they had no record of any reservation for us and were full. Ray was mortified. 'Never mind,' I said, 'the Metropolitan Police will have to pick up the tab. Where's the biggest hotel around here?' Unfortunately, my hopes of staying in the largest hotel (and therefore the plushest) in town were dashed when that turned out to be full too. We found a very basic hotel with cell-like rooms. Oh well.

We stopped in every village en route to the police station. 'We have to,' said Ray, 'you're the day's big news.' People ran forward though the red dust and surrounded the car in amazing welcoming committees, before we'd even had time to stop. All kinds of goods were on sale. Not sure what to do, I refused to buy anything, but Sarah got stuck in and wound up with an armful of souvenirs.

As we drove, we passed mile upon mile of cocoa plantations. I saw many sick people just lying by the side of the road, on the edge of the lush savannah, some too weak to move, but they all, almost without exception, waved and smiled as we shot past.

As dusk closed in and the road wound its way through the scrub, we zoomed past a man sat on a home-made trolley. Both legs were gone below the knees and he shoved himself along the furrowed road with his knuckles. I looked back over my shoulder and he gave me a friendly salute. I watched him until the dust clouds cut him off from view.

'Look, Harry!' Sarah shouted, and I turned round to see a termites' nest bigger than a London postbox. Amazing. But, I reminded myself, we weren't here for the wildlife.

We arrived at the local police station at twilight. Stepping into the police station was like entering a time warp. 'Check it out, Harry,' Sarah said, 'it's ancient!'

The interior was lit by one weak light bulb. Despite the chunks of plaster that fell off the walls and the thick layer of red dust over everything, it actually wasn't that bad. Behind the front counter stood a smiling female constable who turned out to be Ray's cousin, Ameena. As my eyes adjusted I saw a wall of bars to the right. A cage. It was then that I saw their eyes, gleaming softly in the lamplight. Then their hands, about a dozen of which gripped the bars. Faces behind them stared at us with no little interest.

Ameena showed us round proudly, and with good reason. The station was in very good nick. 'Check out the OB book,' said Sarah, 'it's amazing.' Until the late 1990s, every English police station had an Occurrence Book, a written record of the day's events. This station's OB was the neatest I'd ever seen, neatly filled in and religiously kept.

It was very surreal, as if we were standing in an idealized version of a Victorian police station. I had to remind myself that just a few weeks ago I'd been stood freezing my arse off in the January snow in a smart suit in Hackney.

I was brought back down to earth when a drunken sergeant suddenly shattered the silence, emerging from a back room. He marched straight up to me, shouting. My attention was very quickly drawn to the AK-47 he was waving around like he was Rambo.

I looked at Sarah with a 'here we go' expression and readied myself for a fight, momentarily forgetting all the strict instructions I'd been given to behave myself and not start any wars. Luckily, Ray stepped in between us, and the sergeant suddenly calmed down and vanished as quickly as he'd appeared. Ray apologized and politely asked us if we wanted to make an official complaint. Not wanting to make ourselves any more unpopular, we declined his offer.

Eventually it was time. We moved off into the humid night and, after a twenty-minute drive, we arrived on the outskirts of a small shanty town. We left the sanctity of the air-conditioned car and the heat once again slapped us over the head. My face wrinkled at the smell of a stinking open sewer that ran busily down both sides of the road.

People were sat outside huts of varying shapes and sizes, oblivious to the heat and the smell, eating dinner and chatting under the light of the occasional naked light bulb. 'Here we are,' Ray said, as we stopped outside one of the huts. The girls' mother, Jamelia, emerged. She was extraordinarily beautiful; she greeted us warmly, and proudly showed us round her one-room dirt-floor house. This done, we adjourned to the main living area, which was outside, and sat on boxes. We chatted through an interpreter.

She was warm and friendly, very concerned about her girls and very keen to talk.

Knackered, hot and disorientated, I looked into the eyes of this charming, helpful woman. She'd sent her beautiful, intelligent teenage daughters to London to study, to make a success of their lives, to give them opportunities they wouldn't have had here. How was I going to tell her that the man she married had raped both of her daughters 150 times?

I took a deep breath. She remained calm, although tears did fall as I spoke. Step by gentle step, we went through the lengthy formal process of taking a statement. This proved to be a shattering experience for all of us and, exhausted, we decided to pick up where we'd left off the following day at our hotel. Despite the exhaustion, I couldn't sleep and lay there in the hot little box room, staring into nothing; the day's images circling round and round my head in a drowsy merry-go-round.

The next morning we were joined at the hotel by several police officers, including the gun-toting sergeant, the interpreter, Ameena and some of Ameena's relatives. I guessed this might have something to do with the fact that the hotel had a good stash of food and booze. When lunchtime came, I said lunch was on me (i.e. the taxpayer) – that is food and all their non-alcoholic drinks. I didn't want the sergeant to produce a repeat performance and emphasized the phrase 'non-alcoholic drinks' a couple of times, just to make sure.

After lunch, although we soon became immersed in our work, I kept a wary eye on the waiters and what was being ordered. I thought they'd behaved themselves until the sergeant tried to get up and fell over the table. They'd been ordering orange juice but the waiter (who I now noticed was swaying gently behind the bar) had obviously been told to add a decent amount of booze to each order before he brought it over.

I got up, furious, but the AK-47 slung over the sergeant's shoulder gave me pause for thought. He caught my eye. I smiled and asked if I could have a look at his gun. To my amazement, he handed it over. 'Any chance of firing off a few rounds outside?' I asked, pointing the gun and mimicking the kickback. But he wasn't that far gone. He held out his hands, I gave the gun back, and he quietly staggered away to sleep it off.

By the time we were happy the statement was watertight, we were all exhausted, none more so than Jamelia. We sloped off to bed and the next morning we stopped by her house to say goodbye. Jamelia was waiting for us and presented us with some beautiful traditional Ghanaian gowns.

'Thank you,' she said, 'for looking after my girls.' I was speechless. She had so little, yet here she was, handing over what were extraordinarily valuable gifts. We were totally bowled over, humbled and shamed – after all, we'd brought nothing to give her (rules state we can't give witnesses presents). We accepted and promised her that we would do everything we could to see justice done.

Once again, we blasted back along the dust roads on our way back to our hotel in the capital, stopping in villages along the way. We stopped near a school where we saw a child being whipped on the bottom with what looked like a tightly knotted bunch of twigs. Sarah made ready to intervene but I caught her arm. Ray saw us and nodded, shrugging his shoulders. 'Things are different here,' he said.

He was right. Parents from Africa living in the UK were often surprised when they were admonished by social services for hitting a child with a wooden spoon or flex. We have to be a bit careful about knee-jerk reactions – in the 1970s in the UK a naughty schoolchild would have been caned, and most people accepted that as a legitimate punishment, and there was certainly no law against it (caning was eventually banned in 1986, and we were the last country in Europe to do so).

Once we made it back to the capital and collected our keys, I was amazed to receive an enormous phone bill. Someone had snuck into my room and had made a lot of calls! Luckily, the management accepted my explanation straight away and the offending items were struck off.

We had one more day, and we planned to spend some of it debriefing Ray and his colleagues. A smiling Ray was waiting by the 4×4 in the blazing sun when we came down in the morning. 'We have somewhere special in mind for the debrief,' he said.

Outside the hotel grounds were a convoy of four police vehicles full of beaming police officers. 'What the—?' I looked at Sarah and she shrugged.

'Better go with the flow, Harry.'

We travelled for an hour outside the capital, passing through several military checkpoints, until finally we reached our destination. It was a restaurant – with one key difference. It was situated right next to the wall of the Akosombo Dam, the largest man-made lake in the world, with a 5,000-kilometre shoreline. As Sarah and I stood on the dam, looking at the clear, flat water surrounded by low green hills stretching off into the horizon, I said, 'When I joined the MPS, way back in 1989, I never, ever thought I'd have a day like this.'

The food was amazing and in a burst of generosity (which I suspect was expected) I offered to pick up the tab for nine of us, plus take-out meals for those junior police and army officers waiting outside. The bill came to £100. I couldn't believe it. That's what I spend in London at a Middlesex Poly Boys reunion lunch.

Autumn had definitely arrived when we landed back at Heathrow. It was cold, dark, damp and dismal and we were in a sombre mood. 'Well, what the hell's wrong with you guys?' a voice called out as we passed through the Arrivals door. To our amazement, workaholic Rob had decided to pick us up. I don't know of many bosses who would collect their subordinates first thing on a Sunday morning.

After we'd debriefed Rob, I finally made it home to the wife and the kids. My son was duly impressed with the ceremonial gown and begged to be allowed to take them into school. I agreed, and happily, gratefully climbed into bed.

My rest was short-lived, however. I forced myself to sit up straight. It was dark. The phone was ringing. It was 5 a.m. "'lo?" I mumbled. It was Rob. 'We've got a murder case. Get your arse down here asap.'

CHAPTER SEVENTEEN

MURDER

Rob let the bombshells fall one by one to the stunned team. A nineteen-month-old toddler had been punched repeatedly in the head. A neighbour who'd overheard shouting had called the police but by the time they'd arrived, the beating was over, the little boy was out cold and an ambulance was on the way.

So were the police. Paramedics did what they could at the scene before continuing treatment in the ambulance while making a desperate dash for Homerton Hospital.

Doctors had battled through until dawn trying to save the toddler but the news was bad. The child, Tyrell, was hooked up to a life-support machine and had severe brain damage. They planned to wait a few hours for a miracle, but he was expected to deteriorate steadily; the machine would be switched off that afternoon.

'So,' Rob said grimly, 'this is really a murder case. It should be with the murder squad . . . but they've turned it down.'

Several indignant four-letter exclamations followed this statement.

'It's a technicality, but as the victim hasn't been declared dead, they say they can't do it. I've also asked them for a homicide assessment team car but they declined that too. So, we're on our own.'

Fuck.

'Harry, I want you to coordinate from here. Uniform have the scene secured and the parents, Sandra Rowe, twenty-nine, and John White, thirty-seven, are in custody.

'Harry? We need to move fast.' I pulled myself together. Rob was right, any detective worth his salt knows that the first hour, the 'golden hour' after the crime has been committed, is utterly crucial.

But the enormity of the task was truly daunting. The resources available to the murder squad are second to none and normally forty of the Met's most experienced detectives would immediately have leaped into the breach. We had a team of fifteen, including six detectives, three of whom hadn't even been detectives for more than a year.

I tried to focus as I realized that this investigation, a horrific child murder, was suddenly in our hands – and here I was, a humble sergeant who didn't really deserve the title of detective. I tried not to think about the headlines that would surely come once word got out. I failed.

Rob and I had some crucial decisions to make and a mountain to climb. The crime scene needed to be managed, as did witnesses and our suspects. The mother and father had already been separated and taken to different police stations in different cars. These vehicles then had to be taken out of service and forensically examined.

Once Rowe and White had each been isolated in a clean room, they were treated as a crime scene and were processed as such. They were told to strip while standing on a large square of white paper. Any evidence that fell while they undressed would be captured. Their clothes were carefully placed in special breathable evidence bags and labelled.

These would be studied for blood-splatter. We hoped that this analysis might reveal who struck the fatal blow and whether the other person was present and, if so, where they were standing, and how close.

Rowe and White put on white paper suits in place of their clothes, and samples were taken of their hair, nails and saliva. We didn't need their consent for this; it's compulsory – it can be done the easy or the hard way. Blood needs the suspect's consent because it's an invasive medical action that a doctor has to perform. If they refuse, then this decision will be used in evidence against them.

Meanwhile the flat needed to be searched. When the forensics teams arrived they found that the PCs had done a good job; they'd not contaminated the scene and had conducted a flash search. Any uniformed officer's natural instinct is to remove the victim, arrest the suspects and preserve all the evidence by sealing the area as quickly as possible for forensics. But, as has happened before, another room might later be discovered to contain more horror, another victim still clinging to life who dies while the unsuspecting police stand guard outside. So to prevent this, the first officer on the scene always quickly checks the whole premises, while disturbing as little as possible.

Inside, everything was like the *Mary Celeste*: food on the table, cigarettes burned down in the ashtray. It was also filthy. Sticky carpets, dirty, torn and stained furniture; the kitchen black with dirt, oven covered in burned fat.

Bits and pieces of the paramedics' gear were still in the lounge; it was possible to see exactly where Tyrell had lain as they'd worked on him. Everything was videoed and photographed. Outside, officers took down the car registration numbers in the street (the owners could be potential witnesses) and CCTV footage was acquired, as was the recording of the 999 calls from the neighbour and White, asking for an ambulance.

Rob was under incredible pressure; he was constantly being asked to make instantaneous but crucial decisions that would influence the outcome of the investigation. I recorded everything in the decision log; this would be vital when the inevitable inquiry into Tyrell's death began.

Tyrell's body was also considered to be part of the crime scene and it was treated as such. Skin, blood, hair, tiny shards of broken fingernails and clothing fibres from his attacker may have been left on his body and clothes.

The London Ambulance Service often moan when we seize their ambulances. They have good reason – they're a precious resource, but also of significant evidential value. We try to give them back as soon as possible. We needed to search the ambulance for any hairs, fibres, etc., that might have fallen off Tyrell and could be linked to his attackers. A sample of blood, taken before he'd been given a transfusion, was also claimed as evidence. Police officers were dispatched to the hospital to collect and bag his clothes.

I tried not to, but I thought about Tyrell all too often that day, on his back in intensive care, head to one side, his blackened eyes staring sightlessly ahead. He had a broken jaw and nose. Tubes and wires left his body in every direction. Fluids were being fed intravenously through a line in the back of his bruised hand; there was a catheter and another line from his stomach and a tube in his throat because he couldn't breathe for himself.

Being police officers, we were masters of speculation and went through every conceivable scenario, but there was only one possibility: either the child's mother or her current partner or both of them together had beaten Tyrell to death.

But this didn't make our job any easier; in fact there was a very nasty Catch-22, which, as a police officer, if you don't learn to live with it, will drive you mad. We needed to prove who murdered Tyrell but if Rowe and White both denied it and there were no witnesses, and the forensic evidence didn't amount to much, we couldn't prosecute one, the other or both of them for murder.

It's soul-destroying. That's why the pressure was so great to get all the evidence bagged and tagged as fast as possible, without any contamination. It was our best chance of guaranteeing a prosecution. The law has been recently tightened up to make this harder.

We had previously dealt with Tyrell and a quick phone call established that the family had a history with social services. When their file came through, one fact stood clear above all others: Tyrell had been taken off the child protection register just six days before he was murdered.

Shit.

Social services had seen Tyrell four times in the month before he died. White had been made the baby's primary carer as Rowe had been judged to be incapable of caring for the child. A psychologist had warned: 'She cannot be left alone with Tyrell, even for a short while.'

The natural reaction when you hear this is to go mental. But as ever, it's not that straightforward. Up until the day of Tyrell's death, all of his injuries were below the neck. A social worker cannot lay a hand on a child they're visiting; it's the law. So if the child is wearing jumpers at the time of the visit and the parents are clever enough to make all the right noises then the social worker will tick the box and leave, no doubt running with their fat lever arch files full of case info to catch the bus to their next case meeting, to see their third family that day, to stop by a care home to check on a child, to pick up their own kids from school and whatever else was on their impossible schedule.

Information poured in at an overwhelming rate. The office ticked over with silent professionalism as we went about our tasks quietly and steadily. There was no time for emotion, no room for outrage or banter. Finally, Rob finished a call and said to himself, 'This is ridiculous,' and dialled the murder squad.

'I've got fifteen officers on my entire squad,' he told them firmly, 'we're interviewing and searching for witnesses, setting up forensics in six different locations, we've got two suspects denying everything, one of whom I'm sure has a very low IQ and needs a psychiatric assessment, we have officers at the hospital, others trying to find the biological father and any other relatives and you won't even send us a homicide car, so we at least have the right kit to start a murder inquiry. I'm turning this investigation over to you as of now and *if you refuse it, you can explain why to the powers that be.*'

He hung up. I resisted the temptation to applaud. Almost as soon as he placed the phone on its cradle it rang again. He snatched it up. 'What?' he snapped. His face fell. A moment later he said, 'I see, right, well thanks for letting me know.' He looked up at me. 'They turned off the machine. Tyrell died five minutes ago.' Now the remit had been satisfied, the murder squad would arrive shortly.

Tyrell had died needlessly. His death affected everyone, especially the doctors and nurses that had fought so hard for his life, and then had to watch him die.

The question is – would Tyrell still be alive if social services had had more resources? When Tyrell was born, social workers placed Rowe, who was judged to be sufficiently retarded as to be unable to cope as a mother on her own, and her son under twenty-four-hour supervision at a foster home.

The Borough of Hackney had the highest rate of schizophrenia in the UK (three times the national average) and the fourth highest incidence of neurosis.[17] Despite this, there remained a desperate shortage of secure beds available. The pressure to send her out on her own was constant and unbearable. When Rowe started seeing White, it was taken as a blessing and she was discharged. Six months later, after months of savage abuse, Tyrell was dead.

Permit me a soapbox moment. Why is it that children, the most precious, most vulnerable part of our society, are not provided with a five-star service to protect them when things go wrong? Is it to do with funding? If so I know where we can get it from. Why is it that the bureaucrats think it's worth throwing away billions on quangos like the Milk Development Council (MDC) which requires several million pounds so forty-four people can be employed to encourage schoolchildren to drink more milk, partly by producing snazzy poster adverts featuring celebrities?

Back in 1997, the MDC consisted of just four officials employed in a modest central London office. It went on to earn the distinction of being Britain's fastest-growing quango. At the time of Tyrell's death it had extensive new offices in Cirencester and forty-four staff. It levied £7 million a year from dairy farmers, plus a further £5 million from taxpayers and other businesses – and what was it all for? Well, in its own words: '[it's] all about making people feel good about milk, putting milk back on the agenda and in a positive light'.

And yet children are suffering and sometimes dying when we could do better. I wonder which the bureaucrats think is more important? Making milk 'cool' or diverting those funds to improve the fight to try to end the torture of toddlers in the UK?

It's not like the money isn't there. Just staying with the quango example, the government created 113 new quangos between 1997 and 2004. Research by the Economic Research Council, Britain's oldest think-tank, showed that spending on such agencies soared to £167.5 billion in 2006, up from £24.1 billion in 1998. Yes, that's £167.5 *billion*, not million.[18]

The name – an acronym for Quasi-Autonomous Non-Governmental Organisation – covers a host of public bodies such as regulators, trade bodies, advisory panels, museums and art galleries as well as wackily named institutions such as the British Potato Council (winner of the most useless quango of the year before it was quietly merged into a superquango).

Quangos are run and staffed by unaccountable, box-ticking bureaucrats, who are paid huge salaries by the taxpayer. Quango bosses spend hundreds of thousands of our pounds each year on lobbying MPs at party conferences. Tens of thousands of pounds go on dinners and drinks parties at which officials entertain politicians in an attempt to win more public funding. Many of these organizations seem to have been created just to give the impression that Whitehall is serious about doing something.

For example, in 2005, TV chef Jamie Oliver cooked up a storm over the dreadful nutritional state of our kids' school dinners. The Department for Education and Skills, in a desperate knee-jerk reaction to show it was doing something positive, established the School Food Trust with the aim of 'transforming school food and food skills'. It employs ten civil servants, including a chief executive paid £85,000. At least £60 million has already been allocated to the trust.

While NHS trusts and social services were sacking staff, freezing pay, training and hiring due to funding deficits, the public money available to quangos went up, and up, and up. The Training and Development Agency for Schools was behind advertisements designed to lure young graduates into the teaching profession. Their budget was £669 million in 2006, more than three times as much as in 1998.[19]

In terms of child protection, CAFCASS – the Children and Family Court Advisory and Support Service – was set up in 2001 to safeguard and promote the welfare of children; give advice to the family courts; make provision for children to be represented and provide information, advice and support to children and their families. Sounds great, doesn't it?

Alas, CAFCASS has been attacked in several recent Ofsted reports. One 2008 report, which looked at North Yorkshire and Humberside, makes for particularly painful reading. It made it very clear that the lack of accountability over many years had allowed a culture of complacency to develop where there was little objectivity – leading to mass failure. CAFCASS in the south-west was also branded 'inadequate' in 2009 and that 'the views of children are not given sufficient weight'.[20]

Court secrecy, which CAFCASS insisted upon, does not protect the children. Secrecy protects the people who make money out of child protection from being held to account. How did the secrecy of the system protect Victoria Climbié? Secrecy left children at risk by hiding incompetence – all for the princely sum of £100 million a year.

Should these funds not be diverted towards improving the lot of the social services' child protection department? These are real kids dying here, kids in England, in London, the greatest, richest city in the world, dying for the lack of a really effective system, more training, and most importantly, more social workers.

I can hear the stock response: 'It's not that simple.'

Bullshit. I know it is. The Met realized Child Protection was chronically overlooked and underfunded. After the death of Victoria Climbié they had rightly thrown resources at the department. Although we still had a recruitment problem, this was gradually changing as we started to prosecute headline-grabbing cases. Also, management – Rob included – were working hard to transform Child Protection into a serious investigative department. We now chase every single abuser for as far and as long as it takes, whether that means travelling to Africa or Northern Ireland.

The increased funding and value made all the difference; more kids' lives were being saved, more children were being rescued from lives of terror, torture and neglect and we were nailing more and more child abusers. Baby Peter highlights that we are not there yet, but we have moved forward a great deal since Victoria's death, I can assure you.

Right. Sorry about that. As someone who cares about the state of child protection in the UK I simply had to get it off my chest.

The parents 'no commented' most of their way through the interviews. They understood (on the advice of their briefs) that this was their best chance of getting away with murder. The pair blamed each other, before White finally admitted neglect while Rowe was found to be so mentally deficient that she was certified as unfit to plead (her IQ was just fifty, and she had a reading age of five).

They were charged with murder but the lack of evidence meant that they were done for child cruelty instead. This was a slam-dunk case. A post-mortem revealed that almost every bone in Tyrell's body had been fractured. His thigh bone had been twisted, he had seven fractured ribs, a broken collarbone and was covered in bruises. These were all inflicted during the last two-and-a-half months of his life. As Tyrell was in their care, and they admitted that they'd failed to get help for him, they were sent down. White got three years, while Rowe received a supervision and treatment order with Lambeth social services for two years.

I do not know why, and I find it hard to live with the fact that a child can be beaten to death in the presence of its official carers and yet neither of them are prosecuted for the crime of murder or for the fact that the child died while in their care. But they can still be prosecuted for neglecting to seek treatment for injuries (obviously the result of violent acts) sustained months before. New laws have since been introduced increasing culpability in these cases, but this loophole still exists and this case was by no means the exception. In April 2009 Claire Biggs, from Newham, East London, was found guilty of child cruelty while her partner, Paul Husband, was successfully prosecuted for neglect. Rhys, Biggs's two-month-old son, died on 8 May 2006 and was found to have injuries including seventeen broken ribs, a broken shoulder and a fractured arm. Because the cause of Rhys's death could not be established, the pair only faced cruelty charges. Biggs was jailed for eight years for assault.

Is that justice?

Once again, the attacks went unnoticed by health workers despite the fact that they knew the mother had another child taken into care in 2001. Yet again, there were a number of missed opportunities and a breakdown in sharing information.

After the Tyrell Rowe trial, Hackney Council issued a statement: 'The Area Child Protection Committee is concluding its investigation. Recommendations will be implemented by the respective agencies. Appropriate action will be taken as required if individual failings are identified.'

But the results of their investigation were never made public. It's precisely this sort of reaction that increases the public's antagonism towards social workers. I have not read this report, but there is another element here. It may have uncovered good practice by social workers as well. The good work that social services undoubtedly do is rarely revealed. They don't have commendation ceremonies like the police. I am all for lambasting incompetency and serious mistakes, but social workers seem to operate in a world without recognition. This is not good for their morale or their profession – and therefore children. We need to be transparent. It's the public's children we're supposed to be protecting, after all.

CHAPTER EIGHTEEN

'EASTENDERS'

Once again, I was on a long-distance manhunt, this time with Byron on the Caribbean island of Trinidad. We were hunting for witnesses in a case of abuse that happened years ago.

Byron was about to become my new boss; Rob was nearing the end of his thirty-year police career. Once Rob retired, Byron had the almost impossible task of stepping into his shoes – and because the role was so demanding, they had opted for a longer than average handover. He was keen to get his hands dirty and this proved to be the ideal opportunity.

A lone policeman, who was barely out of his teens, drove us straight from the airport to the capital Port au Prince without uttering a word. Our clothes stuck fast in the humidity; we constantly necked a bottle of water as we drove through the insufferable heat. Before us were a mishmash of huts, temples, bars, offices, tower blocks that reflected the carnival-based culture and the heavily industrialized economy. With strong Chinese, Indian, African and British roots, Trinidad's melting pot is just about the most well-seasoned there is.

Thanks to the island's plentiful natural oil and gas reserves, there's never really been a need to woo holidaymakers to bolster the economy. The lack of tourism was plain to see with many poor areas within a stone's throw of modern industrial towers of giants such as Citibank.

As we passed through a poor part of town, our bodyguard suddenly yelled: 'They've got machetes!'

Sure enough, about four men were targeting what looked like an unarmed boy. 'Stop the car!' I screamed, and we skidded to a halt. I saw another machete slice through the air. A man covered in blood was staggering across a patch of grass, machete in hand.

Dodging cars, lorries and ubiquitous squawking chickens, we legged it across the road, bounded up onto the pavement and thrust ourselves into the now-gathering crowd.

Whatever the kid had done these guys were seriously pissed off with him. More people got involved and soon more than a dozen angry men had us surrounded before the bleeding boy was carted away by uniformed officers. The already supercharged atmosphere was stoked up to white-hot proportions when our bodyguard drew an antique pistol from his belt. Not a wise move in a crowd made up of more people than bullets in the chamber.

'Whoah!' I yelled, as the apoplectic crowd hopped up and down, pointing at the gun. 'Put that thing back in your trousers!' I shoved his gun hand down towards his waistband. Things began to calm down a touch, even more so when the mob realized we were police and weren't going away. Byron looked at me and smiled. 'Just like Friday night on the Upper Clapton Road, eh, Harry?' he said. I raised my eyebrows, puffed out my cheeks and laughed as the surplus adrenalin searched for an outlet.

Our bodyguard beckoned us to come along.

'What now?' I asked, thinking that we needed to arrest the attackers, interview witnesses and write up statements.

The police officer shrugged. Christ, if that had happened in the UK, I would have been filling out reports for a week.

'This is going to be an interesting one,' I said to Byron, wondering what else was in store.

Byron grinned. 'Let's just try and focus on the job in hand,' he replied.

'Yeah, right,' I said. 'Just don't go starting any wars!'

Victims of abuse carry the trauma with them for ever. The best anyone can hope for is to be able to accept the fact that they have been abused and that it will continue to influence their faults, feelings and behaviour for the rest of their lives. Some people come to depend on drink or drugs to drown painful thoughts, but memories inevitably force their way to the surface.

Occasionally, people who have locked away memories of childhood abuse suddenly experience a trigger out of the blue. There are many reasons why people suddenly decide to come forward after several years. Sometimes, they discover that their abuser has access to children, whether through a step relationship or new pregnancy, or a new job.

In one case, a woman had been watching *EastEnders* when a storyline about child abuse suddenly stirred feelings that had lain dormant for years. As soon as the programme had finished, she walked to the nearest police station where the station officer filled out a Crime Reporting Information System (CRIS) form (i.e. a crime report). This case became known in our office as 'EastEnders'.

It has been known for CRIS forms that feature historical abuse to become lost in the Intranet ether due to the age of the allegations, which is an outrage. This is mainly because there's often confusion over where cases of historical abuse should be sent.

Normally, any child abuse investigation was centred on the borough where the child was currently living. Historical cases with adults are different. They centre on the Child Protection

Team where the offence occurred, which in this case was Hackney. Pamela's CRIS bounced around the Met's computer system for a couple of weeks before it finally landed in my inbox.

It made for grim reading. Pamela claimed her father had abused her for more than ten years, starting when she was seven years old. I immediately contacted Pamela, apologized for the delay and asked her to come in for an interview.

In historical cases, we usually interviewed the victim using just one officer – this way they are both able to build a rapport, meaning that the victim is more likely to open up. In this case we chose Keira, who'd had her baptism of fire with the man who was being eaten alive described in Chapter Five. Her linguistic and analytical abilities were second to none, and it was this, combined with her youth, that made her the perfect choice.

While they talked, I sat in the control room, pen and paper in hand, taking notes, writing down every place, forensic opportunity, witness and any other relevant detail. This extremely long and detailed interview, which took several sittings, formed the backbone of the investigation.

Pamela's father had brought her to the UK when she was seven, for a 'better life'. In reality he was taking her away from her family and friends so he could abuse her. He started immediately, molesting Pamela on the plane to the UK.

Once they were settled in North London, her father had sexually abused her every day. She tried to resist time and again but her father simply overpowered her. 'I thought, Why bother fighting? He's going to do it anyway. I desperately wanted the abuse to end, but it was easier to just keep my mouth shut.'

It's incredibly hard for a young person to speak out. There are feelings of guilt and shame and fear, and not wanting to make the situation worse or lead to the family being broken up. Sometimes when kids do complain, they withdraw allegations because they want all the upset they've caused to go away. By the time Pamela was thirteen they were in a full sexual relationship.

They lived as if they were husband and wife, rather than father and daughter and, as he grew in confidence, the abuse continued even during regular visits back home to Trinidad.

'Christ, you don't know how difficult this is,' Pamela told Keira, struggling to meet her gaze. 'There's something else.' I held my breath. What new bombshell was about to be dropped?

'I . . . I have a daughter and . . . I've let him babysit for me.'

Sensing there was more, Keira kept quiet.

'And I have a drug problem.'

Putting aside the shocking nature of those admissions, what Pamela had done had taken real courage. Her honesty meant that if it came to a full prosecution, then the defence would grill her mercilessly in open court in an effort to expose her as a bad mother and a drug-addled, unreliable witness. Pamela knew this, but still she ploughed on in the hope that the truth would lead to justice and acceptance. 'I've realized that I just can't live with the fact that no one has ever challenged him,' she told Keira, 'there must be others.'

We usually refer to investigations by the name of the victim or the defendant but occasionally a nickname is used – this label is often the trigger point. The first thing we had to check was whether Pamela's father, Lewis, had access to children. Since turning eighteen, Pamela had lost touch with him and so gave me several possible addresses. I found him at the third house. 'Please, let there be no kids,' I said to myself. But there were. Lewis had a whole new stepfamily, and his new girlfriend was pregnant.

I needed to move fast. The first priority was the kids' safety. Lewis had to be assessed as to whether he should be removed from the family home during the investigation. If he went voluntarily then fine, if not, then it gets tricky.

Before I arrested Lewis, I called social services to let them know what I was up to so we could confirm our strategy. The next call was to the Crown Prosecution Service who gave me the go-ahead to arrest him. They needed to prepare the case so we could make sure Lewis was put on remand rather than on bail, as there was a good chance he'd flee the country.

The target address was perfectly normal, a decent terraced house in a good part of the borough. I placed a car full of officers at either end of the street and waited. This was just like crime squad policing – always fun.

I still wasn't used to the earth-shattering nature of my visits and I took a deep breath as I thought of Lewis's new family and wondered how they would deal with Pamela's accusation. It's a bit of a risk to walk up to the front door; sometimes the accused will see the cops coming and try to flee. If they're successful then this causes untold distress for the victim and is a real pain in the backside for us. I wanted to catch Lewis by surprise, before he could run or slam the door in our faces. No more sieges for me.

After two hours Lewis's car pulled up. I turned the ignition and lifted off the handbrake. A large guy in his mid-forties climbed out. 'That's him,' I said to the other officers. His girl-friend and her kids followed. As he locked his car and she took the kids into the house, I hit the accelerator.

You only get one hit at something like this. He'll know in an instant why we're there and may know that he'll be on remand for some time, so there was a good possibility he'd fight. But, by the time he realized what was going on, the four of us had him surrounded. I arrested him and talked to the girlfriend as the others carted him off.

The next day, with Lewis safely 'in the bin', I got a disturbing call from Keira. 'It's bad news. Pamela's taken an overdose. She's been in hospital but is at home now.' Shit. We shot straight around to see her. The emotional rollercoaster of the arrest after all these years had obviously taken its toll.

After several hours of interviews, in which Lewis steadily denied the charges, I kept him in overnight. An officer was on hand in court the following morning to ensure our reasons for remanding Lewis were properly put before the court. CPS lawyers are massively overburdened; it's impossible for them to get through the thick files of the twenty or so fresh cases they deal with each day; at most they will be speed-read. So if you want your suspect kept in, it's best to send an officer to the bail hearing. If you don't then their victim might well end up with a nasty surprise.

Lewis was indeed remanded. Once he was in custody, we really started to put the job together. We compiled a list of London addresses where Pamela had been abused and visited them, much to the amazement and curiosity of the new occupiers, a sordid episode in their home's past suddenly revealed. The places were searched, photographed and forensically assessed. At one address we found a relative of the accused but they were unable to help, and we uncovered no real forensic opportunities, nor a smoking gun. The equivalent to a smoking gun in this case is an original mattress. DNA can sit in a mattress for decades. A mixed semen/vaginal fluid sample can go a long way towards cracking a case.

Next, we needed to trace witnesses and get statements. Most of them were friends and relatives living in Trinidad. Over a crackly line I spoke to Lorna, Pamela's half-sister. 'I can't believe I'm telling you this over the phone, I've never talked about it with anyone before. But now . . . Well, Dad gave me lots to drink when I was fifteen and made a pass.'

Byron knew the score. 'We go where the witnesses are, Harry,' he told me.

Once we'd been ferried into town and had our machete encounter, we went straight to work hunting down witnesses.

After a long interview with Lorna, we moved on to her mother, her aunt, then her cousins. All of them had compelling and corresponding stories about Lewis. We were even given the name of a man who some witnesses said had helped and joined in with Lewis in abusing young girls. We found him in a house not far from the beach but he denied everything.

Of course, this wasn't terribly surprising but I couldn't help feeling a bit frustrated. I walked to the shoreline where I fretted about Pamela, worried about what would happen if I failed to nail Lewis. As I stood there looking out across the turquoise sea, I decided to call home. Hackney and Hertfordshire felt as though they were a million miles from this hot, sandy beach. 'Harry? Is that you? The line's really terrible.'

After some running around and eventually standing on tiptoe on a breakwater by the beach I was forced to give up. Byron joined me. 'We'll be home soon enough, Harry,' he said, 'our flight's in a few hours.'

We returned to the UK in sombre mood. Pamela had been pushed way beyond her psychological limits. This was her father she had accused, the man who raised her, loved her – and had abused her.

Now, thanks to his abuse, she had even come to question her own existence. The Trinidad interviews made for strong reading; we had written assurances they were prepared to come to the Old Bailey to testify. Problem was, if Pamela wasn't strong enough to carry on, then the case would be dropped in a flash.

CHAPTER NINETEEN

KICKING IN DOORS

I was at home, mulling over Pamela's case, when the phone rang. I looked down and saw from the number that it was the paedophile squad. Byron had gone away on leave and had left me as acting Detective Inspector. Any fast-breaking cases anywhere in East London, then I was in charge.

I snatched up the receiver. 'Yes?'

'Hi, this is DS Robert Jones from the paedophile squad at Scotland Yard. Who am I talking to?'

'DI Harry Keeble, Hackney Child Protection.' (Tip: when you're 'acting', never mention the 'acting' bit!)

'Good. Well, excuse my brevity but we can talk more later. I've just had a call from an officer from the Sex Crimes Unit of the Toronto Police Service, Canada. He's been working under-cover infiltrating paedophile chat rooms.'

The urgency in his voice was clear. I sensed what was coming. My heart rate started to rise.

'He's watching a live-stream video of a man abusing an under-age girl in East London. We've just got a fix from his Internet provider.'

Robert gave me the address. It was forty minutes' drive from my home. I had two options: jump in the Peugeot and 'race' to the scene or coordinate everything from my front room. I sighed. Morse never had this problem. He always seemed to be five minutes from any crime scene.

It's almost impossible to run an operation while bombing down the M11. With hands-free you might be able to talk but hunting through the contacts folder would be a real pain, let alone entering any notes into my decision log. The best option was to orchestrate the operation from home until I had a good detective sergeant or detective constable on the scene. Then I could hop in my car and delegate en route.

I marched out to the car, opened the boot and took out a large bag. Inside was everything I needed: scene logs, evidence bags, exhibit labels, pens, paper and so on; everything you need to preserve and work a major crime scene. I walked back into the lounge, now my centre of operations, and got set up.

The race was on. No time for warrants or explanations. I called Child Protection officers, who scrambled to the address from New Scotland Yard and their central London homes. Now the question was whether to enter with the battering ram or the doorbell.

I opted for the least messy option. It worked.

The officers on the ground told me they had a middle-aged man in custody. 'He's crapping himself,' one of them said, 'saucer-eyed and shaking with fear.' His clothes matched those he'd been wearing in the video. Photos of kids hugging their abusers were on his laptop. His stepdaughter was in another room. He'd been abusing her while her mother was at work.

Outwardly, he was an ordinary-looking bloke with a good job. He lived in a decent, well-kept home. I bet the first thing the neighbours would say was 'Derek? Can't be. He was so nice and quiet.'

Derek was arrested and taken into custody. After talking to

the girl's mother, we were convinced she was not aware of the abuse and so her daughter was allowed to return home. These sorts of cases are fraught with difficulty, especially if the mother won't believe us when we tell her what her husband or lover has been doing to their child. Sometimes, the mother decides to let the bailed father into the family 'for just a bit', which only complicates matters, endangering the child's safety and future with her family. If this turns out to be the case, then we look further afield – but still within the family – for somewhere safe for the child to stay. But of course we can only assess the protective parent to the best of our ability. We can never be a hundred per cent sure, so that is why we always talk to the child. We always include them in any decisions.

I was very grateful to have such a first-class witness. The Canadian officer had started a chat with the man, who professed his preference for five-year-old girls before emailing the policeman indecent images and inviting him to watch his broadcast.

Alas, as the Duty DI I had to leave it there and hand the inquiry over to the local Child Protection team first thing in the morning. My job was to manage the initial investigation, to make it 'safe' and then walk away. What with the constant whirlwind of new cases I faced in Hackney, I never learned what happened to the family in the end.

So many cases like the one just described involved the Internet. We were fighting a constant Internet war against paedophiles – with the invaluable help of our experts from the technical division of the Met's Child Exploitation and Online Protection Centre. Sometimes, when investigating these types of cases, officers soon find themselves deep inside a huge Internet paedophile ring.

In this case, expert technical officers recorded the identities of every paedophile that appeared in the chat room Derek had been using and started going after those who had posted films and photographs on the site showing themselves abusing their own children, from babies to teenagers. Some children had been raped live on the web while hundreds of men watched online.

Using these methods, the officers rescued at least fifteen children from a terrifying life of abuse and, in a joint investigation with Canadian police, the source of the broadcasts was tracked to a Suffolk farmhouse. Brewery worker Timothy Cox, twenty-eight, who called himself 'Son of God', was the man at the top of the pyramid; he ran the chat room from his parent's house in Buxhall.[21]

Cox spent several hours every day sending out more than 11,000 images to other users from 35 countries. He'd gathered nearly 76,000 images, including 1,100 videos containing 316 hours of footage. One video of a child being abused was ninety minutes long. More than 200 people were investigated as a result. There were at least 700 users of the site across the globe, some as far away as Australia and Canada.

Cox admitted six offences of possessing indecent images of children with intent to show them and two of distributing them, all carrying a maximum ten-year sentence. The judge told Cox that he would have got seven years but reduced the sentence by a third to the equivalent of a concurrent four years and eight months on each charge because of his guilty plea. Cox would be eligible to apply for parole in just nineteen months.

Fortunately, Judge Peter Thompson also imposed an indeterminate sentence, meaning that Cox could only be freed when he was no longer considered a danger. I hope that the parole board will not even think about letting him out for a very, very long time indeed.

After this raid I went to visit Pamela. She was going to make it. She was also determined to see justice done once again. I assured her she would have her day in court, the biggest court in the land, in fact – the Old Bailey.

Several cases our unit had worked on were nearing trial at the Old Bailey, but still the fax machine whirred and rolled; a never-ending list of children that needed saving.

CHAPTER TWENTY

ALTERED IMAGES

As much as I wanted to, there was no time to put off viewing them, no chance of passing the buck on to someone else. It was my case. I just had to get on with it. Our private tender experts had recovered 7,500 images of child pornography from a laptop and I needed to examine them.

These images are graded using an official scale (called the Copine Scale) of seriousness – naked kids photographed having a bath or on the beach, right up to kids having sex with animals. We had to go through all of those images and pick one or two from each category as evidence; these would be shown to a jury, if the case went to trial.

We never, ever went through these sorts of images on our own, always in pairs. You have to look out for each other when looking at them, otherwise there's a danger of losing it – you see all of the abusers' knowing, smiling and ecstatic faces, their vile bodies and the horrible things they do to tearful children, torturing them, scarring them for life. Once you've seen this, it's hard to repress the desire to beat the suspect to death in the interview room.

It's even worse when viewing films with sound; then it's possible to hear the screams of the children and the slaps as they're being hit, as well as the voices of the paedophiles. One video had the soundtrack from 'Walking in the Air' dubbed over it. Understandably, the officer who viewed that video developed a real aversion to that particular song.

I sat down with Simon. 'Right then,' I said, 'let's have a look,' and opened the first folder. I'm not going to detail the images here but it's essentially everything you'd expect to find in hard-core adult pornography, everything you can possibly imagine – and then some.

'Look at those curtains,' Simon said.

'What?' What could curtains possibly have to do with this case?

'They're just like one of my granny's old dresses. Same pattern and everything.'

I looked. It was true. God, they were awful. Whoever owned this house had the worst taste in home furnishings I'd ever seen. 'Well we'll have no trouble linking other crimes to the same house,' I said, 'this is pretty damn unique!'

Simon started to laugh; it was completely inappropriate for the images we were staring at but it was infectious. 'Shut up, you muppet,' I said, trying not to giggle. 'Oh God, look at that wallpaper. Austin Powers would be proud of that.'

'Yeah, what would you call that pattern? Psychedelic vomit?'

'I bet he's got a collection of amusing bow-ties as well.'

Our humour was as black as could be and totally inappropriate, but poking fun at the paedophiles' awful taste in home furnishings did help. It's a process of desensitization, much like what doctors have to go through to acclimatize to blood and gore. In fact we were in stitches when Rob suddenly thrust his head in the door.

'What the hell's up with you two?' he demanded.

Unable to speak, Simon and I tried to swallow our laughter and wiped the tears from our eyes. As usual, the sheer breadth and pace of the work left us very little time to reflect on our bizarre afternoon. Rob had interrupted us to tell me that I was needed on another urgent case: a man who'd married a vulnerable woman for his own selfish reasons – so he could abuse her son.

The child, who also had learning difficulties, had told his schoolteacher that he'd been shown cartoons depicting child abuse and had named a famous Disney character.

Problem number one was that the child had special needs and was not considered a reliable witness. I could see a defence barrister rubbing their hands with glee at the prospect of an easy win. Problem number two was what the hell was he talking about? We'd never even heard of Disney cartoons that featured child abuse.

As usual, Rob put everything into perspective for me. 'Remember, Harry, first things first. Always follow the investigation right to the end, no matter how weird it gets. Once you've reached the end, then you can start making life-changing decisions. Secondly, this is child protection in inner-city London. You'll never stop being surprised. Don't forget your pagan encounter.

'Thirdly,' he went on, 'abusers are abnormal; they'll get sexual gratification in ways that you and I will never, ever understand. So grab hold of the case and push it through to the bitter end.'

The first step was to interview the boy. Craig and I got clear disclosures about actual abuse and the Disney cartoons. So, as per normal, the suspect was removed from the family home and we seized his computers.

When the report came back from our own lab, we were in for a surprise: they'd found dozens of Japanese child porn cartoons. I found it very hard to believe that, at the time, these videos were perfectly legal. They were horrendous, blatantly paedophilic, but there was nothing we could do.

We were very concerned about the boy's ability to give evidence but at least we had his disclosure to his teacher regarding Disney porn. If we could find this on the stepfather's hard drive, then we would still be in with a shot.

The lab report also told us that there was an encrypted file on the laptop that they'd not been able to access. 'I'm betting that's the one we want,' I told Craig and Rob.

Craig nodded in agreement and then voiced our fears. 'Do you think he's out-geeked the lab guys on this one?'

Just then, I received a tip-off that the mother had been letting the suspect back into the family home. No time for messing around, Craig and I went straight round.

As soon as I spoke to the mother, any anger I felt towards her evaporated: she also had learning difficulties. This was why she'd been targeted. Evil bastard.

I was polite, but very firm and we eventually came to an agreement.

The investigation plodded along. It was extremely slow, thanks to the encrypted hard drive, but we knew there was something in this. After some research we approached another, even more 'specialized agency' to see if they could access the hard drive. Once they knew what it was for, they went at it day and night and, eventually, they cracked it.

It was sickening and utterly, utterly devious. Someone had painstakingly redrawn and reanimated scenes from a well-known Disney cartoon, transforming them into child porn. That way, a child could be sat in front of the telly to watch a 'Disney' film and they would be introduced to child abuse through the altered images – and the paedophile hasn't even committed a crime.

This is what police and social services are up against. There are no lengths to which a paedophile will not go to groom a child. What frightened me about this guy in particular was the psychopathic but sophisticated way he had constructed the abuse: the mother with special needs who had a child with special needs who was groomed for abuse by a defaced Disney cartoon. This guy had invested years of time and effort.

As did we. It took us two years to gather the evidence and find the guy (as there were no police bail conditions available in those days, he was living abroad). At one point I had to exert serious pressure on the detective sergeant who had taken over the case to keep it alive. It paid off. He was brought to trial and given seven years.

After this case I wondered whether paedophiles who were that devious could ever feel any genuine remorse. I never personally encountered a paedophile with that disposition but, apparently, while they are very rare, they do exist. Rob mentioned one case he knew of where a paedophile had actually wanted to get caught, so he could be cured.

'Peter was an IT security expert and had been downloading child pornography at work,' Rob said. 'He'd left one page of a pornographic story on his desk. A cleaner had found it. Another IT expert had been called in to examine Peter's hard drive and discovered several images of young children. Amazingly, his wife, Amanda, stuck by him. They were both middle-aged, active members of their local neighbourhood watch, volunteered at church helping the homeless and elderly, real pillars of the community. There was nothing one could say about their appearance or manner, a completely melt-into-the-background couple.'

I'm paraphrasing, but the way Rob described it, their interview went something like this: 'Married for twenty years,' Amanda had told their interviewer stoically, 'I'm not about to throw it all away now.'

'So,' the interviewer said, 'you know your husband has been accessing illegal material.'

'Yes, although I thought that was all over.'

Peter interrupted. 'Believe me, being arrested is the best thing

that could have happened to me. It started when I fell for a girl
a few years younger than me when I was in my early twenties. I
never did anything, never even told her. Since then I've always
been . . . interested.'

'So, it's little girls then?'

They both nodded.

'I never thought he'd do it again,' Amanda said. 'We've seen
doctors, psychologists, counsellors and therapists.'

'But no one could stop my urges,' Peter added. 'My GP told
me that the most effective treatment was only available to convicted offenders.'

That was quite true. It's all a bit late by that stage of course
but the treatment, such as it is, for convicted paedophiles in UK
prisons is world class. Offenders are shown how to challenge
their behaviour and how to put the needs of victims before their
own desires. The method isn't foolproof by any means; there is
no 'cure' and there are doubts as to its effectiveness, but it does
at least offer a practical strategy for those who claim they want to
try to change.

When Rob told me about this case, I thought of the other
men who'd accessed porn online that we'd caught before they'd
gone a step further. It seemed as though Peter was yet another
man on the edge, on the verge of living out his fantasies. At least
I hoped he had remained on the verge.

Amanda was then asked how she would have felt if they had
daughters; how would she feel if she were here having this conversation after Peter had assaulted a young girl?

'My husband is a decent man. He wouldn't take it that far.'

'But he's already lied to you.'

'I'm hurt and sickened,' Amanda said, 'but I know he gen-
uinely regrets what he's done. When I found out the first time I
was totally disgusted, but it wasn't anything like the revulsion he
felt towards himself.'

They'd got rid of their computer to try to remove the temptation. It wasn't to last. It didn't help that Peter was an IT expert responsible for advising companies on Internet security.

He asked the company to increase its security, so that sites of a sexual nature couldn't be accessed, but his bosses decided not to bother. The urge overtook Peter soon after and he started surfing for child pornography on his work computer.

Unable to resist the lure, he made up computer viruses so he had to work late. He used his expert knowledge to bury his trail and he often wiped his hard drive. Eventually, addicted yet remorseful, disgusted at himself for his sick desires and the betrayal of his wife, Peter tried to kill himself.

'Do you think you're in danger of acting out your fantasies?' the interviewer asked.

Amanda tried to answer for him: 'He could never hurt a child. I know him that well.'

Peter broke in. 'Why do you think I tried to kill myself? Videos didn't do it for me any more. I'd . . . I'd started to consider . . .' He broke off sobbing. Amanda put an arm over his shoulders and hugged him.

Peter pulled himself together. 'I hear the support available inside is first class,' he said. 'I need to be able to talk to a professional. I could never consider telling anyone else. A professional might be able to help me.'

He also argued that there should be longer prison sentences – decades long, if not lifelong post-prison community supervision.

It was extremely odd to hear a criminal demanding tougher sentences, but I had to agree. The guy who'd abused his daughter and 'confessed' during my interview in Chapter Seven got two years. He was free in one, released from our overcrowded jails early for good behaviour and returned to the real world – still sexually attracted to children. Although he was now on the sex offenders' register, I personally didn't feel as if enough had been done to protect other children from him.

Peter was sentenced to sixteen months. I hoped that it would prove to be long enough for the specialist doctors and therapists to work a miracle. I was very sceptical, however; paedophilia is at the core of these sex abusers' personalities, something that's impossible to change – like being heterosexual or gay.

By this stage I had a rudimentary knowledge of how paedophiles used the Internet and how the Internet had helped feed previously unknown desires. I believe that tough legislation should be passed to force Internet service providers to clamp down on child pornographers.

They've been telling us for years that it's too big a job, but that's not true. The Internet service providers simply have to monitor the smaller servers, and if they discover that much of their content is illegal they could shut them down. It wouldn't catch everything, but that, combined with stiff penalties for those providing or promoting illegal material, would help to make a significant difference.

There remained a constant stream of painful reminders of how far many men like Peter, who had started out viewing illegal material on the Internet, eventually went.

One evening I received a phone call from a local businessman. His voice trembled as he spoke: 'Someone's left a . . . er . . . strange message on our computerized answerphone,' he said. 'I had to report it because it er . . . well, perhaps you should hear it yourself.' He emailed it to me straight away.

The voice was of a middle-aged woman and she spoke in an absolutely deadpan tone, which along with the poor-quality recording, made it seem all the more sinister. I can still recall it word for word.

'Yeah, it's £100 for ten minutes. You can do what you like to him as long as you don't hurt him. He's only five. Oh, and make sure you bring him a McDonald's Happy Meal for after.' The voice told me a lot. A smoker, East End accent, £100? It had heroin written all over it.

No time to waste. I sent an urgent request for officers from Territorial Support Group. Why? If drugs were involved and if this was part of some horrific organized child prostitution ring, then any surprise visit from the cops may turn nasty very quickly. If the address was a rancid council flat on a large estate where there was no love lost on the police, then I didn't want to be caught out screaming for back-up when it all kicked off. I was playing to win, to get the child to safety.

There was no doubt in my mind that this was going to be hard for the officers. If they crashed through a door to find a man with a gun or a knife on the other side, then they are trained and professional and can deal with the situation. But what if they found a man in the process of abusing a five-year-old boy?

I had to make sure I got there first. TSG officers' adrenalin leaps through the roof in the time it takes for the sirens to be switched on and the van's engine to roar. If they saw what was on the other side of the door before I did, then there was a chance they'd beat any paedophile they found to a pulp.

I missed kicking in doors and, although it was rare for me to feel like committing righteous retribution on some of the unpleasant characters we arrested, the answerphone message had really got to me. I was looking forward to kicking the door in personally.

It was not to be. Our intelligence came back with the address. Not my area. This meant I would have to hand the job over. Shit, I really wanted to see this one through. Now, I would never even get to hear the outcome.

I still have the recording and I sometimes play it to people who join us on attachment and are thinking of joining Child Protection. This job attracts remarkable men and women with great compassion – these are also the sort of people who some-times find it hardest to live with the horror and sense of helplessness you're forced to endure. I tell them if they can live with hearing that tape, knowing that there's nothing they can do to save that child from what's already happened to them, then they can live with the job.

CHAPTER TWENTY-ONE

FROM ONE EXTREME

Pamela survived her overdose and, as the trial began, her half-sister Lorna arrived from Trinidad. I collected her from Gatwick and as we walked through the airport she asked me: 'How will I survive? I have no money for food or anything.'

Oops.

The Crown Prosecution Service would cover the cost, no problem, but I should have filled out the forms a long time ago as they take weeks to process. Fortunately, I'd just been paid and so I nipped across to a cash machine, withdrew £300 and handed it over. I also gave my credit card details to the hotel.

The next day I got a phone call from Lorna. Can I have some more money?' she asked.

'What on earth happened to the £300?' She eventually confessed that she'd been unable to resist the lure of Oxford Street and had blown the lot on clothes.

I could hardly blame her. She lived in poverty in Trinidad and now suddenly she was in one of the richest cities in the world with cash to burn. It had been all too tempting to get presents for everyone back home. Needless to say, Lorna had to make do with a much smaller allowance after that.

I was so nervous about this case. Normally I was unflappable in court but I was scared for Pamela. She'd already come so far and been through so much. To now spend three weeks in the courtroom with her father and accuse him of abuse and to then face cross-examination – the inevitable questions about her own drug addiction and parenting skills – well, I wasn't sure she could handle it.

I half-expected to get a call at some point saying that she couldn't go on. The CPS had done Pamela and their department proud by getting the case to court. They really wanted to show that they were not afraid to invest the time and resources to investigate and prosecute abusers, no matter how long ago it took place. Time should in no way be a barrier to justice, a view held by Katherine, our tenacious prosecutor in this case, who'd helped send many rapists to prison.

Most of the three-week trial involved Pamela giving testimony in harrowing detail of the abuse, confirming times and locations and frequencies and the form that it took. She spoke clearly, with dignity and complete honesty, impressing both judge and jury. She looked much healthier and happier. I could see something had changed, but I didn't know what.

Lewis, her father, continued to deny everything. I had held out a small hope that, if he were guilty, he'd break down and confess. This had happened in a handful of isolated cases where the accused, finally confronted with the damage they'd done, suddenly found themselves momentarily overcome with guilt and changed their plea.

Alas, in this case, it was not to be. When it came to cross-examination, Lewis's defence barrister grilled Pamela relentlessly. He constantly referred to her drug addiction and made sure the jury understood that she had left her own daughter in the care of her father on more than one occasion.

I was in court when the jury emerged to give their verdict.

Not guilty.

The case finally over, I prepared myself to console a distraught Pamela. I was worried that this might have pushed her over the edge again and back into depression. But I was wrong. Pamela told me she had got almost everything she wished for.

'We didn't fail,' she said. 'I have closure. I've stood before my father and told him exactly what he's done to me. I can move on. Besides, everyone's now watching him closely.'

This brought it home to me that trials and investigations can be worthwhile even when the accuser walks free. Sometimes victims feel that finally people had taken them seriously, were prepared to believe them – and still did believe them even after the verdict. This often came after years of fear of what would happen to them if they ever spoke out, whether they would be ridiculed as vain attention seekers or would get into trouble for making 'false' accusations.

Pamela had bounced back after her overdose. In the run-up to the trial she had broken free from her addiction and found a job. Facing up to her past had tested her to the limit but now she had the strength to live with what had happened and everything was in place for a bright future.

As far as I was concerned, trials like this one were a turning point in the history of child protection. It had shown me the value of investigating cases of historical abuse and the positive effect it had had on Pamela's life. Of course, there were still some mixed emotions as Lewis was free and had access to several children – but as Pamela said, at least all eyes were now upon him.

I thought about the jury too. They had been presented with a case of testimonies. No DNA, no fingerprints, no confessions, just Pamela's words against Lewis's. By law, jurors cannot talk or write about their experiences. As police officers, we owe them a huge debt of gratitude. All officers appreciate the dilemmas jurors face and know only too well all the emotions they take away with them once these very difficult trials are over.

Not long after Pamela's trial, I received a referral that stated that a teacher had assaulted a child. I drove to the school for the strategy meeting with Terry, a social work manager, and the head teacher.

I listened as the head teacher explained the case.

'The boy had been eating crisps in the playground. He was asked to stop by the teacher, twice. When the boy continued, the teacher snatched the crisps away.'

'And?' I asked.

'We received an official complaint of assault after school when the boy told his mother what had happened.'

So, you're saying that having his crisps taken away—'

'Snatched—'

'Right, yes – snatched away, in the eyes of the parent, constituted assault.'

'Yes, that's right.'

Terry and I exchanged glances. He was as robust an investigator as I was and I knew we were thinking exactly the same thoughts.

What on earth were we doing at this meeting? This was utter crap, a total waste of our time. I fumed quietly, not wanting to lose it with the teachers. But they had done exactly the right thing. A child had been assaulted and a strategy meeting convened. It was imperative to maintain a good relationship with the school. Most of our referrals came from teachers and there was no way we wanted to put them off telling us about potentially serious cases in future. Besides which, the school had obeyed the rules in this case.

Terry spoke for both of us by making this clear, as politely as possible. Nonetheless, the head teacher was still worried about our reluctance to get involved. I suspect that my body language was giving too much away. Rein it in, Harry, I told myself.

Afterwards, Terry told me: 'I have four children at risk to see today, and this is bollocks.'

I agreed. Unfortunately, while Terry was able to escape, I still had to investigate and write up a report because a formal allegation of assault against a child had been made.

I tried to relax. I tried not to think about all the worthwhile cases I could be working on instead. I gave myself a moment, took a deep breath, puffed out my cheeks and blew. I reminded myself that this mother did not realize the repercussions of her accusation and in some way believed her allegation to be serious. Nevertheless, I had to wrap this up quickly. I was needed elsewhere.

I called the mother, who was still highly indignant. I realized that I'd changed. The old Harry would have said exactly the same words as I did then – but in a much harsher tone. Now I spoke softly – the new, improved Harry.

'So what you're saying is that your son's teacher snatched away his bag of crisps when he refused to stop eating them?'

'Yes, but—'

'Now, does that sound like assault to you?'

'Well, it's not that simple.'

'I know that. If you go ahead with this allegation, your child will be officially interviewed, as will all the children who witnessed the event. There will be a lengthy investigation and tribunal in which you and your son will play a key part and most likely have to give evidence. The teacher's career could be damaged and he may be suspended. If you do go ahead then you can, but you must understand the impact of what you're about to do. I will have to balance what is in the best interests of your child.'

Luckily she took the hint and dropped the allegation. This at least saved me from refusing outright to investigate, which would have been my next move.

I was still fuming from this waste of time when an exasperated James called me. 'You'll never guess what, Dev's been suspended for indecent assault.'

'Oh *God*,' I replied with total exasperation. Dev was the stand-up guy who had opened my eyes to the world of social services. He was wise, sympathetic and tremendously experienced, a real safe pair of hands. 'What the hell happened?'

Within the hour I found out that his accuser was a mother currently under investigation for neglect who had a long history of false accusations. Despite this, Dev was suspended immediately and I still had to investigate, even though the case would never go anywhere near a courtroom. This was yet another part of the job which was incredibly hard to live with.

Taking Dev out of the job was kicking the whole department of social services while it was down. Dozens of cases would have to be picked up by his co-workers. No extra staff would be brought in. Once again, workers would be forced to neglect the children they were there to protect. Once again, it would be the children who suffered, this time because of a false accusation made by an abuser, designed to try and get her off.

Of course, the argument quite rightly goes that social workers, the police and anyone who works with children has to be above reproach. Every allegation has to be tested to the full letter of the law if we are to have any hope of maintaining the public trust – but we have to be proportionate.

Dev was torn apart by the accusation. As a cop, I'm well used to being falsely accused – criminals accuse us of lying all the time and it's sometimes quite funny when we have conversations with the accused solicitor that go along the lines of: 'That's not what happened, is it, Officer Keeble?'

'Yes, it is.'

'No, it isn't.'

'Yes, it is,' and so on.

You then think: Tell you what, why don't we let a jury decide?

Innocent teachers and social workers find it much harder to cope. Few can imagine the upset caused to decent teaching staff when they're faced with allegations, especially of a sexual nature.

For some, the trauma can simply be too immense; a false accusation can ruin a teacher's or social worker's health and psychological well-being and destroy their life. One teacher was told he couldn't even be with his baby daughter unless her mother was present, for as long as he was under investigation. He was found to be innocent.

Even if it's completely unfounded, rumours still persist and even when acquitted, they feel as though their colleagues – and in some cases their pupils – still believe that they're guilty.

Sometimes they never recover and very often leave the job – but by then their chances of finding another have already been reduced. In July 2009 the cross-party Children, Schools and Families select committee reported that future employers were able to see whether a teacher had been under investigation even if they were later found to be innocent. The same committee also reported that authorities tended to believe pupils over teachers and that '95 per cent of claims' are false and are often found to be malicious. We don't as yet know how many false allegations are made against teachers each year.[22]

While Dev's case was still meandering its way through the system, Rob sent me to investigate an allegation of assault at a children's refuge in Stoke Newington. All too often secure refuges tend to have all the charm of small Victorian prisons; they are grim and frightening places for anyone, let alone troubled children. The home in Forest Road, Hackney, was an infamous example. The building radiated coldness. Children with mental and/or drug problems were stacked like goods on bunk-bed shelves in tiny rooms with miniature windows covered in grime. The furniture was outdated, torn and scored with graffiti; fist and knife-sized holes peppered the plasterboard walls. Of course, the poor state of the furnishings was not necessarily the fault of the council. Troubled children inevitably cause damage and destruction, and homes like this one bore the brunt. Fortunately the home in Forest Road was eventually closed but of course this by no means fixed the problem.

When I pulled up outside the home Rob had sent me to, I was pleasantly surprised. Although Victorian, it was clean and pleasant and its period features were intact. Once inside, it felt like a good youth hostel. I couldn't hide my admiration as I shook the hand of the accused, a large Rastafarian man called Lionel. 'This makes a pleasant change from the other accommodation I've seen in Hackney,' I told him.

He beamed back at me. 'Yeah, well, you do what you can with what you got, you know?'

I spoke to the fifteen-year-old boy, David, first. When I entered the room I was immediately taken aback by his size. He was over six foot tall and built to match. I'd checked his history. Unsurprisingly, it was complex and deeply troubled.

I pulled up a chair. He sat calmly on the corner of the bed. The room was a good size and was warm, despite its high ceilings. The house was quiet.

David told me there'd been some trouble with another lad on the landing and he'd used half a snooker cue to defend himself. Then Lionel intervened and that's when the assault had happened.

'Do you have any injuries?'

'No. But I don't want to stay here any more. Can't I be moved somewhere?'

Ah. This was the most likely motivation behind the accusation. That was beyond my power but I told David I'd talk to social services and would be in touch.

I interviewed Lionel in his office over a cup of coffee. Many professionals become angry or distraught when allegations are made against them, but Lionel seemed to have taken it in his stride. He talked about David positively, telling me his strengths and weaknesses. I was very impressed; he was talking about a child who had made allegations that could see him suspended, arrested and put on trial. He really cared and was totally committed to the kids he worked with. He left me feeling humbled; he had a difficult job that required exceptional skills but his salary was probably a great deal less than mine.

Although I was certain Lionel had done no wrong, leaving David in his care was probably not a good idea in case the teenager reported another incident or made a more dramatic attempt to get moved. I sought the advice of Terry and, because he was technically a child from outside of London, we managed to place him with foster parents from the South Coast that evening.

Two days later, the eleven-year-old daughter of the foster parents made an allegation of indecent assault against David and he was moved immediately. His troubled past continued to influence his future.

The traumatic effect upon this foster family must have been massive. After going through a long and complex vetting process, they had offered their home to protect vulnerable children. They had trusted David and this is what they got in return. We desperately need foster carers – they're a vital part of child protection, so when children abuse the foster system, the knock-on effects for other children can be enormous.

Every time an allegation was made against anyone who worked with children, be it a teacher or school worker, no matter how ridiculous it sounded, we always ran a criminal record check on them. We shouldn't have had to because the Criminal Records

Bureau (CRB) would have cleared them, so they should have had no criminal past, right? Wrong. The CRB wasn't a slick and omniscient fact-checking machine. It consisted of underpaid clerks overwhelmed with a hundred requests for background information every day.

In one case, a teacher was accused of inappropriate behaviour and because the results were so serious I sent a detective constable to the school to get him off the premises, not after the lesson but asap.

But how do they get away with it?

Anyone applying to work with children must be vetted by the CRB. Names are run through the police national computer, which records convictions and cautions. The CRB also checks forces' intelligence records and the Protection of Children Act (1999) List (the Secretary of State has a duty to record the names of individuals who are considered unsuitable to work with children on this list) and reports back to employers. Employers then decide whether an applicant's record makes them unsuitable.

The CRB does generally work but people still manage to slip through the system. The classic example was Ian Huntley, the murderer of schoolgirls Holly Wells and Jessica Chapman. He lied on his application and got a job as a school caretaker.

When I was called to a school after a pupil accused his teacher of assault, the teacher responded by making a vigorous counter-allegation against the pupil. A criminal records check on the police national computer into the teacher's background revealed a number of convictions from about twenty years ago, including an assault on police. I then asked for his job application form to be faxed over.

The form had questions where the applicant could cross out the things that did not apply – it was 'yes' or 'no'. This teacher had crossed everything out clearly, except for the question 'Do you have any previous convictions?' where he'd ticked between the boxes.

It went on to say, 'If yes please state what they are'. He'd left it blank.

I called him up and asked him to come in and make a statement.

'Of course,' he replied, before going on to practically accuse the teenager of attempted murder.

As soon as he arrived I arrested him for pecuniary advantage – obtaining employment by falsehood.

The interview was entirely predictable. 'Well, that should read "yes",' he told me when I asked about the form.

'If that's the case, then why aren't your convictions listed below?'

He seemed to think they weren't terribly important and instead demanded that I investigate the assault. He'd even brought photographs that showed his injury, an ambiguous-looking bruise.

I needed to end this mess once and for all. 'Look,' I told him, 'you have no realistic prospect of a conviction, as you lied on your application form. No jury is going to stand for it.'

The school sacked him, the pupil and his parents were satisfied with that and all the investigations fell by the wayside. Job done.

It wasn't just teachers that lied on their job applications. A school caretaker was reported by a colleague for looking at indecent images on a school computer. When I ran the checks, I found he had undeclared juvenile convictions. So, one evening I took a team of computer experts with specialist gizmos into the school and we spent the night scanning the hard drives of almost a hundred computers. We found nothing. It was a strange one; there was plenty of reason to be concerned, but there were simply no hard facts and so the case evaporated.

Amazingly, although I never saw it in Hackney, some London councils managed to recruit convicted child molesters, one of whom worked as a bus driver for kids with learning difficulties in the neighbouring borough of Haringey. He was eventually arrested for pecuniary advantage and sacked. By then he'd been working with children for years.

Unsurprisingly, I spent a great deal of time visiting schools and I'd only just dealt with the snatched-crisp incident when I was called back to speak to a young, inexperienced teacher. She'd just returned from a five-day field trip, during which a pupil told her that their father had sexually abused them.

'When did you learn about this?'

'Three days ago.'

'Why didn't you call us then?'

'We were in the Lake District, it seemed better to wait until we returned.'

'Where's the child now?'

'Well, she's back at home, the trip's over.'

I think my sigh said it all.

'Have I done something wrong?'

'We need to know as soon as humanly possible after the child has confided in you. It doesn't matter where you are. We've lost forensic opportunities and a chance to talk to the child before she's gone home. Not only has she been potentially exposed to fresh abuse,' I said, 'she may no longer want to talk about it, especially now she's back at home and under the control of her abuser. We can't simply pluck a child out of the family home on your say-so, which is all we have now.'

To my profound embarrassment, the teacher started to sob right in front of me. She'd tried to do what she thought was the right thing and I couldn't really blame her. What she had in compassion, she lacked in training.

This was undoubtedly one of the most difficult areas of child protection. Teachers know their pupils pretty well and often meet the parents. This makes them an absolutely vital part in child protection. Teachers are responsible for saving thousands of children from further sexual abuse and neglect but still, in my experience, they remain woefully uneducated in the way child protection works. They need to attend regular courses in child protection; one day at teacher training college just doesn't cut it.

Each school has a designated representative who is responsible for referring potential cases to the police and social services but the effectiveness of this role varies from school to school. I've been in some schools where a teacher has simply been given a folder and the title. As is the case with many aspects of child protection, its importance is only realized when it's too late.

At least two teachers need to be made child protection representatives. Schools need to have a big child protection poster up on the school wall, which states the duty of teachers to report concerns. It must be made clear to parents that this is part of the teacher's responsibilities. Teachers can learn pretty much all they need to know about the basic practicalities of child protection by taking a one-day course (which should be refreshed each year).

Sometimes, teachers are under the impression that parents must be told if a referral to social services is made. This is WRONG. I cannot stress this enough. If it's a case of the child being smelly or other minor examples of neglect, of course tell the parents. If it's a case of indecent assault or an explicit disclosure, then don't. Refer the matter to social services, but be clear that you have not told the parents. Ask for instructions as to what to do. Telling the parents of children who are being sexually abused would almost certainly lead to the loss of forensic evidence and would give the abuser time to influence their victim's testimony.

If you're not sure what's been said, just ask the child to say it again. Ask open questions without putting ideas in their heads.

If you ask: 'So was it Uncle Billy who touched your privates?' then you've probably blown the prosecution and hampered a chance to make the child safe. Instead, just ask: 'What happened? What are you worried about?' Never, ever, suggest a name of an abuser or an act. Remember children often use words to mean several different things; by using the word 'sex' they may mean kissing, for example. You can ask 'What do you mean?' if it seems unclear.

Once you've finished speaking to them write down the day, date, time, place and what you and the child said. Then ring social services immediately, not at the end of the day, immediately.

The sobbing teacher kept an eye on the child and eventually we got her away from her abuser. 'Thank you,' she said to me afterwards.

'I don't need thanking. You did it,' I replied. 'Despite the mistakes, you've saved a child from hell on earth and given her a shot at recovery. You can't ask for more than that.' The same teacher eventually became the school's child protection representative.

CHAPTER TWENTY-TWO

OFF THE SCALE

The young barrister looked me dead in the eye. 'Detective Sergeant Keeble,' she said in a slight cockney accent, 'you called my client a paedophile.'

'Yes, I did,' I replied, staring straight back, 'and had he stolen a car stereo I would have called him a thief.'

'You also told my client that he couldn't see his grandchildren again.'

So many powerful emotions threatened to overtake me that I had a sudden rush of blood to the head.

Her client had been accused of trying to fondle a nine-year-old child and it was just the alleged victim's word against his. There was so much more to the case than that. I knew far more about the accused than anyone else in the courtroom and I was struggling not to blurt it all out.

What the court didn't yet know was that the environment in which he'd kept the child was truly disgusting. Would you leave a young girl with a man who had a bucket half-filled with vomit and spit in the lounge that appeared to be days old? No, I thought not, and that's what I meant when I said he would never babysit again – the alleged abuse was not the only reason.

I glanced at my counsel. I fought my natural instinct to let this slip and held fast, for now. Outwardly, I remained the model of calmness.

'No. What I said was that he couldn't *babysit* his grandchildren again.'

A few moments later, the judge halted the increasingly acrimonious cross-examination and called for an interval.

I told my counsel about the ace up my sleeve. 'Should I play it?' I asked. He shook his head. I knew he was right. This sort of thing doesn't matter so much in a burglary trial, but it does with children. Every conviction has the potential to be a landmark case, to set the legal standard for similar cases in the future. If I blurted out something that was (legally speaking) irrelevant to the charge, such as the living conditions, then the trial could have been stopped and the accused might have left the court a free man – after all, he wasn't on trial for neglect.

Even so, when the judgement came, we didn't get the result we wanted. Severely pissed off, I stepped out of the rear entrance into the courtyard where I saw something that brought me up short. The defence barrister was walking hurriedly to her car.

She was in floods of tears.

I watched in amazement as she sat in her car and sobbed. She had gone into the courtroom, had done her job and had successfully defended her client. But she'd also ended up with a result that her heart didn't want.

She was young and something told me she wasn't your average barrister (it was the first time I'd ever been cross-examined by someone with a cockney accent). She was going to have to cope with this part of her job, otherwise it was going to drive her mad.

Seeing her this way after having faced her fierce cross-examination brought home to me how deeply child protection trials affect us all. All of us – police officers, barristers, judges and juries – are fighting a personal battle, in the face of wanting to do what's obviously the right thing for the child, to remain professional. We have to work within the justice system to see that justice is done.

Of course, this doesn't make it any easier when someone we believe to be guilty walks away after having played the system, free to abuse or attack someone else again.

Fourteen-year-old Rita arrived at our interview room after her mother called the police. She said that her daughter's employer, a thirty-something Iraqi man who ran a pizza and kebab joint in Hackney, had indecently assaulted her. As the accused had a longstanding employer–employee relationship with the child, we got the case.

In the interview, Rita told Craig she'd been pleased to get the part-time job. The owner had been friendly and welcoming. 'Business is booming,' he told her and boasted that he occupied all three storeys of the building, with the pizza/kebab shop on the ground floor, a flat above and a 'staff room' in the basement.

Although small, Rita thought the basement looked quite cosy; there was a stereo and plenty of soft cushions to lie on; a great place to relax on a break. The business owner was always friendly, but asked Rita very personal questions, which became so personal that she started to feel uncomfortable – and then he indecently assaulted her in the basement.

'I think he videoed me,' Rita told Craig. A records check revealed that her boss had previously been accused of rape. Although the charges were later dropped, our own inquiries led us to become seriously concerned that we might be dealing with a serial sex attacker.

'We need to find that tape,' I told Craig. Unfortunately we didn't know where he lived so we set up an observation point in front of the shop, with two of the lads keeping an eye out for when he left. They then radioed the surveillance team, who shadowed him home.

As soon as we had his address we planned the hit; a simultaneous double-whammy on his home and pizza bar. I led the raid on the pizza bar while Simon took the flat. Nothing. No video, no child pornography.

I didn't give up that easily. Some serial sex attackers are very sly and take precautions in case their home is raided, so I'd booked a POLSA team. These are the guys in navy outfits who take the rigorous searches of premises to the next level. Their work is crucial in catching killers and rapists. I have the utmost respect for these guys, mainly because I believe they have the most boring job in the entire police service.

But when they were finished, several hours later, they told me they'd found nothing. It came down to Rita's word against her employer's at the trial.

Rita was incredibly brave. By this time she'd turned fifteen and was heavily pregnant to her thirty-something boyfriend – obviously not the best way to present a child witness to a jury. Despite this, she gave evidence with integrity and conviction. Sadly, I think her condition and current relationship turned the jury against her and the accused was acquitted. While I understood their decision, it was once again terribly frustrating.

Almost exactly one year later, as part of a separate investigation, the same man was given a long sentence for rape.

It was dawn and five of us were standing outside a large Victorian house in South Hackney. A few early morning commuters passed by and looked at us curiously; it was obvious that we were the police. I rang the doorbell and tried to see through the mottled glass door. Eventually, after a few more rings, a shadow appeared in the hallway.

This one had been on our books for a while. It was part of

Operation Ore. As we worked our way through our credit card
list of people who had downloaded child porn from the Internet,
we often found that a suspect had moved home, which meant we
had to spend more precious time tracking them down.

The door was opened cautiously and the head of a man in his
mid-forties peered through a small gap. I shoved my warrant card
firmly under his nose and did the intros. After checking the
man's ID, it was clear he wasn't the one we were after.

'So who else is in the house?' I asked.

'There's a couple of blokes upstairs,' he said. Great. Worried
they had awoken and might be deleting or destroying evidence,
I bounded upstairs and burst into their room. As the door flew
back, there was a flurry of movement from the bed – the two
men were together, naked, baggy-eyed with crumpled hair. They
reeled from my rude awakening.

The guy on the right recovered first and yelled: 'Who the fuck
are you and what the fuck are you doing here?!'

As he gathered the covers protectively around him, an enormous black dildo rolled off the bed and onto the floor with a thud.
It rolled to a halt at my feet, its tip pointing accusingly at me.

This took the man's wind out of his sails; well, what could you
say after that? I suppressed a grin. The other guy had stayed quiet
and looked at me blankly. I wondered whether he was the one
who had something to worry about.

'Get dressed,' I said, 'we need to talk to you both.'

Mr Angry continued to rant. 'Why is it that the cops are
always targeting gay men? Leave us the fuck alone!'

People who rant at the police about injustice can be guilty or
innocent; it's a symptom of both. It's the quiet ones you want to
watch.

We started the search. The computer was photographed, as
were all the leads before we carefully took it apart, placed exhibit
labels on each individual piece and locked them in the car boot.

While we searched the rest of the house, Mr Angry continued to rant about the police targeting gay men. One of our gay officers took Mr Angry aside and had a quiet word. It shut Mr Angry up completely but not before we received a mumbled apology.

We found a video entitled 'Cock Hungry Schoolboys'. We thought we had something there but its title was slightly misleading in that it featured grown men. However, I was convinced that we were on track and their names were on our list, so I arrested the couple.

During the interviews, they denied all knowledge of child pornography and were bailed while I waited for the report on the computer to land on my desk.

When it did, I called Simon over before taking a look. 'It's your lucky day,' I said sarcastically as I waved the DVD, 'let's see what they found.'

A minute later, we were totally stunned. The images were off the scale, absolutely horrific. Suddenly, something I'd never seen before flashed on the screen. 'What the hell was that?' Simon said. I paused and rewound the slideshow.

'Is that an ultrasound scan?' Simon said. Having seen several as a father, I nodded. It was of a mature baby still in the womb.

'Someone's actually getting off on this?' I said in disbelief. 'This can't be sexual, can it? Ultrasound pictures?'

There were loads more on the disc. This was so weird that it wasn't even an offence; no one had even considered that such images could be misused in this way.

It was frightening stuff. Such warped minds are hard to fathom. This, combined with the other truly horrific material, made us all the more desperate to put the culprit away for a very long time indeed.

Sadly, there was a major problem and it remains a common one: three people in a house with access to the same computer. The owners of the PC denied everything, along with everyone else who'd ever been in the house. So the next step was to examine what was viewed either side of the images. If a suspect had accessed their secure online bank account and had then gone on to view child porn immediately afterwards, then this could help us convince a jury. Alas, it was not to be in this case.

I checked with the Crown Prosecution Service but I already knew the answer. We could never prove who the images belonged to. All I could do was log the criminal intelligence we'd recovered from the computer and hope that the images would help us crack other cases and save other children.

'Christ,' I said to Rob, 'there's someone out there who needs to be put away badly but what can we do?'

Rob just nodded. What else could he say?

CHAPTER TWENTY-THREE

OBSESSION

It was a fresh spring morning. Karl and I were stood on the Hackney doorstep of yet another suspected child molester; we were ready to do battle once more. As usual, we hoped for a quick resolution so we could get ourselves down to Bodrum's at a reasonable time for a Turkish breakfast.

As usual, it wasn't going to be that straightforward.

While he looked like a teddy bear, Karl, who was on the verge of drawing his pension, had a good dose of the Gene Hunt from the *Life on Mars* school of policing about him. An utterly devoted officer, he had seen everything it was possible to see in Child Protection. But this case would soon show us both that no matter how long you'd done this, there would always be some new challenge to be met – and in rising to this one, Karl would be pushed to the absolute limit.

Nine-year-old Janine had gone to her doctor and complained of 'problems down below'. When the GP examined her he was horrified to discover that Janine had gonorrhoea. He referred her to social services and they faxed the case straight over.

Karl was on the receiving end and pulled it out of the machine. He spoke to the mother first and then interviewed

Janine. She told him her uncle, whom she named, had abused her and possibly her two sisters while he babysat her. Karl then brought in her siblings for interview and spoke to the doctor. While this was going on, I tracked down the suspect and checked whether he had access to any other children. Luckily, he was unemployed and lived at home with his mother.

So here we were, on the uncle's doorstep in a typical Hackney terrace bright and early the next morning. Our policeman's knock brought a quick answer from his mother. Once she got over her surprise, she told us that her son wasn't there and that she didn't know where he was. A quick look round the house confirmed this.

Karl and I looked at each other. 'Right,' I said. 'Where would a lowlife like that be at 8 a.m.?'

'Well,' Karl said, 'he's unemployed, has nothing in particular to do. There's no signs of excessive booze or drugs in the house, so he's probably not out trying to get an early morning fix.'

We thought for another moment before the penny dropped: 'Doctor!' we said simultaneously.

His mother refused to tell us who his doctor was; hardly a sign of her belief in the innocence of her son.

Karl returned to the hallway and suddenly scooped a letter off the table by the phone. 'Harry! Letter from the doctor's surgery here.'

Without so much as a goodbye, we dashed out to the car and drove straight round to the Hackney surgery. I flashed my badge and beamed at the receptionists.

'Can we have a quick word in private?' I asked.

After confirming our target had indeed booked an appointment for that morning, I asked if they minded if we waited in the surgery. 'We might spook our suspect if we're waiting by the doors,' I said. 'We'll watch the street through the window and will grab him before he gets through the doors, so we won't disturb your morning routine.'

The manageress kindly agreed and Karl and I took our seats with a clear view through the glass door. The surgery was already pretty full; lots of sad-looking kids down with the latest bug.

'I bet we can spot this one coming straight off,' Karl said.

He was dead right.

Two minutes later, Karl tapped my shoulder and pointed to the door. 'There's our man.' Sure enough, there he was, getting off the number 38 bus. He looked exactly like the stereotypical abuser: thinning and lank hair, bad teeth, patchy stubble, grubby clothes and a shifty expression on his pockmarked face.

We left the surgery and marched up to him. 'Hello,' Karl said, showing his badge before confirming the man's identity.

'We'd very much like to have a chat with you,' I said. He said nothing so I pressed on.

'Why have you come here?'

'To see the doctor,' he said.

'We know that. *Why* have you come to the doctor? What's wrong with you?'

'Err . . . I've got a follow-up appointment for gonorrhoea.'

'Scratch that appointment,' Karl said, 'you're nicked,' and we drove down to the station.

'That should sort the case,' Karl said. 'They've both got gonorrhoea and he babysat. We might even spare Janine a court appearance.'

Alas, it was not to be. I had hoped the same as Karl but unfortunately the entire case once again came down to the child's word against the adult's. There are more than a hundred different strains of gonorrhoea and there were no identifying tests for all the different varieties. It seemed as if no one had even thought of the possible implications for sexual abuse cases. Besides, our suspect had already been treated and no longer had the disease. So the fact that they'd both once had gonorrhoea wasn't enough, it was circumstantial, never enough for a conviction.

Then we also had the difficult decision to make as to whether it was in the child's best interests to face a lengthy court case and cross-examination. Time does heal, and in the months it took for the case to come to court Janine's memory would fade. Was it really in her best interests to have to give evidence all over again, to reawaken those terrible memories? She was such a sweet and smart girl. Her mother seemed far more distraught. There was always a danger that the mother would drop the charges to spare her daughter the ordeal of a trial.

'I'm not giving up that easily,' Karl told me as we let Janine's uncle go, our breakfast all but forgotten. The suspect had hardly spoken, just enough to ask for a solicitor and to deny everything. He had a record for other crimes and he behaved as if he'd been through this a million times before. He wasn't troubled at all by our fancy interviewing strategies.

As our suspect strolled away, we walked back to the office. 'Each time I see the damage done to a child,' Karl said, 'I know that there's someone close by who will continue to hurt them. Unless someone does something he's going to do it again and again. How can I not try? What if we *could* match the same strain of gonorrhoea that Janine had on his clothing? There must be *someone* out there doing research.'

'If there is then I reckon you'd be the man to find them.'

Karl nodded and put his shoulder to it. As the days went on and he continued to work into the evening, trying to find a medical specialist somewhere in the world who might be able to help, I did start to worry that he was becoming dangerously obsessed.

By then I had my own obsession to worry about: a case had finally reached the Old Bailey – that of Sylvia and Alison, the girls from Ghana.

It was an extremely harrowing trial for the jury; four weeks of witnesses, evidence and expert testimony. They heard everything from the sisters, every last detail of the abuse.

'He raped us separately at first, then together,' Alison told them quietly. The look of horror on the jurors' faces told me all I needed to know. They were utterly convincing. No one would think for a moment (as their father Omari's new girlfriend did) that the sisters were making it up.

Between them, the sisters coped magnificently; in contrast, their father was a constant pain, often refusing to come to court. I felt totally humbled at how they coped with putting themselves through this trauma once more. It's almost impossible to describe their bravery; they were after all in the Old Bailey, in front of judge, jury, solicitors, barristers and journalists.

When Sylvia, the bolder of the two sisters, ended her testimony with a heart-felt message, I don't think there was a dry eye in the house. Gripping the rail, tears on her cheeks, she looked across the dock at Omari and said: 'He's still my dad and I still love him.'

If anything, this magnified her father's betrayal a hundredfold. His daughters were incredible young women who would have provided all the love any father would ever need. Now he had robbed them of their childhood, of their right to be raised safe, secure and happy. Instead he had forced them to live in terror for years and now, even though they were facing up to the past, they still bore the mental scars he'd given them.

It may have been wishful thinking on my part but I'm sure Sylvia's words affected even the judge. Omari collapsed when the jury found him guilty. He repeated the performance when the judge gave him twelve years.

The girls now had to try to rebuild their lives. I thanked them for what they'd done. Not only had they achieved justice, they'd helped to protect other victims from their dad and men like him.

*

By now, many of my early cases were reaching various courts and conclusions. As ever with child protection, they proved to be complex prosecutions and some outcomes surprised me. In the case of Hannah, Serena pleaded guilty on the basis that she did *not* cause the injuries, but *had* failed to treat them. She was sent to prison for a year. Although this was frustrating, it was far better to know that Hannah had been rescued from becoming another grim statistic. She'd remember little of the trauma she went through as a four-year-old.

The end result of Salma's case, the baby with the fractured skull, was a bitter pill. To me, and any other person with half a brain, it was a clear-cut case. The parents had confused their stories during our interviews. We'd proven that the father had lied about his employment, the mother about her understanding of English. Two doctors, one who had treated the girl and another who was a world-renowned radiologist had told me that it was almost impossible for a baby to receive a 3mm skull fracture from falling out of bed.

While it may have seemed cut and dried to me, there just wasn't enough evidence. Suravinda had hardly opened her mouth since the investigation had started and, to add to the drama, had since become pregnant.

Neither parent was prosecuted for child abuse.

It was desperately infuriating. Something bad had happened and I was sure some intangible threat was still there. I was reminded once again that in this case the victim would never be able to tell us what happened and by now quite probably had no recollection of her injury.

There was no denying it. This troubled me and I told Rob as much.

'You have to let it go, Harry. Remember, thanks to you the child is safe and well and should remain so.' Social services would watch the family until all the children had turned eighteen. I hoped it would prove to be enough.

'That's the point of these cases,' Rob continued. 'That's what it's all about. They're successful because we've saved kids and people are looking out for them. It's not often you get the perfect outcome, and without you pushing the investigative boundaries, some may have ended in tragedy.'

Despite these difficult cases and some setbacks, it felt as if we were 'winning'. As the various trial dates of my cases started to merge with ongoing investigations, I was stretched to my absolute limit but at the same time I'd never felt so confident in what I was doing. I suddenly realized that, like Karl, I was obsessed with the job, and there were no limits and there was nowhere either of us wouldn't go to do it to the best of our ability.

In fact, I almost didn't recognize myself any more. I was nowhere near Rob's level but I was now an all-round officer – able to bust through crack-house doors, stare down paedophiles in the interview room and stand up under cross-examination in the most intimidating courtrooms in the country. This was no longer a world about which I knew nothing but, as Rob took pleasure in often reminding me, I never knew what would happen from one day to the next. I was yet again about to be taught a lesson, this time by social services, in what was yet another murderously difficult case.

CHAPTER TWENTY-FOUR

SMOTHERED

I was trying not to lose my temper with the social worker but was failing badly. While on a routine inquiry, a constable had found a baby girl tied to her cot. She'd obviously been left alone for some time as she was covered in her own faeces.

The PC had quite rightly removed the baby there and then and called us immediately. A quick check told us the child was already on the child protection register. Obviously anxious to make her safe, I'd taken the child into police protection. This lasts for seventy-two hours. The problem was that the social worker disagreed as to what we should do next.

'I've interviewed the mother,' she told me over the phone, 'and she says that her daughter had got into the habit of climbing out of her cot and had almost fallen. The mother was just trying to make her secure by fastening her to the bars of the cot. The ties weren't taut.'

'And the excrement?' I asked.

'The child's nappy had simply been left too loose. There's no reason for us to remove the child.'

'Yes, there is,' I replied, absolutely furious and struggling to keep a lid on it. 'That cock-and-bull story might barely be acceptable from a mother if her child was not already on the child protection register. If we return that baby now, she'll go straight back in the cot and will continue to be neglected.'

I couldn't believe the social worker's attitude. For some reason she'd decided to put a positive 'spin' on the mother's interview when to me it was obvious the baby was in real danger. I had a feeling that she was inexperienced and was struggling to cope with the caseload and/or was under pressure from someone senior to stop putting so many kids into care. Still, her decision was unacceptable; sure you can be overworked and under pressure but to leave a child on the register with a parent in those circumstances was, in my mind, unforgivable.

I usually admired the commitment and passion with which some social workers argued their case. But that was because I could understand their argument. In this case I didn't have a clue why she was being so bloody obtuse.

Byron had told me to stick to my guns, so I did. 'She's wrong, you're right,' he said, 'it's your duty to make sure they don't get away with making a stupid mistake.'

'That PPO may run out Sunday night,' I explained to social services over the phone, 'but I'm so concerned at your stance in this case that I will reapply to the court so that the girl will remain in my care for another eight days.'*

'But you can't reapply.'

'Not as a police officer,' I shot back, 'but I can reapply as a private citizen.'

This was met with silence. Chew on that, I thought, hoping that this would make them see sense. It didn't and I should not have suggested something I was never going to do.

After the discussion was over, Keira called me. She'd received

---

* PPO is a Police Protection Order – the power to remove a child or keep a child in a place of safety for seventy-two hours if they are at immediate risk of significant harm.

an urgent referral from a doctor at Homerton Hospital. 'Looks like a grey case,' she said, 'the doctor claims a patient has tried to kill her baby. She's on the record with social services.'

'Who took the case originally?'

'Norman.'

As Keira and I went to get the details of the case we met Dev in the corridor, who'd just returned to work after being cleared. He was a changed man; he looked weary and lost. Over time I'd come to notice that he no longer chased his cases with the same determination and strength he used to; yet another non-civilian casualty in the war against child abuse. I wondered how long he would last before he decided to chuck it all in and try something else. It wasn't long.

A few weeks earlier, 'Jenny', a single mother, had walked up to the front desk of Hackney Social Services with her daughter and told the startled receptionist that she didn't want her baby any more: 'You have to take her for me, I can't cope.'

Norman realized that Jenny was suffering from chronic depression and believed that with the right kind of treatment there was a very good chance she'd overcome it. I agree that this was a much better option than leaving the woman depressed and putting her baby into care. After all, by going directly to social services, she had put the baby first, so there was hope. Jenny was later hospitalized for her depression and, as part of her treatment, she was allowed to keep her daughter with her.

That night a junior doctor entered the ward and, to her horror, saw a pillow lying across the baby's face. She snatched it off, checked the child – she was fine – and then called us.

'I'm convinced she tried to smother her baby,' the young doctor told me. 'She's suffering from severe depression.'

Keira spoke to Jenny. 'No go, Harry,' she said, 'adamant denial. She won't look me in the eye but I don't think that means she's lying. She's quite confused but does understand that she's in a very serious pickle. She's very frightened.'

'Do you have CCTV?'

The doctor shook her head. 'Only outside the ward.'

She hadn't seen Jenny place the pillow over the baby's head and there was no physical indication that the baby had been deliberately smothered.

But how did the pillow get there? It was a toddler's pillow, so the baby could have pulled it across – or it could have wriggled underneath. It was unlikely but by no means inconceivable. I remembered the child that had fallen six floors from a supposedly secure tower-block window and had nothing but a bruised back to show for it . . . anything was possible.

There was DNA from the mother on the pillowcase but this was of little help evidentially. DNA is extremely helpful in stranger cases but with families it's often of no use as their DNA is expected to be all around their children. So it came down to the doctor's word against Jenny's. Not enough for any jury. I noted that the doctor had become increasingly traumatized by the whole event and started to doubt her decision.

'Could I have been mistaken?' she asked.

'Don't worry,' Keira said, 'you've absolutely done the right thing. Try not to think about it too much, that's our job.'

As we left the hospital I said, 'She's either going to drop her accusation or be shaky on the witness stand. We need more.'

The next step was to get an official statement from Norman, the social worker who had initially dealt with Jenny's case. He'd since left Hackney Social Services and had moved to Northern Ireland. After getting clearance from Special Branch, Keira and I flew from London to Belfast International, and hired a car.

To do this unescorted would not have been possible before the Good Friday Agreement, signed only a few years previously. Things really had changed. We lunched in Londonderry and then strolled up a hill. Directly below us was the 'Bogside', an area ingrained in Northern Ireland's history, the site of Bloody Sunday and the Battle of the Bogside. It all looked so peaceful. 'Amazing really,' I said, 'you'd never think this was once the epicentre of the Troubles.'

We dropped in at the local police station to let them know what we were up to. We were met by a friendly uniformed sergeant, and after a brief chat about the state of policing today, I asked, 'So, do you think we could go on a patrol with you guys?'

'Sure, no problem at all. Hop in that Land Rover over there and a couple of the fellas will be over in a minute.'

'It's pretty well armoured, Harry,' Keira said as we clambered in. 'Perhaps it's not as peaceful as it looks.'

She wasn't wrong. I noted when we got in that chain mesh covered the inside of the Landy. There were bench seats in the back and we settled into these as two young constables and a sergeant joined us.

After a round of 'hellos', I asked: 'What's the chain in aid of?'

The two men looked at each other. One of them turned in his seat to look at me and said, 'You'll see,' with a rueful grin.

It was then that I noticed that they weren't wearing body armour. 'That's amazing,' I said, 'back in Hackney the beat officers look like paramilitaries. You guys are just in jumpers and shirts!' They smiled at my disbelief; I simply couldn't get over the fact that patrolling officers in Hackney wore more protection than officers in Londonderry.

Darkness was falling as we set off towards the top of the hill; the exact same spot where Keira and I had stood earlier. The sergeant gave us a run-down on the Troubles, pointing out some of the key parts of the Bogside. 'Let's have a closer look,' he said, and we drove off into the estates of Londonderry.

As we entered the first estate there was a sudden bang as loud as a shotgun, right behind my head. 'What the f—!' Missiles of every description, bricks, bits of metal and wood, hit the side of the Landy. Someone lobbed a few sawed-off sections of scaffolding poles; these made the greatest racket of all. 'Before you say it,' the sergeant yelled over the bedlam, 'we do get the odd kitchen sink thrown at us as well! That's what the chain along the roof's for, so you can hang on!'

I was going to ask if there was any chance of petrol bombs, but I was interrupted by Keira. 'Christ,' she said, looking through the mesh-covered windows, 'they're tiny!'

I turned and saw about a dozen kids; almost all of them were aged about nine or ten. Unbelievable. 'They hate the cops already?' I asked.

'We're reaping what's been sown,' the sergeant said. 'The battles and injustices are still fresh in their parents' minds.'

I glumly observed that most of them would have been in nappies when the Good Friday Agreement was signed.

Their hatred of the cops would remain for years, if not for the rest of their lives, and may even be passed on to the next generation. I wondered what kind of parent allowed their kid to do this. And then I thought about the 'occupation'. I guess it's not hard to pass the hatred down but I couldn't imagine letting my kids get away with this sort of thing. They were attacking us in front of the entire estate. Everybody could see what was going on.

Perhaps this was just the equivalent of the Hackney parents who unleashed their young children into the estates and surrounding streets, bored and unsupervised. Or in some way similar to the hopelessness of the Jamaican ghetto where kids join gangs and die young, fighting gun battles with the cops.

Why was it that wherever I went, it was always the same? Kids running wild, already disenchanted, raised to hate the police and wanting to find criminal means to beat poverty because they believed they had no chance of a fair shot at life?

The sergeant broke in on my thoughts. 'So what brings you to our fair town, then?'

I explained what Keira and I did. They wrinkled their noses in disgust. It was plain to us that they were exercising some restraint; they didn't know us well enough to lecture us on the pros of the conveniently straightforward philosophy of castration and hanging for child abusers.

Finally, it was time to leave our colleagues to their adversity. Their disgust at what we did turned to shock and amazement when we told them where we were staying. Concerns of officers' security while abroad sometimes led to unexpected perks – like highly secure, well-equipped hotels.

We interviewed Norman at the police station. 'I feel terrible, Harry,' he said, cradling his coffee. 'If Jenny had killed her baby . . .' His voice tailed off. I knew exactly where he was coming from. This is one of the reasons why it's incredibly tough being a social worker – you live in fear that a case will come back and bite you.

Norman continued. 'The jobs I've covered, sometimes even the ones I've forgotten about, literally haunt me in my dreams. I ask myself what have I forgotten to do. What did I miss? I have days where I wake up with a feeling of utter dread.'

We took Norman's official statement; as far as we were concerned, he'd done all he could and our investigation told us he'd made the right decision. But of course, if Jenny had killed her baby then the media would have vilified him. This is just the way the job is. The police and social services have to make life-changing judgements based on the available evidence. The problem is, of course, we can never be a hundred per cent sure that we have all of the evidence or that we have successfully judged the mental state of any one individual. The prevailing view was that the best approach was for the child to stay with the family whenever possible and Norman had gone along with this.

Keira and I returned to London the next day. At one of the hearings we saw Jenny. She was pale, even thinner and clearly still clinically depressed. I was almost relieved that, thanks to a lack of evidence, the charges of attempted infanticide were dropped.

It's a big ask to expect Joe Public to find Jenny guilty when it's her word against the doctor's and the case boiled down to the issue of intent. The doctor could not say what was in Jenny's mind, only Jenny knew what really happened. Once a jury understood the extreme ramifications of a guilty decision (Jenny would go to jail for a very long time, she would never see her daughter again and her daughter would be taken into care), I doubt whether many would have found her guilty.

I just hoped that Jenny's denial was truthful and if it wasn't that she would at least get enough of the right treatment to overcome her depression. It was strange to see the child go back to the mother in this case, as this was a potential attempted murder, as opposed to the example of neglect described at the start of the chapter. But it all comes down to what's in the best interests of the child, based on the available evidence. The neglect was systemic and, in my opinion, life-threatening, whereas the depressed mother had tried to put her child first and sought help for her condition.

At least there was hope. For many others, help had come too late.

CHAPTER TWENTY-FIVE

INJUSTICE

I was sitting in Bodrum's with Patrick, discussing his latest case. He waited until the waitress had plonked down our refills before continuing. 'This guy's been getting away with it for such a long time, there's no way he would have limited himself to just one child,' he said.

Patrick had just been through a horrendous memorandum interview with a young victim of child abuse. He'd claimed that a close relation had systematically assaulted him for years.

Sarah joined us. She'd just picked up a historical case. 'I reckon it's the same with mine,' she said. 'A Scout leader involved with the local amateur dramatics society. He won the trust of a child *and* his parents before he started abusing the poor kid. He's been a Scout leader for decades, so I reckon there must be others. Why is it that so many paedophiles manage to find work with children? Is it really so easy?'

It is. Paedophiles carefully search out any opportunity they can. Unfortunately, there seem to be far too many prospects open to them and a shocking number of paedophiles manage to worm their way into jobs that require constant contact with children.

We see the stories all too often – Scout leaders, teachers, doctors, nurses, etc., facing trials for child abuse. Invariably, a long and disturbing history of abuse emerges during their trials, a history peppered with 'second chances' and 'missed opportunities' where their bosses have fallen for a paedophile's appeals for mercy; that it was a momentary lapse and will never happen again.

Take Stephen King, for example, a former youth worker and self-styled expert in child pornography who advised police and criminal prosecutors on how to protect children. He also gave advice on sentencing paedophiles to the independent Sentence Advisory Panel. His work was credited in the final recommendations made in the panel's report, which was used by the Law Society, the Bar Council and the Probation Service. He attended meetings where police and other bodies discussed tactics for tackling paedophiles.

He'd also been quoted in and contributed to several newspapers, including the *Guardian*, as an expert on child abuse. For example, after the conviction of Howard Hughes for the rape and murder of seven-year-old Sophie Hook, King had argued that demands for a sex offenders' register were over the top. A 20 July 1996 letter from King about calls for a sex offenders' register states: 'A far more sensible approach would be to include on such a register the names of those who have reoffended . . . as the proportion of recidivists seems to be nowhere near the practically hysterical levels claimed by some apparent experts.'

Nothing could have been further from the truth: burglars can reform, paedophiles cannot. Make no mistake, when they are released back into society, they are likely to reoffend.

King proved himself to be the living embodiment of this rule. He was jailed for six months in 1989 for gross indecency with a child. Fifteen years later, in 2004, King, now fifty-four, pleaded guilty to twenty-one counts including sex with a girl under thirteen years (she was ten years old), ten counts of indecent assault, six charges of indecency with a child and four counts of taking indecent photographs of a child. The youngest of his victims was nine years old.

He kept a diary for nearly a decade in which he catalogued the abuse of his young victims. He bragged how he 'got away with it' when police officers decided not to press charges after an earlier inquiry.

He lured children to his flat by posing as a tutor. He set up a photographic studio in his bedroom with blacked-out windows. He tied the girls up and took hundreds of photos and filmed dozens of videos of them engaged in sexual acts alone, with each other and with him. King even filmed himself 'grooming' them, prior to the physical abuse. One of his victims had since attempted suicide by slashing her wrists with broken glass, while another had developed learning difficulties.

Judge Fabyan Evans sentenced King to seven years for 'systematic sexual abuse'. Speaking outside the court, Detective Inspector Neil Thompson from the Met's Paedophile Unit said he believed there were many more victims and urged them to come forward.

Many people felt the sentence was far too light. Speaking to journalists outside the court, a victim's father said: 'I left the court screaming, "Stop, this is not a deterrent." We're still very angry about what happened. His sentence is disgusting. He'll be out in a few years. The worst thing is, you can't protect your child. Everything you have striven for has all gone. Her innocence has been stolen.'[23]

King is by no means the exception.

Bernie Bain, a notorious paedophile who was head of one of Islington's care homes in the seventies, targeted boys of seven or eight and was described by police as 'extremely violent' and 'sadistic'. He was never brought to trial in Britain. Detectives did not discover the full extent of Bain's activities until 1995, by which time he had abused children for three decades. Police eventually found seven people willing to testify against him in court. He was living in Morocco at the time, having served a prison sentence there for abuse. He was deported to Holland, but an attempt to extradite him to Britain failed. Despite an international warrant for his arrest he disappeared again. He escaped justice by committing suicide in Thailand in May 2000.

The *Evening Standard* and the BBC's *Today* programme had both launched investigations into Bernie Bain and the Islington Care Home scandal, the most recent of which came in 2003, when Margaret Hodge was appointed Minister for Children. Hodge was the head of Islington Council at the time concerns about Bain had first been raised. The *Evening Standard* called for Hodge to resign following their publication of a 'killer memo', which showed she was warned by senior social workers about the sexual abuse in Islington, but failed to act on their advice.

One of the victims, Demetrious Panton, had written a six-page letter to Hodge, detailing the details of his abuse at a residential unit in Elwood Street, Islington. Bernie Bain had sexually assaulted him, he wrote, 'three or four times a week for over a year'.

Hodge dismissed Panton's claims and labelled him an 'extremely disturbed person', a comment she was forced to apologize for publicly after Panton consulted lawyers and after he received a glowing public testimony from a senior police officer.[24]

Hodge has since argued that she 'regretted what happened in Islington children's care homes' adding that she had 'learned the lessons' and that her experience put her 'in a better position to be Minister for Children'.

I'm sure that's of little comfort to those who suffered under Bain. Council administrator Yvonne Williams was in Islington's care from the age of eight to eighteen. She was sexually abused every day from the age of ten for six years.

Liam Lucas, twenty-six, was raped as a nine-year-old boy by an Islington care worker. He told the *Evening Standard* that he still suffered from nightmares and flashbacks.

Ann Belcher, twenty-eight, was raped by a man who visited her bedroom almost every day for two years.

Michael Fitch spent ten years in an Islington care home that turned him from a happy boy of nine into a tortured adult. He had made more than a dozen suicide attempts.

His brother Douglas was abused by the same man for four years, from the age of thirteen. 'If Michael had been believed,' he told the *Evening Standard*, 'if Hodge had listened, I could have been saved from abuse.'

Yet nobody stepped in – despite being asked to investigate.

And so it continues.

Catholic leader Archbishop Cormac Murphy-O'Connor agreed to pay compensation to victims of Father Michael Hill, given a five-year prison sentence in 2002 for a series of 'disgraceful and disgusting' sex attacks on three young boys aged between ten and fourteen. Hill would ingratiate himself with families, befriending young boys with treats and outings before assaulting them. A further eight similar charges were left on file and not proceeded with, due to their historical nature.

He had previously been jailed in 1997, also for five years, for ten offences against eight boys. Before this he had worked as a priest in Sussex where he committed two more assaults. Following complaints, he left the parish in 1983 and received treatment at a church centre while temporarily suspended.

Hill went on to become the chaplain of Gatwick airport. Two of his subsequent victims included a child who missed his flight and a thirteen-year-old boy who was in a wheelchair. He systematically abused children while he was supposed to be a trusted spiritual guide, yet he had been forgiven and treated with leniency time and time again. And even with this record, the judge only saw fit to hand out the same sentence of five years that he had received in 1997.[25]

Anthony Barron, fifty-four, was the image of respectability – a bank manager, Scout treasurer and member of the parent–teacher association. He was also a predatory paedophile who carried out sex attacks on girls as young as three, using them as 'toys' and storing film of his acts in an extensive video library.

He was arrested after a five-year-old child told her mother what had happened. At his trial in 2007, Barron was found guilty of the rape and attempted rape of a twelve-year-old girl and admitting eighty-seven offences against another ten girls between 1995 and 2006. They included assaults on two sisters on the same day, one after the other. He even abused another child while her mother was elsewhere in his house.

Andrew Bright QC, defending, told the court that his client was 'capable of reform' and hoped to be allowed back into the community one day to 'do what he sees as his duty to go some way to putting things right'. Let's hope he is never given the chance. In 2007, he was given a minimum term of nine years before he can apply for parole. He will also spend the rest of his life on the sex offenders' register.

Judge Julian Hall told jurors in the case – who had to watch some of the video footage – that he would excuse them from jury service for the next ten years because of the trauma they'd suffered. 'Once is enough for a lifetime,' he said.[26]

Interestingly, the same judge had previously been accused of being too lenient on paedophiles. He once described a girl of ten, raped twice by a window cleaner, as 'provocative' because she wore frilly underwear. And in an earlier case, the same judge told another paedophile to buy his child victim a bicycle to cheer her up.[27]

In 2007, another interesting sentence came from Judge Jim Spencer, who fined Kevin Harrison £500 and ordered him to pay

£190 costs after Harrison, fifty-one, admitted paying for the sexual favours of a girl aged sixteen who needed the money to fund her drug habit. This offence, which outlaws sex with prostitutes under the age of eighteen, carries a maximum sentence of seven years' jail. The judge reportedly warned Harrison to 'keep himself to himself'. He also said: 'Why should a girl of sixteen who wants to sleep with him not be able to – it is not a crime, is it?' He was referring to the fact that the age of consent for sex is sixteen.[28]

Harrison already had no less than eighteen sexually motivated offences on his record. He had been jailed for two years in 1977 for enticing two girls into his car and abusing them. He was then jailed for seven years in 1980 for a number of sex offences against children, and was given community punishments for further sexual offences against young girls in 1991 and 1992.

His 2007 crime carries a maximum sentence of seven years' imprisonment. By freeing him, Judge Spencer had sent out a message that the sexual exploitation of children is not a serious offence.

Also in 2007, Judge John Rogers suspended Derek Williams's six-month sentence for downloading child pornography, saying that he had to consider a Home Office request to jail only the most 'dangerous and persistent' offenders. Williams had downloaded 200 images, some of which were given the serious 'level four' grading.

The judge clearly didn't grasp that consumers of child pornography are very dangerous and very persistent offenders – after all, they supply the demand for this most evil and depraved of markets. Instead, Judge Rogers's judgement indicated the exact opposite: that downloading child pornography is not linked to the production of child abuse films and pictures, but is in fact a minor offence. Judge Rogers had only served to help other viewers of child pornography excuse their behaviour.

Luckily, Williams was required to register with the police as a sex offender within seventy-two hours and missed the deadline by eighteen hours. He blamed the unrelenting press who had surrounded his house after the judge's comments. This time Judge Rogers activated the suspended sentence of six months and gave him an additional two months for failing to register.[29]

Even more seriously, a serial paedophile escaped with a one-year jail sentence in 2004 for the attempted abduction of an eleven-year-old girl while posing as a child protection officer. Gary Brown, thirty-two, was convicted after he targeted the child as she waited at a school in St John's Wood in North London. Detective Constable Mark Gladman was stunned at the result. He said: 'We can't believe it. He has a record of offences against children going back to 1993.'[30]

Even serving police officers who have been found guilty of offences against children have been treated leniently. Richard Curry, a police sergeant praised for bravery and his work in anti-paedophile operations, was jailed for just six months in 2003 after downloading child pornography. Curry, thirty-nine, admitted six charges of possessing 1,300 pictures of children as young as seven in pornographic poses.[31]

The following year, the first serving Metropolitan Police officer was convicted for incest (he cannot be named for legal reasons). The father of two, forty-eight years old, sent a video of himself sexually abusing his underage daughter to an Internet paedophile. He was arrested after detectives discovered the film of him with the fifteen-year-old girl on another paedophile's computer. Officers found over 300 photographs of young children – and thirty-two videos – some involving babies. He also confessed to having abused his daughter for about a year and having had sex with her up to six times. He was jailed for six years.

Based on my own experiences of working with criminals, sex offenders have a compulsive nature and are very likely to reoffend. The sentence they receive needs to reflect this. I am not saying that lengthy prison sentences alone are the answer but abusers must be pilloried by the courts. Not to do so gives the impression that sexual assault is not really a crime; that it's practically acceptable.

It's tragic that so many in authority fall for paedophiles' fake contrition. I've interviewed many and so understand only too well just how plausible they can be. But paedophiles who sincerely don't want to reoffend wouldn't try and retain or find positions which put them in constant contact with children. As one journalist put it: 'Recovering alcoholics don't look for work in breweries.'[32]

In my experience it's very much a case of 'once a paedophile, always a paedophile'. Paedophiles will always be dangerous, and the best one can hope for – given that they're almost never locked up for life – is that they'll apply behaviour modification techniques they learn in prison in real life.

'I'm not very optimistic about therapy,' Patrick said when this topic came up. None of us were, and with good reason. If anything, therapy brought paedophiles together. One case involved four paedophiles who met on a counselling course in prison. They founded a charity for Romanian orphans and used this as a way to abuse them. They told detectives their charity work was to 'repay their debt to children'.

And they'd talked themselves into believing it. That's what makes paedophiles so incurable – their mind-boggling level of self-delusion. They believe children want them, 'provoke' them, and that adult–child sex is natural, harmless – even beneficial. It's this conviction, mixed with their extreme deviousness and crystal-clear awareness of what normal people think about paedophiles, that helps them to escape detection for so long.

They're very careful. Sudden snatches of children are very rare indeed: paedophiles often spend months targeting a future victim and gaining their trust before committing the abuse. True remorse and insight is extremely rare. Remorse, if present at all, is a tiny part; you can't work on the principle that a paedophile is feeling guilty and might confess. Any shame they feel doesn't last very long before their survival instincts take over, especially if they think there's a chance of getting away with it.

It doesn't help that we still seem determined to help them escape justice, thanks to some ludicrous loopholes. In 2003, Simon Moore, who was from Hackney, contacted two thirteen-year-old girls via the Internet after logging on to a children's homework chat room used by his daughter.

The father of four travelled to Scotland to seduce his first victim after exchanging explicit emails with her. He told her he would kill her mother if she told anyone during the five months he spent abusing her. It was only when his horrified wife found his emails that she alerted the girl's mother and Moore was arrested.

Moore, a labourer, thirty-seven, appeared at Paisley Sheriff Court but successfully demanded bail under the European Convention on Human Rights. Only weeks later he abducted and had sex with another thirteen-year-old he met through the same chat room. She was naked in his bed when police arrived to arrest him. It was later discovered he had been in contact with more than 200 girls.

Moore was sentenced to six years at Southwark Crown Court for the first abuse and three years for the second. The latter girl's furious father said: 'Scottish justice failed my little girl. What they are saying is that the rights of filth like Moore matter more than the rights of my little girl. He had sex with a thirteen-year-old girl, repeatedly. My daughter is a nervous wreck.'[33]

The three years (which will probably end up being eighteen months) seems to be extremely lenient – especially as this is someone who has clearly demonstrated they are an extremely persistent offender.

Moore's deviousness suggested he was also familiar with the law. Until 2004, the maximum sentence for unlawful sexual intercourse with a girl under thirteen was life, but the maximum sentence for a girl aged thirteen or over was two years. Thankfully this was increased, albeit belatedly, to fourteen years as part of the Sexual Offences Bill 2004, the first radical overhaul of our outdated sex laws for fifty years.

So we have paedophiles in trusted positions in society escaping with light sentences time and again. The cases described here are not that exceptional. Behind every one of them lies a terrible history of abuse and a lifetime of damage for the victims.

Cases don't come much worse than those of Dr Timothy Healy, fifty-six, who was jailed for twelve years in 2002 for a ten-year period of abuse. The GP drugged some of his victims (two of whom were aged eleven) before filming himself abusing them. Although eleven of his victims were in court to see him sentenced, some have never been identified.[34]

Although teachers are vital in the fight against child abuse, very occasionally they're found to be the perpetrators. In 2001 Judge David Selwood called Paul Tramontini, a maths teacher of thirty-four who ran off with a fifteen-year-old schoolgirl, 'Every parent's nightmare'. He also said: 'You were in a position of trust and also in a position of power and this offence represents a gross breach of that trust.' He jailed Tramontini for eighteen months after hearing that the girl's mother could never forgive him.[35]

It was quite right that Tramontini was jailed. As a teacher, he had betrayed his profession, using it as a means to seduce an underage teenage girl. Although he had broken the law and the girl was only fifteen, he was not a paedophile. The law says that anyone under eighteen is a child. A paedophile is someone who has a sexual interest in a child. So does that mean that a nine-teen-year-old who sleeps with his seventeen-year-old girlfriend is a paedophile? No, of course not. The term 'child' is a legal one. A paedophile would not find a mature-looking fifteen-year-old girl attractive. They much prefer pre-pubescent kids. There is a difference between underage sexual activity and paedophilia. This is why the law has specific offences regarding under-thirteens.

Judge Selwood, on the other hand, *was* attracted to children under thirteen. In 2004, the day before he was due to preside over the trial of a man accused of indecent assault, Selwood, sixty-nine, was arrested for downloading child pornography. A married father of four, who retired from the army a major general (just two ranks from field marshal), he had a lengthy entry in *Who's Who?* After leaving the army he became a circuit judge in 1992 before becoming a resident Crown Court judge in 1996.

Operation Ore detectives were very surprised when his name appeared on a credit card used to buy and download child pornography. The images were considered to be level one, of naked and semi-clad children, the least serious of the five categories.

When confronted, Selwood claimed he was curious to see how difficult it was for someone with few computer skills, such as himself, to find such images. In a statement to police he said he never had any sexual interest in young children but admitted it would be difficult to describe his actions as 'research'.

At his trial, he admitted twelve counts of making indecent images of boys aged eight to fourteen and one count of possessing seventy-five indecent pictures in his computer.

Now, reflect on Judge Selwood's own words when, in 2002, he oversaw the trial of Paul Hobbs, who was found guilty of being in possession of hundreds of indecent images of young girls. 'Those who search for and download images of this kind,' Selwood told the court, 'create a market which encourages the abuse of young girls.' He sentenced Hobbs to seven years, a decent sentence.

Selwood was given a twelve-month Community Order. He was excused from working in the community as part of the Order, because of his age and health. He also didn't have to attend a programme for sex offenders because, the judge said, the advice and guidance he needed could come from a probation officer. He was put on the sex offenders' register for five years.[36]

A year's community rehabilitation order in cases like these simply does not represent an effective deterrent. Remember, behind these indecent images are real children who will have suffered immense trauma. Remember also that Selwood admitted twelve counts of 'making indecent images of boys'. Experts condemned Selwood's sentence as 'little more than a slap on the wrist' and demanded a major overhaul of punishments for Internet paedophiles.

There can be no sympathy, no matter how glowing the guilty person's record might be. We have to send out a strong warning to everyone, in all walks of life and in all professions, that they cannot escape the law by using the Internet to access abusive images of children.

In Judge Selwood's case, children's charities demanded a review of any cases involving offences against children that he'd heard. Before Selwood's disgrace, two men he dealt with for offences involving children had their sentences increased on appeal. Selwood also cleared a world authority on child abuse of having criminal intent when he downloaded child pornography. He described the accused as 'naive' for not seeking legal advice or consulting colleagues before accessing the computer images. Nevertheless, when the Crown Prosecution Service reviewed Selwood's history, they found 'no obvious pattern of inappropriate sentencing'.

Just twenty-four hours after Judge David Selwood escaped a prison sentence, Eton College master Ian McAuslan, fifty-eight, also avoided jail even though he admitted possessing over 2,000 images of children, 200 of them described as indecent. IT staff at the school, whose past pupils include Princes William and Harry, discovered the images when McAuslan handed the computer in for a routine upgrade. McAuslan pleaded guilty to two charges of possessing indecent images of children and fourteen of making indecent images of children. He was sentenced to nine months, suspended for two years.[37]

And so it continues – the children suffering, those responsible escaping time and again with light sentences, they and others utterly undeterred.

We could only speculate on what sentences Sarah's and Patrick's suspects might receive. All we could be certain of was that we would follow each and every case to the very end in our effort to protect children and present the best possible evidence in court. Obviously, there was a limit to what we could achieve if the courts weren't able to put these people away for long enough. Of course that wasn't going to put us off – no matter how difficult or delicate the case might be.

CHAPTER TWENTY-SIX

OUT ON THE INSIDE

I was in the midst of an urgent inquiry. A grandfather had been accused of abusing two teenage granddaughters and the entire family had gone on the run. I'd never encountered anything like this before – siblings, parents and grandparents all on the lam – supposedly an entirely respectable middle-class family had upped sticks and vanished into the ether.

Tanya, who had recently joined the unit, and I were screeching round Stamford Hill in the Peugeot, hunting for clues as to their whereabouts, when a cold wave of panic suddenly overtook me: 'Oh shit, no!'

'What the hell!?' Tanya yelled as I skidded to a very abrupt halt in the middle of the road.

'The 101 Book! Oh bloody hell, no, please, no.'

The 101 Book is a soft-backed A4 booklet which contains tear-out forms that we hand over to the occupiers of any home we've searched, as well as pages where we note what we've found, where and when and so on. We'd been searching houses all day and I'd forgotten the book at the last address. There was one serious catch: we'd just interviewed a prominent rabbi and Passover was imminent.

As I looked out of the window, I saw the last few people in traditional dress jogging anxiously homewards. I checked my watch: two minutes to go.

The family we were looking for was from an extremely traditional and secretive Hasidic Jewish group called the Haredi. The 20,000-strong Jewish community in Stamford Hill, North London, was probably the last place in London I'd expect to uncover a serious crime as they were famous for being just about the most law-abiding citizens you could ever meet.

To say that this investigation was delicate was a massive understatement.

I'd dealt with the Hasidic community only once before. A child had been seriously scalded. Once again, I'd pushed my poor old Peugeot to the limit to get to the scene but Sarah and I were somewhat taken aback when we found the house full of ultra-Orthodox Jews. There was nothing wrong with this, of course, but their world was normally closed to outsiders and here we were about to trample all over it.

I kept reminding myself of Rob's golden rule: 'If it's in the child's best interests, get on with it.' Cultural sensibilities be damned, I thought, protect the child, just protect the child and everything else will take care of itself.

The Haredi have their own independent systems in place that are similar to our state systems of justice, health and welfare and so a Jewish ambulance, called *Hatzola* – the Hebrew word for rescue – was already in attendance, as was a Jewish social worker and the local rabbi.

'They're quick off the mark,' Sarah said.

'Let's hope they haven't ruined the scene,' I replied, and sought out the parents.

The mother and father were clearly distraught as they watched the paramedics tend to their child.

'It was the bathwater,' the father told me, 'there's something wrong with the immersion heater.'

As the ambulance left with their son, Sarah and I went to have a look and took photos of the heating system. The water was indeed scalding hot. A quick check revealed that the settings were too high. My gut instinct told me this was an accident.

Nonetheless, we would be as thorough as ever. I explained this to the family, the social worker and the rabbi, adding that we needed to conduct background checks and would have to speak to 'mainstream' social services before we could officially close the case. Fortunately, it turned out to be that straightforward.

During this case I learned that the Haredi community as a whole tries to avoid contact with modern society. Television is frowned upon. They are very much of another time: the dress code for men, for example – long black coats, tall black hats, white stockings on the Sabbath – is imported from eastern European ghettos of the eighteenth century.

So, while this was a useful, if brief introduction into the workings of the Hasidic Jewish community, I still felt a little apprehensive when the report into the allegation of abuse first came in. This only increased when Simon took a call from social services and yelled across the office: 'Better take it up a notch, Harry, Granddad's entire family have gone on the run!'

Never being more than a desk or two away, Rob had heard everything. 'Right!' he shouted. Everyone automatically stopped whatever it was they were doing.

'I want everyone on this,' Rob said. 'It's Thursday, so we've not got long before the Sabbath and it happens to be Passover. Fortunately, it's a whole family we're looking for, so they shouldn't be too hard to find.'

This was top priority. As far as we were concerned the girls were in real danger. I alerted the rabbi and the Jewish social worker that I'd met before as I drove to the family house and asked if they knew of anywhere the family might have gone, but they were unable to give me any possible leads.

The house was deserted. Apart from a few essentials, the sort of things you'd think about grabbing if your house was on fire, everything was still there, all the furniture, much of their clothing, books, kitchenware and so on. I noted that this large house must have been a pretty busy place; some of the bedrooms were shared – how could someone hope to get away with sexually abusing two teenage girls in this house without everyone else knowing? Our search proved to be fruitless; there were no immediate clues that suggested where they'd gone.

Thoughts raced through my mind. What drama had unfolded here? So much had been left behind. Had they gone for good? Why did the whole family vanish? Were they under the spell of the grandfather? Was he an influential member of the community? Was the problem of living in such a close-knit community that the shame, whether guilty or not, would be too great?

The whole team charged around Stamford Hill. Tanya and I bounced from one address to another, speaking to rabbis, friends and neighbours of the family, pleading with them to help. They were not always the easiest people to interview. At the first address, although the Haredi man who answered the door shook my hand, he ignored Tanya, while his wife wouldn't speak to me. A Haredi man will not shake hands with a woman who is not his wife. This would be impropriety verging on lasciviousness and, besides, she might be menstruating, which under the strictest interpretation of Jewish law makes her unclean. Haredi women usually avoid eye contact with strangers.

And then came the final address, that of the most prominent and senior rabbi, who was the same size, shape and volume as Brian Blessed, the boisterous booming-voiced actor.

He'd been very courteous. 'Come in!' he'd said with a roar and a smile. 'You'll have to be quick, Passover is nearly upon us!'

I'd gone and left my 101 Book on his kitchen table. I really, really needed it. It was too important to leave for Passover. I checked my pockets, my bag and the car once more. Nothing. Damn, damn, damn.

Tanya glared at me in disbelief: 'You fucking idiot!'

I couldn't argue. I had to make a decision.

'You can't leave it,' Tanya said.

'Oh, for God's sake.' With a huge cloud hanging over me, I swung the little Peugeot around and screeched back to the rabbi's address.

We stood at the beautiful Victorian coloured-glass door and rang the bell for the second time. I could hear angry shouting coming from within the house; clearly the occupants were not at all happy about my insistent ringing.

I looked at Tanya. She was grinning at me.

'What the hell are you smiling at?' I demanded.

She pointed at my jacket. The 101 Book was poking out of my inside jacket pocket.

'What the—? How the hell did I miss that?'

The shouting grew louder as the shadow of the angry rabbi appeared in the hallway. The door rattled as he stormed towards it.

Bollocks.

I looked at Tanya and thought about making a run for it. The rabbi wouldn't follow because it was Passover, but Tanya was in heels. Besides, if I'd tried to run she would have felled me with a single precisely placed blow.

Guessing my thoughts, Tanya folded her arms, looked at me sternly and said: 'It's your stupid mess, you carry the can.'

'Oh crap!' I exclaimed, just as the door was thrown open.

'Whaaaat?' the Rabbi thundered angrily.

'Ah, er . . . sorry. We wanted to ask you something else . . . so sorry to disturb you but it's very important.'

What could I say now? I had to think of something important, a great question, more than enough reason to return – just deliver a simple line with humbleness and save the day.

'Errr . . . Can you, can you . . . think of anything else?'

Oh good grief. What had I just said? I could feel Tanya's incredulous eyes boring into me. Here is a man vital to police community relations on a vital case, one of the biggest, most urgent cases we've ever undertaken and I'd just screwed it all up.

He looked dumbfounded; his face turned deep red and his mouth fell open.

'Look,' I continued, 'I'm really, really sorry to disturb you, but are you absolutely sure there's nothing else?'

With that, I deployed the only weapon I had left: puppy dog eyes.

Tanya coughed.

The rabbi's expression softened into genuine bewilderment. 'No!' he boomed, and slammed the door. I breathed out as we walked down the path.

'I think I got away with that one,' I said with no little relief.

'Yeah, right,' she said, 'I can see it now.' She impersonated the tone of a prize-giver at the Oscars: '*And the award for police community relations goes to Harry Keeble!* We'll let everyone else be the judge of whether you got away with that once we get back to the office.'

'You wouldn't!'

This was a major screw-up and I deserved the ridicule. The Haredi are extremely protective about their image, which is entirely understandable. That's why police relations are so crucial. Although my incident with the rabbi appeared quite amusing, it could become deadly serious if we'd lost that rabbi's full trust and cooperation in a future case.

The longer we looked, the more worried we became. Was it already too late? I wondered. Might we never get a result? Perverts always look for and exploit weaknesses in whatever community they happen to be a part of, whether it is the English village or the ultra-Orthodox Haredi. As far as the Haredi are concerned, a child abuser would be able to take advantage of the fact that Haredi girls almost never speak out about abuse. If they admit to being raped, their chances of finding a husband are pretty much reduced to zero.

As the investigation progressed, I learned that they rarely allowed people from 'mainstream society' into their world. Social workers are sometimes called 'child-snatchers' while the police may be referred to as 'Cossacks', harking back to the nineteenth-century pogroms against Jews in Russia, so the chances of us getting to hear about some crimes are slim. Instinctively, a victim is far more likely to approach a rabbi than the police – and that's as far as their complaint might ever go. This is partly why they came across as so utterly law-abiding – many crimes were dealt with internally.

The Haredi in Israel have recognized the problem of sexual predators; the Shlom Banaich Fellowship (SBF) is the only organization that treats paedophiles and their victims. In Bnei Brak, a predominately Haredi city near Tel Aviv, SBF social worker Doron Agasi told a journalist from *Time* magazine that one young Haredi man had confessed to molesting more than a hundred girls. Agasi convinced the young man to turn himself over to the police. Unfortunately, this wasn't enough for the authorities, who didn't bring charges because none of the parents of the alleged victims filed complaints. The rapist remained free.

There is no organization like the SBF in the UK; I can only

hope that the Haredi communities here will recognize this, even if the problem only exists on a tiny scale – after all, the Haredi consider themselves defenders of morality in Jewish society.

Our breakthrough finally came from Heathrow Airport, once the cops there had checked the manifests for the family name. They'd fled to New York. As usual, I was up for the chase but this time Rob decided Simon and Lucy should go. They found the family, who greeted them with surprise and no little horror. When Simon and Lucy got to speak to the girls they said they'd since withdrawn their allegations.

'You see, everything has been dealt with internally,' their father said as he escorted Simon out.

The door slammed behind them and, with that, the case was closed.

CHAPTER TWENTY-SEVEN

THE BALANCING ACT

I was back in the Jewish community not long after the case of the disappearing family, except that this time it proved to be a very sombre investigation.

'I don't think you should tell the parents,' the rabbi told me quietly, shaking his head.

'But we need to get their signed consent,' I replied, perplexed.

'They're ultra-Orthodox; they need to bury their child within twenty-four hours,' the rabbi said, looking back down the hallway towards the parents.

'There are sometimes exceptions – if it's Sabbath, which it's not, or if relatives have to travel a long way to attend – which in this case they don't. I'm sure they'll permit a post-mortem if it's legally required and as long as I'm able to attend but they must have their child back in time for burial.'

That wasn't going to give me enough time. I looked over the rabbi's shoulder. I could see the young parents, obviously devastated, standing outside their baby's room; someone was reading Hebrew prayers aloud.

It was a tricky situation. Any sudden, unexpected death is devastating. When the death is that of a baby, without explanation, it's not difficult to imagine the effect on the bereaved family. In this case the family had returned from a visit to Israel to their home in Stamford Hill; the next morning they had awoken to find that Marnin, their six-month-old baby, had passed away.

The last thing I wanted was to make the mum and dad feel as if they were under suspicion, or trample over their deeply held religious views. Normal procedure is to treat the area as the scene of a serious incident, to interview the parents and any other witnesses before taking their baby to hospital for a post-mortem. My job was to collect every shred of detail surrounding Marnin's death, which would be added to the cot death data register, part of the ongoing worldwide hunt for explanations and preventions.

Any cop will have seen plenty of dead bodies in their time. Usually, freshly graduated PCs are charged with breaking into homes where an old person might have died. You'd get at least two or three of these a month. You kind of get used to it after a while. With babies, you never do. Marnin looked as if she were still asleep; her skin still appeared to be flushed with life.

Looking closely, there seemed to me to be no evidence of smothering; no sign of scratches, bruises or imprints to the face or neck, no little red dots around the eyes where pressure caused by suffocation has caused the tiny veins to pop.

In babies under a year old, there's not likely to be much of a struggle or much pressure applied to smother them, so it's still very hard to judge. Sometimes there are traces of milk on and around the lips, usually a consequence of death rather than any indication of cause.

The mum and dad were very withdrawn. They were clearly in the first stages of grief, shocked and numb. There was a possibility they would become angry or very emotional – especially if I mishandled what should be a routine investigation.

'My wife is worried Marnin suffocated,' the father began, 'or . . . choked. Is this what happened?'

'Well,' I said as reassuringly as possible, 'it is possible but very, very rare.' I didn't mention that the pathologist would try to determine cause, along with the coroner. It was still too early. I felt they needed a few more minutes to get used to my presence. Events and words greatly influence how a family deals with their bereavement in the long term. It helps, at this early stage, to still refer to the child as if she were still alive – and to use their name.

After speaking to the rabbi I was really worried. Tests had to be carried out on Marnin's brain before we could release her for burial. Doing this would take us beyond the twenty-four hours.

In the end, the parents decided to sign over their consent to the rabbi, so they were free to grieve while he continued negotiations on their behalf. I was slightly surprised by this. Although I could see it was the right thing to do, it was a big ask. Reading my expression perfectly, the rabbi took me to one side. 'It's better for them here,' he said, pointing to his heart, 'and here,' pointing to his head. I nodded. He was my kind of rabbi. Child protection was full of delicate balancing acts; I could appreciate that being a rabbi in Hackney required a fair bit of tightrope walking.

We eventually managed to broker a compromise between the rabbi, the pathologist, the coroner and the Jewish Burial Association, so with some very careful coordination, the parents' religious needs were realized.

CHAPTER TWENTY-EIGHT

NEVER LET YOU GO

Jane alleged that her father had abused her for a number of years. She'd decided to come forward, she told us, after she'd moved out of the family home to a different part of the UK, and with the encouragement of her half-sister. At just over sixteen years old, Jane was, legally speaking, an adult for the purposes of a memorandum interview. Nevertheless, Keira and I agreed with Byron that the legislation for children still applied and we should treat her the same as we would as if she were fifteen.

A quick search revealed that the suspect had since moved up north. Even though the accused and the accuser no longer lived in Hackney, it was where the abuse had taken place, so it was down to us to investigate. I filled out a referral and sent it to local social services and the police in the area where he lived. We needed to establish whether her father had access to children. If not then fine, if yes, then social services would pay him a visit to make an assessment and speak to the children.

This part would be very softly, softly. It wouldn't go beyond asking the kids questions like 'Are you happy?' or 'Is there anything worrying you?' If the children appeared to be OK, and if police checks revealed nothing else, then that's all we can do until the victim can be interviewed. To my relief, there was no evidence of any access to children.

Keira and I went to Jane's home for an informal chat to introduce ourselves properly; this was a much better option than asking her to come down to the police station, an intimidating place at the best of times.

Jane was timid, yet very collected and very calm. We'd started with a cup of tea and a friendly chat about nothing in particular. Keira and I made no mention of the evidence, not yet. Instead, we gradually began to discuss the procedure: detailing exactly how we expected her case to develop. We made it absolutely clear just how much we intended to support her.

Although Jane seemed pretty resilient, I wondered whether she really knew what she was getting into. I admired her courage but wondered how she would react once the darkest days of her life were exposed in the blinding glare of the Old Bailey.

Jane arrived at our interview suite a week later in high spirits. 'Wow,' she said with admiration as I showed her around, 'this place is all right, isn't it? Not like a police station at all.'

I left her with Keira to conduct the interview and took my seat in the control room. I placed my coffee next to the monitor, and fanned myself with my notepad. The room was tiny and poorly ventilated; there was really only space for one. If anyone joined me we'd be forced to leave the door open.

I soon forgot the heat as Keira began. Memorandum interviews are fascinating to observe, they're almost like a form of hypnosis; the isolation of the subject in a neutral room, followed by a period of acclimatization and relaxation, gradually leading to the reliving and exploration of past events before the subject's carefully orchestrated return to the present.

First, Keira set the scene, describing the purpose of the interview. Next, she built a rapport with Jane by talking about anything that put her at ease. Soon they were discussing some of the everyday things in Jane's life. After a few minutes, Keira gently steered Jane towards her relationship with her family, nudging her towards the main topic of concern.

Hesitantly at first, Jane started to talk. It was clear she found the going tough but her voice stayed steady as she described how her father had first abused her. 'He'd keep finding these pathetic excuses to enter my bedroom, like checking whether I'd switched off the lights, or wasn't still reading, listening to music.' Jane had spent hundreds of sleepless nights watching the door handle, waiting in terror for it to turn.

Once Jane had finished this first telling, the first time she'd spoken in such detail since the abuse itself, Keira had to decide whether she was still fit to continue. This was always a delicate moment. Thinking about the crimes in such detail for the first time in all these years had taken Jane right back to when she was a terrified teenager in her bedroom; unsafe in her own home, under threat from her own father. Suddenly, after years of repression, she was once more very close to her mental state at the time of the abuse. Her emotional condition would lead to the return of all the physiology of the 'fight or flight' response and the paralysis many experience of being unable to do either. Some victims experience a physiological or psychological breakdown at this point.

I peered at the screen, looking for the physical signs; an alternation of paling and flushing of the skin, faster breathing, pupil dilation, sudden and jerky movement. I didn't see any of the above; neither did Keira.

Keira went back over Jane's account and started to build on her story, picking up on key points. We needed to know every detail about where the crimes happened; rooms are often redecorated and properties redeveloped. We always attend and photograph the scene, no matter how old the crime. DNA can remain in place for years and if, after the interview, we thought there was a chance it was still there, then we'd go looking for it.

This done, Keira moved on to the human element. Most importantly, we needed to know whom she spoke to first about the abuse – they're obviously a key witness. Also, did anyone else see the abuse happen? Did other family members recall the excuses her father used to make so that he could sneak into her bedroom? Who else was living in the house? Were there any regular visitors?

Once we were sure we had a full list of names, we'd trace and interview every one of them. It didn't matter whether the abuse happened years ago or just the previous week. Every stone was overturned without question. Of course, inquiries where a child is in immediate danger had to take priority over historical cases, but we always got there in the end.

Eventually, Keira briefly left the room to ask me if there was anything I'd spotted that she needed to go over. As usual she'd done a brilliant job and had completely immersed herself in Jane's most private life. I told her she'd missed nothing.

She returned to Jane for the 'cool down'. This was another crucial part of the interview. The small break enabled Keira to change the subject and once again start talking about something that Jane felt good about; there was no way we'd leave her in the traumatic world that we'd just forced her to revisit. Once Keira was certain Jane was back to her present-day self, she wound up the interview. Even so, it would still take time for both Keira and Jane to settle back down completely. These long interviews have a significant psychological impact.

We examined and photographed the crime scene; the suspect was arrested and his first statement was taken. Keira also interviewed Jane's half-sister, Sam, as a witness. Keira did such a good job bonding with Sam that she got the feeling Sam was holding something back. Eventually, Sam confided that their father had also abused her. 'I can't accuse him in court,' she said, 'but I will support Jane, I'll give evidence.'

Some weeks later we were sat in the corridor of the Old Bailey, waiting to be called into the courtroom. There was a great deal of legal interest in this case as it was the first ever at the Old Bailey where an 'adult', Jane, was allowed to give evidence via video link. I was chatting with our barrister about this when he suddenly said something quite chilling.

'You know, DS Keeble,' he said quietly, 'I don't think victims share everything with us. I think that it's often the case that they've gone through so much more, but keep it back, releasing only what they feel consciously able to deal with.'

His comments left me feeling extremely uneasy. Had we missed something? Should we have probed more into Jane's abuse? His statement proved to be prophetic. As it turned out, we hadn't missed anything from Jane's testimony. It was Sam, her half-sister, who revealed more.

As our barrister took her through her testimony, she suddenly broke down. 'There's something I'd like to add,' she said, speaking through tears. She pointed at her father and said, 'He did much worse to me.' Gasps of shock spread through the courtroom.

My blood ran cold. I shared a shocked glance with the barrister. This was really bad. Until that point, Jane and Sam had told us about sexual abuse but had not mentioned rape. Rape carries a heavier sentence. If this allegation has not been made to the defence before the trial (so they could prepare to defend it in court), then the defendant cannot be tried for it. The trial collapsed under a torrent of objections from the defence.

Waves of guilt crashed down upon me. We could have done better here, I thought. Maybe if we'd done more, had paid more attention, spent more time, we would have pressed the button that would have released Sam's disclosure before the trial. I'd never felt so gutted. Two so very brave young women, so very helpless, and we'd let them both down.

I visited them at home immediately after the trial. Sam welcomed me with a smile. 'I'm so sorry,' she said.

She'd been so brave and had put herself through an ordeal she did not want to go through and was not ready for, not for herself, but for her sister, and *she* was apologizing to *me*?

'I should be apologizing to you,' I said. 'I've let you down. To have brought you so far and to have let it end where it did is unforgivable.' Sam and Jane did their best to reassure me that despite the end result the experience had been very positive for them both, in that they had confronted and dealt with the past.

I still felt awful. Sometimes a bad case just gets hold of you and simply won't let go and I carried this one around with me for a long time afterwards.

Back at the office I spoke to Byron, who told me we'd done all we could and that no one could have expected more from us. I shook my head. No matter how anyone rationalized it, I still felt as if I was responsible for messing it up. We were supposed to be bringing child abusers to justice, not putting the victims through hell only to see their tormentors escape.

I was still going over and over this case a few days later when the office door flew open with a crash. I looked up. Karl strode into the room and marched to his desk.

Sarah and I looked at each other. Something was up. I'd never seen Karl looking that flushed before. I'd been worried about him. He'd refused to give up on the Janine case and worked like a man obsessed, so much so that I wanted to pull him off it.

Rob had advised me to let him be. 'He'll have to find out for himself if this case is going nowhere,' he said sagely. Nevertheless, I was still worried how Karl would cope if he hadn't cracked the case by the time he retired. Would it mar the end of what had been an amazing career? Would he spend the rest of his life traumatized by the memory of this 'failure'?

He sat down at his desk, punched his computer into life and started typing furiously. I was about to ask him what was up when, without turning away from the screen, Karl said: 'I've got the bastard!'

I was amazed. Karl had been ringing hundreds of doctors and researchers all over the planet but to no avail. 'How?' I asked.

Karl replied, 'Someone's finally gone and cracked it, and they're only bloody right here, in the UK.'

A group of molecular scientists had had some success identifying different strains of gonorrhoea. The problem was that because their cutting-edge research was so groundbreaking it was going to be difficult to make the case work, let alone get it through the courtroom.

Karl had a sample of gonorrhoea from Janine and he hoped to match that to a sample taken from her alleged abuser's clothing. First, biochemical and immunological tests revealed that both samples were *Neisseria gonorrhoeae*, a general umbrella term for this particular kind of bacteria. Next, the scientists went deeper and searched for gonococcal-specific DNA from the clothing and compared their results with Janine's sample.

The results were printed on two transparent films. Karl had watched, not breathing as the two films were placed on top of each other over a light box. All he could see at this point was a jumble of colours, bars and dots. The scientist moved them up and down and side to side and, a bit like one of those magic eye paintings, they suddenly became one.

'They share the same sequence type, number 403,' the scientist said. 'It worked.'

'You mean this ties up my case?' Karl asked.

The scientist nodded. Needless to say, Karl was ecstatic, but it wasn't over yet.

A nerve-wracking few weeks followed as we waited to see whether this groundbreaking research withstood expert medical opinion and cross-examination under the court's spotlight.

It did.

When presented with the evidence, the paedophile did the only thing he could and pleaded guilty. Janine, much to the joy of her mother, didn't even have to testify.

This was a stunning result all round. Without Karl's determination to get the case to court, Janine would have been forced to testify about a traumatic event that time would have already done much to heal – her old wound would have been reopened. It was very likely that this paedophile would have walked away a free man, to abuse again, knowing he had already beaten the cops once. Instead, Janine's uncle went to prison for two years and was placed on the sex offenders' register. He would be closely monitored for more than a decade once he was released.

Karl's case made the *Lancet* and the police magazine the *Job*. It was a genuine scientific landmark – the first time that molecular detection and genotyping had ever been tried on clothing. Thanks to his intelligent and dogged detective work, Karl had changed the policing of sex crimes across the world.

This case also highlighted the important fact that the medical profession has long neglected its duty to research child abuse. This is partly because this type of work doesn't attract drug-company funding. It's also a sad reflection of the historical attitudes within the medical profession.

Just fifty years ago, many doctors and many textbooks failed to recognize child sexual abuse as important in the transmission of gonorrhoea in children. No mention is made in any of the textbooks of the 1950s of the possibility that it may be passed on through incest. The same textbooks acknowledged sexual transmission of gonorrhoea in adults and denied contact transmission (e.g. picking it up from a toilet seat), but maintained the exact opposite as far as children were concerned. How could they have been so blind?

Neglect and the physical, sexual or psychological abuse of children is one of the biggest public-health challenges we face today, yet any research into this area is dwarfed by work on more established childhood ills – in particular those that lend themselves to drug treatment.

When he wrote his report on Victoria Climbié, Lord Laming highlighted the poor response of the medical profession. He was surprised and disturbed to discover that it was difficult to find doctors who wanted to work in child protection. 'One might have expected that the scale of the problem would act as an inducement to those doctors who wished to make a significant impact on the health and well-being of the child population to enter the field. In such circumstances it is vitally important that those practitioners who do work in the field are adequately equipped to do so effectively.'

An editorial in the *Lancet* put it best. 'The true scandal is not the failure of a handful of individual professionals in notorious cases [such as Victoria Climbié, Baby Peter and Tundé], but the failure of the medical profession towards the generations of children at risk to come.'

Karl's success gave the whole office, especially me, a huge boost. In our never-ending quest for justice, we felt that far too many perverts had managed to beat the system. I sat down and wrote up Karl and the scientist for commendations.

And there was more good news to come.

The cases that Sarah, Patrick and I had discussed in Bodrum's cafe had spiralled into significant investigations. Sarah's hunch about the Scout leader abusing more children was correct. She discovered another child protection unit in the north of the UK was also investigating him. He'd been a Scout leader for more than twenty years and had abused several young boys during this period. Incredibly, the other unit was actually looking to trace Sarah's victim. So thanks to her determined research, two jobs in two different parts of the country were fused together. Eventually, the Scout leader rolled over and admitted several counts of indecent assault and gross indecency. He was sentenced to six years.

Meanwhile, once Patrick had memorandum-interviewed the young victim of child abuse who'd claimed a close relation had assaulted them for several years, he threw himself into the investigation. He managed to find a further seven victims from the same family – he even found one family member who was living abroad. By the time the trial came round, Patrick's evidence was so strong that the suspect pleaded guilty. On the day of sentencing, I was walking along the high street when I saw an *Evening Standard* banner outside a newsagent's. It said: *Paedophile Gets 14 Years*.

'Nice one, Patrick!' I exclaimed, unable to contain myself. I marched inside and persuaded the shop owner to hand the banner over to me and I stuck it up on our office wall. This became a constant reminder of how fantastic it felt when everything worked and when justice was done. Karl, Patrick and Sarah had shown us just what we were capable of achieving if we did everything we could and pushed a case right through to the very end.

CHAPTER TWENTY-NINE

A DAY IN THE LIFE

A Hackney flat: every piece of furniture smashed, every pipe bent, twisted and pulled from the wall. The terrifying result of a sudden teenage breakdown.

The crematorium: a handful of boys mourn one of their own, murdered over a drug debt, all of them thinking, It could've been me.

The B&B: a crack-seller stops by to pitch his wares to the lost and lonely teenage residents.

Behind the crime scene tape: a teenager who'd slept with knives under his pillow stabbed his stepfather without explanation.

Inside the crack house: a girl on her back on a filthy mattress. Men doing what they liked, as long as they paid for her £10 fix.

On the street: the thirteen-year-old stuffs lethal packages in his mouth – heroin on one side, crack on the other, ready to spit them into customers' hands.

The social service visit: the social worker turns a blind eye to the mental problems of a fifteen-year-old. He'll soon be sixteen and somebody else's troublesome statistic.

The police interview room: a cop pretends to care but he's

seen too many troubled teenagers like the one sitting opposite him to know there's no hope.

The pub: a barman picks up a forgotten mobile phone and finds hundreds of pictures of child pornography. It belongs to a local GP.

The public toilet in a supermarket: a fifteen-year-old boy rapes an eleven-year-old girl.

The squat: a teenage kidnap victim held for twenty-four hours. Burned with lighters, ribs broken for losing drugs.

Our interview suite: a violently abused seventeen-year-old girl tells us she's ready to confront her drug-dealing father in court.

The semi-detached house: a father batters his underachieving twelve-year-old son.

The church hall: a minister tells anxious parents their 'difficult' child is possessed by demons.

The chat room: a father uploads an image of his daughter in the bath.

The estate: the starving nine-year-old scavenges in bins for food.

The withdrawal: a parent throws their child against the wall in a fit of rage, then collapses, crying in despair at what they've done.

The school toilets: a girl slices steadily down her arm with a razor, feeling no pain.

The cot: too weak to cry any more, the baby lies wet with an agonizing rash.

Coming home: the twins share the floor of their furniture-less flat with a family of rats.

The pavement: a bleeding victim, their purse hot in a running teenager's drug-addicted hand.

The hospital: the doctor stops short as he lifts the child's top and sees dark, angry bruises covering her ribs.

*

The police investigate 8,000 cases of child abuse every year in London; that's twenty-two every day. All of the cases listed above could happen in just one day. This is *not* a small problem.[38]

These are just the cases that we know about; in 2006, the head of the Child Protection Command at New Scotland Yard, Detective Chief Superintendent Peter Spindler, told journalists that it was likely that 95 per cent of incidents of child abuse go unreported.

Of those cases we did know about in London in 2006, 20 per cent had been abused sexually, 50 per cent physically, while 30 per cent were down to neglect. DCS Spindler said that in terms of background, 38 per cent were white Europeans, 27 per cent from African or Caribbean families, while 10 per cent had an Asian background. In 19 per cent of cases the heritage was unclear.

Across England and Wales, the number of children under sixteen who have been raped (again these are only the cases we know about) comes to 5,000 cases per year.

This last set of terrifying figures were a recent discovery – the Home Office only started recording the ages of rape victims for the year 2004 to 2005. In that period, 974 girls under thirteen and a further 3,006 under sixteen were raped, while 293 boys below thirteen and 320 aged below sixteen were raped. Only one in fifteen assailants (a total of 303) was ever found guilty.

Home Office figures show that girls under sixteen made up 31 per cent of the 12,867 females who were raped in 2004 to 2005, while boys of the same age comprised 54 per cent of the 1,135 males raped in the same period.

The Metropolitan Police investigated 793 rapes of children in 2005 to 2006. Again, it is likely that the true number of rapes is far higher because so many children do not feel able to report the crime.

Every day, children are being raped in toilets, phone boxes, cars, bedrooms, bushes and parks, in their homes, in their bed-rooms. Most of them are raped by someone they know. The number of 'intra-familial rapes' in London of under-sixteens by close relatives, carers and professionals such as teachers and Scout leaders (which is what the CPU – the new term for CPT – specifically investigates), rose from 282 in 2002 to 2003 to 392 in 2005 to 2006, a jump of 35 per cent (this may be because as we get better and awareness spreads, more people have started to come forward). Over 90 per cent of the attackers were male.[39]

One worrying trend is the rise in the number of attacks on girls under sixteen involving more than one male assailant, one of whom is often known to the victim. This may be a sign of pae-dophiles 'inviting' others to join in via Internet chat rooms, as well as the rise in sick gang initiation rituals and methods of intimidation.

But what about all the kids we never get to find out about? How can we possibly guess at the true extent of the problem? One indication comes from the remarkable charity called Kids Company, founded by Camila Batmanghelidjh in 1996.

It was set up to provide practical, emotional and educational support to vulnerable inner-city children and young people. Kids Company operates in one small area of south-east London and works with teenage mothers, young offenders, kids excluded from school, school leavers without training or employment as well as victims of abuse and/or neglect, and those with severe and often complex mental health needs.

The kids self-refer – i.e. they just show up as and when they like. These are very often the most vulnerable kids, the ones too afraid to go somewhere 'official', the ones who've fallen beneath the radar of social services and the police. Kids Company offers unrelenting love for every child, whatever it takes: no matter how disturbed a child is, they will never be turned away.

Their figures are stunning: 12,000 kids turned up at their door in 2008. Over 1,800 children with nowhere else to go turned up at the centres on Christmas Day in 2008. This is just in a small area of South London. To put that in perspective, 30,000 children are on the child protection register nationwide.

With annual running costs of about £4.5 million a year, Kids Company is amazing value for money, although raising those funds isn't easy. Although a lot of money comes from private investors and businesses, too many of them 'want to engineer specific social changes which are quick, easy and measurable', says Camila. 'I have had someone from a major company refuse to give me the £50,000 they were looking to donate because, in her words, "Your kind of children don't look good on our annual report."' These are the kids that nobody seems to want to know about, let alone help.

A remarkable study carried out by the University of London on 1,500 children of Kids Company revealed that over 80 per cent of them had experienced severe and multiple traumas in childhood. These were 'lone children' living in chronic deprivation, with little or no support from the adults in their family.[40]

Some were young carers struggling to look after younger siblings or with parents who were unable to care for them, and many had been forced into drug-running, gangs or prostitution as their only means of survival.

Amazingly, thanks to the support of Kids Company, 77 per cent of these kids managed to return to education, training or employment. When asked, dozens leap forward to testify to how Kids Company did so much to help them.

'Basically, if I hadn't found Kids Company I'd be dead, or back in jail,' one teenager said. 'Kids Company and their staff like kept me out of trouble, and changed the direction of my life. They put a roof over my head and done everything basically. Like, not everything, 'cos I've had to change and do stuff myself, but like [they] helped me get along. If I didn't have them I'd be back in jail for sure.'

A twenty-year-old man said: '[Kids Company] gives me something to do in the day. It stops me doing crime, you get me? Instead of going out there to do crime or sell drugs to get money, I'd rather come here and get a bit of an education for life later, you get me?'

A woman of twenty-one said: 'Yeah, I love them. I ain't got no siblings and my mum is like really dependent, so I feel very alone and feel vulnerable. But I always feel that there's Kids [Company].'

Younger children had plenty to say as well. One eleven-year-old boy said: 'Kids Company is different as it's always available. You talk to them [the staff] and they always listen to you.'

A girl, also eleven, added: '[I came with my friend] 'cos he told me about it and he told me it was like a place to come and it was fun.'

A twelve-year-old girl said: 'The staff is nice to you, they talk to you when doing key working and ask other kids to move away if you is having a meeting so they can talk to you about it.'

A seven-year-old told her interviewer: 'Social workers are different because they work somewhere else. My social worker, like sometimes he comes around and talks about different stuff. I like Kids [Company] though 'cos I like being spoken to better, properly at Kids [Company].'

Kids Company also supports kids with emotional and behavioural problems in schools, giving the teachers time to focus on education. Being in school is often the only opportunity the kids get for adult support and direction as their home life is often unstable, with numerous families sharing the same home or so many brothers and sisters that they're lost in the crowd.

Again, dozens of schoolchildren who have been helped this

way leaped forward when asked to say what they thought of Kids Company. For example: 'Life would be more difficult [without Kids Company]. Some people might kill themselves because they wouldn't have anyone to talk to, to get their anger out.'

And: '[Without Kids Company] I would probably be permanently excluded.'

Kids Company works hand in hand with social workers on many cases after children at risk self-referred. Rachel came to Kids Company after she became pregnant. Her mother had died and her father was in prison. She had been through several unstable foster placements and had started smoking crack.

Kids Company provided her with constant daily help in person, supported her with raising her child, getting her off drugs and getting her back to college. Rachel eventually got one of the highest marks in her year, now works as a PA and is planning to study accountancy. So much was gained by Kids Company's intervention. I'm certain that Rachel would have become a crack prostitute without their intervention and goodness knows how many children she may have given birth to that would have to be taken into care.

Camila says: 'The children who come to Kids Company are dignified individuals making their way back from emotionally dark places. These youngsters may never be Olympic heroes or business leaders, because their starting point was so horrific. They deserve medals because they're surviving their experience of childhood, because they battle every day against the will to commit suicide. Every day they balance the struggle between wanting to die and struggling to live.'

Social services from one London borough cannot hope to come close to helping 12,000 kids. In inner-city boroughs, so few are put on child protection registers that research carried out by the University of London suggests the system only registers children it has the resources to handle. In one typical poor borough where 4,520 children were referred to social services in a year, only half received even an initial assessment. Only 3.5 per cent reached the child protection register. It's impossible that only 160 children in this poor borough needed protection.[41]

I believe that many social workers would be the first to agree that our current system is old and outdated. Too many good social workers have become demoralized working for a department that mimics business models and ethics. Our social care system needs a massive overhaul. Wherever you look there is a chronic shortage of almost everything that works to stop children turning into hellish teenagers.

Kids Company's programme for the most neglected children – those with addicted or mentally ill non-functioning parents – shows what it takes. It collects children from home before breakfast, feeds and clothes them, takes them to school and afterwards helps with homework, psychotherapy and supper before taking them home – where there is often no food, clothes or sheets, only filth and squalor. This kind of intensive support works – but it costs.

We've been ignoring what is an enormous problem for far too long – we have to accept that there is a significant proportion of the population who abuse thousands of children every day. Until we do, and until we start changing our attitudes towards troublesome children, we are all guilty of neglect.

Normally when you ask eight- or nine-year-olds if they had the opportunity to ask the prime minister for anything at all, they say things like more lollipop ladies and parks. You ask the children at Kids Company and they ask for no more killings, drugs or gangs.

'It is our belief that the public need to be frightened for these children, rather than frightened of them,' Camila says. How right she is. Kids Company is the first, very tiny step in the right direction.

There will always be cause to be worried for our children, but as long as Cardigan Squads up and down the country are in existence, and as long as we have dedicated officers, then there's every reason to expect that hundreds of kids at risk will be rescued and given a second shot at life. Kids can recover . . . it's up to us to get to them early enough and to provide them with the right kind of intervention.

CHAPTER THIRTY

A NEW WAR

Courtrooms are busy places; they're full of barristers, various assistants, stenographers, numerous courtroom staff, security guards and reporters packed into tiny benches. The courts of the Old Bailey are surprisingly small and usually, despite everyone's best efforts, there would be some bustle, shuffling of papers, documents being passed, hurried whispering and tiptoeing between benches during proceedings.

But not today.

The judge, Christopher Moss, had taken the unprecedented step of removing his wig and had ordered the barristers to do likewise so they appeared less intimidating. He had also asked, as if it were needed, for total silence.

As soon as the video monitor was switched on, the face of a nervous little girl looked out at us. The court fell totally still. What we were seeing was live. And it was two-way. She saw the court as clearly as we saw her. No one moved a millimetre or made a noise as, in a small but clear voice, Tundé began her testimony: 'I will never forget what happened,' she said.

When she got to the bit where she described how Sita

Kisanga forced her to take her jumper and vest off, I studied the faces of the jury.

'She pulled a little knife and she did little marks,' Tundé said. 'I was bleeding.'

They were struggling to contain themselves. They twisted uncomfortably in their seats, more than one of them glared at the accused. Tundé told them how she was cut time and time again, how she was beaten with a shoe, temporarily blinded by chilli peppers because she 'had witchcraft' before she was put in a plastic laundry bag.

Nobody doubted Tundé was telling the whole truth.

Tundé's dignity was in stark contrast to the defendants, who argued and bickered throughout the trial. They blamed each other in turn and had quarrelled on their way to the dock that morning – this was after Tundé had to wait for more than four hours for an interpreter to be found for her aunt.

As part of her evidence, the prosecution played the video of Tundé's interview.

'My aunt said that my mum and me have got witchcraft . . . They said today you die . . . One kicked me, one slapped me and one pushed me. I asked myself, "What have I done?" . . . She says if I tell anybody she hits me, she will take a knife and stab me.'

It was then that the judge spotted that Tundé, still clearly traumatized by her experience, had started crying. He ordered the video be stopped and adjourned the court.

When Sita Kisanga testified, she said she still believed that Tundé was a witch. She said she felt betrayed by her co-accused. Apparently, she didn't hear the beatings taking place in the room next to hers.

'On one occasion I heard the child crying,' she said, 'and I asked her aunt what the problem was. She said to me, "Sita, this child is talking about serious things, things relating to witchcraft."

She started to explain that the girl goes to Africa in the night to do bad things.

'I know it's not easy for people to believe there is the spiritual world and the material world. She was beating her like that because she believed in witchcraft. Our church pastor confirmed that the girl was a Kindoki.'

When Judge Moss announced that her cross-examination would not be completed that day, Kisanga buried her face in her hands and mumbled, 'I am not coming back tomorrow.' She received scant sympathy.

Our prosecutor, Patricia May, summed up with no little eloquence: 'There is no doubt a feeling among you all that in Britain such an accusation would be incredible and that no adult would believe it. This child was treated as a scapegoat by family members, tormented, subjected to all sorts of assaults which must have caused her considerable pain, fear and distress. If the abuse hadn't stopped, it would have led to fatal consequences.'

The jury were utterly convinced. There was simply no doubt about child cruelty. There was, however, some question over the attempted murder. It may have been an empty threat; no matter how traumatic the effect of that threat was, it did not necessarily mean that the accused were planning to carry it out. For this reason, the jury could only find them not guilty.

When it came to sentencing, the judge said that the accused trio had mounted a 'campaign of cruelty that amounted to a campaign of torture . . . It is the very pinnacle of cruelty to a child that demands the maximum sentence.'

The girl's forty-year-old aunt was convicted of four charges of cruelty. Sita Kisanga was found guilty of three charges of aiding and abetting child cruelty. They were each sentenced to ten years. Kisanga's brother Sebastian Pinto was found guilty of one charge of aiding and abetting and was sentenced to four years.

At the end of the trial, the Metropolitan Police announced

the formation of Operation Violet, a five-strong team set up to target abuse committed in the name of religion. It included a detective inspector who was also a Christian pastor. James, who'd led the investigation to catch Tundé's abusers, was chosen to front it. I could think of no one better.

Tundé's high-profile case had drawn a great deal of attention to our squad and it was at the forefront of our appeal to the entire Metropolitan Police to try to get as many police officers as possible to come to our careers fair. The idea was for us to pitch all the benefits of our department, hopefully persuading officers to apply for positions throughout SCD5, the Child Abuse Investigation Command.

The event was held on 21 July 2005, in a swish conference room at the brand new Emirates Stadium in Highbury, North London, home to Arsenal Football Club. Just about the whole of the Child Abuse Investigation Command was represented there, each with our own stall and own presentation. There was the Paedophile Unit from New Scotland Yard, James and Operation Violet, and me there to dispel all the myths that had gone into creating the label of 'Cardigan Squad'.

When it was time for me to give my presentation, I went through all the major cases I'd worked on. I spoke with no little enthusiasm about rescuing Hannah, the elation I'd felt at preventing another Climbié.

I also focused on Pamela's story, how my understanding of justice was altered by this case – how I came to realize the amount of good we did even when we didn't get the result we wanted in court. 'Despite Pamela's brave struggle against her past, and despite the extraordinary lengths we went to to get evidence, her father was acquitted,' I explained.

'But Pamela told me that we hadn't failed. She had stood before her father and had told him exactly what he'd done, the damage he'd caused. She had some kind of closure and was able to use this as a point from where she could move on with her life. Facing up to her past had pushed her to the limit but she came through. She had broken free from her drug addiction; she had a job. After the trial, she had the strength to live with what had happened. She had everything in place for a bright future.

'Victims feel that, finally, after years of fear and repression, that here is someone who will at last take them seriously, who will believe in them whatever the judgement might be in court. People like Pamela encourage others to come forward, others who'd kept quiet because they were afraid of being ridiculed as vain attention seekers or in case they got into trouble for making "false" accusations.'

I also covered the Jamaican job as well as our trips to Africa and Trinidad, knowing that foreign travel would get their interest: 'If you feel a child is at risk,' I told them, 'no matter where they might have been taken, no manager in the world is going to stop you on the basis of cost.'

Several heads nodded enthusiastically. Like so many detectives, I'd had several investigations cut short due to the cost – but that was before I signed up for Child Protection. I had so much to sell. It was easy to dispel the false image of the Cardigan Squad.

'*You* are in the driving seat when it comes to investigations,' I said, emphasizing the 'you'. '*You* take the case and you are responsible for seeing it through to the end, no matter where it might take you. Remember,' I said, playing the ace up my sleeve once again, 'there's no question of overtime when a child's safety is at risk. It will be approved.'

Afterwards our stand was swamped with interested detectives and I was soon running low on business cards. I was delighted and continued to sell my job enthusiastically. It was then that I noticed that people's attention was being drawn elsewhere. I tailed off in mid-conversation and looked around. Everyone was staring at the giant plasma TV screens. Sky News was on. The ticker tape flashed across the screen: 'BREAKING NEWS: Four explosions in London. Four suicide bombers on the loose'.

We'd been hit again. The second attack in only three weeks. Was this the beginning of a new sustained campaign? How many more attacks might there be? I looked around the conference room and out through the window into the stadium. Imagine Arsenal were playing at home. Tens of thousands of people; whole families, young and old. I couldn't bear the thought.

People were already calling their loved ones when the most senior officer present, Superintendent Chris Bourlet, called for everyone's attention. 'I am sure you are all aware of the serious-ness of the situation we're currently facing,' he said gravely. 'I'm calling on volunteers who can be deployed from here if the need arises.'

I felt no little pride when the whole floor stepped forward as one, without a second's hesitation. Officers from across the Force, of all ranks and departments, were united with the same simple thought in that instant; we were ready to do whatever was nec-essary to defend London. After all, no matter where our careers had taken us, this was the core reason for signing up for the police in the first place. I could see the superintendent was pleased, although I'm sure he would've expected nothing less.

In the event, we were not needed that day but a seed had been sown, reinforced by the then chief, Sir Ian Blair. 'This is a campaign we are facing – not a one-off event,' he told reporters. 'The second attack on July 21 should not be taken as some indi-cation of weakening of the capability or the resolve of those responsible. This is not the B-team. These are not amateurs. They made a mistake. They made one mistake. We are very, very lucky. The carnage that would have occurred had those bombs gone off would have at least been the equivalent to those on July 7.'

Over the following few days, Sir Ian said that there were many 'tired faces' at Scotland Yard. He said that a thousand officers were involved in the inquiry but that the extent of the threat would mean the Yard's resources would need to be extended. 'We will have to strengthen in the next year the firearms capability of the Metropolitan Police,' he said. 'We have to give people rest.'

The time had come for me to move on. Sir Ian had issued a call to arms and I felt as if it were my duty to respond. Many Londoners lost friends and relatives on 7/7 – and to have this followed by another attempt just two weeks later, well, it was just impossible for me to ignore.

I'd loved what I'd achieved over the past four years. I'd learned so much and the Child Protection Team, under Rob's guidance, had been totally transformed. Our knowledge and operational techniques had improved massively. This was reflected by the fact that after our careers fair we were overwhelmed with applications.

Rob had already gone by this time. He'd served his thirty years but he wasn't about to settle down into quiet retirement; men like Rob can't. He would work until he could work no more; he felt there were still so many things he could achieve – and in so little time. He'd always, without fail, been at the office at 6 a.m. and had never left before 6 p.m. It wasn't just because we were overloaded with work. It was because he cared; he was determined to see that there would never be another Victoria Climbié in Hackney.

He applied for and was immediately welcomed into the Serious Crime Review Group as a child protection case reviewer. Following every death or – if deemed necessary – serious injury, an independent investigation is launched by this independent agency. I couldn't think of a better role for Rob. Once he got his teeth into someone else's investigation he'd pull it to pieces for the benefit of all. He soon proved his worth and went on to lead the Serious Case Review into the death of Baby Peter.

I did worry that he was pushing himself too hard in the twilight of his career but he tried to reassure me during Karl's retirement do: 'This is my life, Harry, it's what keeps me going. It's simply impossible for me to not do this. I have to keep going until we're protecting kids properly – until there are no more Baby X, Y and Zs, and to make sure that kids will always get justice.'

I nodded. 'Rob, I've got the call. My transfer's approved. I'm off to Special Branch.'

'Harry, that's fantastic.'

I'd even been apprehensive about telling him I was moving on. I didn't want to disappoint my mentor.

'No regrets about leaving, OK?' Rob gestured towards the rest of the squad who were busy toasting Karl. 'Hackney's in good hands with Byron. Be proud of what you've accomplished here. Now you have to go where the fight takes you. Mine will always be in this department. Right now, with these attacks, I can't think of a better place for you to go.'

Rob, as ever, had said exactly what I needed to hear. I looked back with great pride at my time at Child Protection. I hoped that I had been one of many who had helped to transform its image and improved its effectiveness. Clara, Sarah and Patrick were still there, and you couldn't hope to have a more dedicated bunch, fighting for justice for Hackney's most vulnerable kids.

By the way, Karl, who was presented with a much-deserved commendation at his retirement do, left the Force a happy man. Sadly, neither of us can remember much about his speech – I would have loved to have quoted some of it here, but it was all a bit of a blur after the first few pints.

NOTES

1. 'Social workers in Climbié case are fired', Terri Judd, *Independent*, 13 November 2002.
   'Police "cancelled visit to little girl's home for fear of catching scabies"', Matthew Beard, *Independent*, 25 November 2000.
2. '15 children died in care of Haringey', *Society Guardian*, 2 February 2001.
3. 'Scandal of Paedophile's School Jobs', Tim Miles, *Evening Standard*, 21 November 2001.
4. 'UK Child Poverty – The Facts', Bob Roberts, *Mirror*, 17 October 2006. See: endchildpoverty.org.uk for the latest figures.
5. *Protecting Children: Working Together to Keep Children Safe*, Heather Flynn and Barbara Starns, Heinemann, 2004, p.13.
6. '"Sarah's Law" moves a step closer', Alexandra Topping, *Guardian*, 16 March 2009.
7. 'No one mourns and no one talks – A community closes ranks after a paedophile is shot dead', *Independent*, 29 May 2000.
   'We'll shed no tears; murdered sex fiend who lived in the shadow of hatred', Gary Jones and James Fletcher, *Mirror*, 19 February 2000.
8. 'Jamaica Riot Erupts After Police Shooting', Vivian Tyson, Associated Press, 26 October 2003.
9. 'Vicious circle; Jamaica. (Police and crime in Jamaica)', *Economist* (US), 1 November 2003.
10. 'One in 10 passengers on flights from Jamaica could have drugs: diplomat', AP Worldstream, 3 January 2002.

11. 'Police crackdown in Jamaica nets 51 "drug mules", 2,502 cocaine-filled condoms and nearly $1 million in suspected drug funds', David Paulin, Associated Press, 19 April 2002.

12. 'The Devil's Work?? Burned, beaten, cut with knives . . . a new police report claims that child abuse, and even murder, is practised in some of Britain's African churches. But what IS the truth?' *Daily Mail*, 17 June 2005.

13. 'Torment of Africa's child witches', *Sunday Times*, 5 February 2006.
'Witchcraft child abuse trail goes from London to Congo; church is facing new allegations over violent exorcisms', *Evening Standard*, 31 March 2006.

14. 'Accused pastor did not break law', bbc.co.uk, 25 January 2007. http://news.bbc.co.uk/1/hi/uk/6297279.stm

15. 'Child Abuse Linked to Accusations of "Possession" and "Witchcraft"', Eleanor Stobart, Department for Education and Skills, Research Report RR750, 2006.

16. 'Police "cancelled visit to little girl's home for fear of catching scabies"', Matthew Beard, *Independent*, 25 November 2000. And: Neil Garnham QC, opening statement to the Victoria Climbié Inquiry on Wednesday 26 September accessed at http://www.victoria-climbie-inquiry.org.uk/News_Update/ nov.htm

17. Hackney Borough Profile 2006, Chapter Three, p.53, accessed via http://www.hackney.gov.uk/xp-boroughprofile.htm

18. 'Boom in quangos costs us five times more than Forces', Robert Watts, *Sunday Telegraph*, 19 August 2007.

19. 'Quangos: the runaway gravy train', *Sunday Telegraph*, 19 August 2007.

20. 'Ofsted says Cafcass South West is "inadequate"', Thursday, 20 August 2009.
http://www.thisisnorthdevon.co.uk/court/Ofsted-says-Cafcass-South-West-inadequate/article-1265903-detail/article.html
'Cafcass are "inadequate" it's official – Court secrecy hides incompetence and leaves children at risk', John Hemming MP, 17 February 2008.

http://westmidslibdems.org.uk/news/001653/cafcass_are_
inadequate_its_official__court_secrecy_hides_incompetence_
and_leaves_children_at_risk.html

21. 'Depraved web of the "Son of God"', *Daily Mail*, 19 June 2007.

22. Allegations against school staff, House of Commons children,
schools and families select committee, 6 July 2009.
http://www.publications.parliament.uk/pa/cm200809/cmse-
lect/cmchilsch/695/69502.htm

23. 'Paedophile masqueraded as child protection expert', Ben
Taylor and Duncan Gardham, *Daily Mail*, 17 March 2004.

24. 'Another victim says he will sue Hodge; Margaret Hodge's
attempts to defend her position lands her in more hot water',
David Cohen, *Evening Standard*, 12 November 2003.
'Hodge Apologises in bid to save job', Patrick Hennessy,
Evening Standard, 14 November 2003.

25. 'The cost of a silent betrayal; Quiet surrounding the abuse com-
mitted by Father Chris Clonan could be an expensive lesson
for the Church', *Coventry Evening Telegraph*, 27 November
2002.
'Archbishop let paedophile priest return to work', Ian Burrell,
Independent, 20 July 2000.
'Cardinal denies ignoring paedophile priests', Pat Hurst, *PA
News*, 21 November 2002.

26. 'Evil of a child predator; Barron's home: Girls lured there: The
face they trusted: Parents let Barron spend time with their children', *Daily Mail*, 31 August 2007.

27. 'Judge's mercy for the man who raped girl of ten; Under fire:
Judge Julian Hall said he faced a "moral dilemma"', Sam
Greenhill, *Daily Mail*, 25 June 2007.

28. 'Anger as pervert escapes with fine', Neil Hunter, *Northern
Echo*, 16 February 2007.

29. 'Memo to Reid and Falconer', *Sunday Mirror*, 28 January 2007.
'Joke Justice (except it's not very funny, is it?)', *Mirror*, 26
January 2007.

30. 'Anger as sex pest gets one year', *Mirror*, 6 January 2004.

31. 'Sergeant gets six months for possessing child porn', *Evening Standard*, 25 July 2003.

32. 'Thanks, judge, for making paedophiles feel less guilty about downloading porn', Deborah Orr, *Independent*, 27 January 2007.

33. 'Paedophile groomed new victim while freed on bail; Internet pervert sent to High Court as sheriff rules his powers are inadequate', *Daily Mail*, 29 April 2005.

34. '"Evil doctor" jailed for sex abuse', bbc.co.uk/news, 20 September 2002.
    http://news.bbc.co.uk/1/hi/england/2271415.stm

35. 'Teacher jailed after fleeing with pupil', bbc.co.uk/news, 19 September 2001.

36. 'Outrage as he walks away with community order', *Daily Express*, 14 July 2004.

37. 'Eton master admits 16 child porn charges', Stewart Payne, *Daily Telegraph*, 23 April 2004.
    'Child porn teacher spared prison', bbc.co.uk/news, 14 July 2004.
    http://news.bbc.co.uk/1/hi/england/berkshire/3893257.stm

38. 'Church workers need to be monitored', Dominic Bascombe, *The Voice*, 17 July 2006.

39. 'Revealed: the horror of the 5000 children under 16 raped every year', Denis Campbell, *Observer*, 14 May 2006.

40. Kids Company research and evaluation programme, Doctor Carolyn Gaskell, Queen Mary University of London, April 2008.

41. 'Our nation of obsessive teen-haters must wake from its complacency', Polly Toynbee, *Guardian*, 3 November 2006.

END NOTE

If you have been the victim of sexual abuse, whether yesterday or twenty years ago, it's vital to report it. Even if you don't want to follow it up with a police investigation, you hold valuable criminal intelligence that could be used to help protect other children. Also, by coming forward, you will have taken the first step on the road to achieving some kind of closure.

You can do this by contacting your local police (alternatively, this can be done anonymously by calling Crimestoppers), local social services and various voluntary organizations. You are also more than welcome to approach me directly via my website: harrykeeble.com

Harry

Crimestoppers: crimestoppers-uk.org Telephone 0800 555 111

Help and information for adults can be found via the National Society for the Prevention of Cruelty to Children (NSPCC): www.nspcc.org.uk Telephone 0808 800 5000.

For children see ChildLine: childline.org.uk Telephone 0800 11 11.